bc

Jim –

T'was a mighty struggle –

Wept word and meaning –

but – here at last is Ralph.

Read in good health.

Edward Charles

Ralph
FIRST DUKE OF MONTAGU
1638 - 1709

Edward Charles Metzger

STUDIES IN BRITISH HISTORY
VOLUME 2

THE EDWIN MELLEN PRESS
LEWISTON/QUEENSTON

Library of Congress Cataloging-in-Publication Data

Metzger, Edward Charles.
    Ralph, first Duke of Montagu, 1638-1709.

    (Studies in British history ; v. 2)
    Bibliography: p.
    Includes index.
    1. Montagu, Ralph Montagu, Duke of, 1638?-1709.
2. Great Britain--Court and courtiers--Biography.
3. Ambassadors--Great Britain--Biography. 4. Great
Britain--Politics and government--1660-1714. 5. Art
patrons--Great Britain--Biography. I. Title.
II. Series.
DA437.M66M48   1986   941.06'092'4 [B]   86-23797
ISBN 0-88946-452-9

This is volume 2 in the continuing series
Studies in British History
Volume 2 ISBN 0-88946-452-9
SBH Series ISBN 0-88946-450-2

All rights reserved. For information contact:

The Edwin Mellen Press   The Edwin Mellen Press
Box 450   Box 67
Lewiston, New York   Queenston, Ontario
USA 14092   L0S 1L0 CANADA

Printed in the United States of America

CONTENTS

To Roe

without whose constant encouragement
this work would not and could not
have been written.

ACKNOWLEDGMENTS

While this book was written by one individual it would not have been possible without the generous assistance of the following individuals, institutions and publishers who granted permission to quote from the various works and manuscripts: Clerk of the Records, Record Office, House of Lords, for permission to quote from the Bromley Precedent Book in the Record Office's collection; Public Record Office, Chancery Lane, for the use of their valuable manuscripts; The British Library for graciously allowing the reproduction of the plates found in the Appendix - the Gardens at Boughton and two prints of Montagu Houses; The Royal Commission on Historical Manuscripts for allowing the use of their published manuscripts; the Bodleian Library, Oxford University, for kind permission to reproduce the protrait of Ralph, First Duke of Montagu; the Marquess of Bath, Longleat House, for his gracious permission to quote from the Longleat Coventry Papers; The Houghton Library, Harvard University, for permission to quote from "Lachrymae Musuarum"; Yale University for permission to quote from two letters of Ralph Montagu found in the Osborn Collection (Beinecke Rare Book and Manuscript Library); Yale University Press for gracious permission to quote from the publication Poems on Affairs of State: Augustan Satirical Verse - 1660-1714, Vol. II, 1678-1681; John Murray (Publisher) Ltd. for permission to quote from Christoper Monck: Duke of Albemarle by Estelle Frances' Ward; and Curtis Brown Group Limited for kind permission to quote from the Way of the Montagues by Bernard Falk. To any contributors whom I may have inadvertently overlooked I render a sincere apology and sincere thanks for their help.

CHRONOLOGY

1638?	Birth of Ralph Montagu (date unknown) Dec. 24, 1638...baptised at St. Bartholomew-the-Less in London
1640?	Birth of Elizabeth, sister of Ralph Montagu. (Date of birth is unknown but is estimated from reference to her found in letter of 1648 written by Lady Winwood to her son-in-law, Edward, Ralph's father).
1661, July 23	Appointed Joint Keeper of Hartleton Lodge in Richmond Park
1665-78	Master of the Horse to Queen Consort, Catherine of Braganza
1668	Marriage of Elizabeth, sister of Ralph Montagu, to Sir Daniel Harvey, Kt., ambassador at Constantinople
1669-72	Ambassador Extraordinary to Paris
1671-1685	Master of the Great Wardrobe (by purchase)
1671/2, Jan 2	Member of Privy Council of Charles II
1673, Aug. 24	Married Elizabeth, Dowager countess of Northumberland, and daughter of Thomas, Earl of Southampton
1673, Dec.	Montagu sent to Tower for

	quarrel with Duke of Buckingham in front of King
1676, 1677–78	Ambassador Extraordinary to Paris
1678, July 12	Montagu removed from Privy Council by order of Charles II
1678, Oct. - Dec.	Member of Parliament for Northamptonshire
1678, Dec. 19.	Montagu's papers seized by order of Charles II
1679, Feb. - Jul.	Member of Parliament for Huntingdonshire
1679, Aug. - 1681, Mar.	Member of Parliament for Northamptonshire
1679, Aug. 8	Birth of first son, Ralph, died before his father was created Earl (1689)
1681 or 1682	Birth of second son, Winwood, styled Lord Monthermer, Died, unmarried, in Flanders about May 1, 1702, - age about twenty years
1683/4, Jan. 10 Self imposed of is exile in France	Birth of a daughter, Anne. Date 'of' her birth is unknown as the date of her first marriage to Alexander Popham
1683	Self imposed exile in France Created 3rd Baron of Montagu
1685	Montagu returned to England from his selfimposed exile. Removed from office of Master of the Great Wardrobe by James II

1687, Feb. 6	Death of young Ralph Montagu, aged eight
1688/89, Feb. 14	Once again a member of the Privy Council - William III and Mary
1689, April 9	Created Viscount Monthermer and Earl of Montagu; reinstated in office of Great Wardrobe
1690, March 29	Birth of third son, John
1690, Sept. 19	Death of first wife, Elizabeth
1692, Sept. 8	Married his second wife, Elizabeth, Dowager Duchess of Albemarle, and daughter of Henry, 2nd Duke of Newcastle
1693-95	Captain of the Band of Gentlemen Pensioners
1695	Commissioner of Greenwich Hospital
1695	Entertained William III at his country estate Boughton, Northamptonshire
1697-1702	Appointed Lord Lieutenant of Northamptonshire
1702, May 1	Death of Winwood Montagu, second son of Ralph Montagu, in Flanders
1704/5, March 20	John, only surviving son of Ralph, married Mary, fourth and youngest daughter of John (Churchill), First Duke of Marlborough

1705, April 14   Created First Duke of Montagu

1707, May 6   Marriage of Lady Anne Popham,
                      daughter of Ralph, Duke of
                      Montagu, widow of Alexander
                      Popham, to Major-General Daniel
                      Harvey, Governor of Guernsey

1708/9, March 9   Died of pleurisy at Montagu
                      House, Bloomsbury, London

     When dealing with English history, there is
the necessity to remember the problem of dates.
England did not officially accept the Gregorian
Calendar until 1751, hence, the calculation of
calendar dates differs in England from that commonly accepted in the rest of Europe. Prior to 1700,
the English used what is commonly called the `old
style' date, which was ten days behind that of the
Gregorian Calendar. Up to the year 1751, England
began the New Year on the twenty-fifth of March,
while the Gregorian Calendar commenced the New Year
on the first of January. Hence, there is the
difficulty of a time difference when calculating
dates; between January 1 and March 25, the English
calendar calculated from the year previous rather
than from the Gregorian Calendar. Because the
research done for this work bore the dating of athe
`old style', any dating used will remain in the
`old style' in order to keep a note of consistency
throughout the work.

ABBREVIATIONS

Many sources, particularly archival sources, have been consulted in the preparation of this biography. For the sake of ease and brevity in citing 'of' these sources, a system of abbreviation of the said sources has been employed.

Baschet Transcripts	Baschet Transcripts - P.R.O./31/3/138 (Vol. 127) - 155 (Vol. 155). Copies of the correspondence of Barrillon, French Ambassador to London, preserved in the Ministere des Affaires.
Bath MSS.	Manuscripts of the Marquess of Bath, Longleat, Warminster, Wiltshire.
B.M. Add. MSS.	Additional Manuscripts Collection, British Museum, London.
B.M. Egerton	Egerton Manuscript Collection, British Museum, London.
B.M. Loan 29	Portland Manuscript Collection (on loan), British Museum, London.
B.M. Sloane	Manuscripts of Sir Hans Sloane, British Museum, London.

B.M. Stowe	Stowe Manuscript Collection, British Museum, London.
Bodl. MSS. Add.	Additional Manuscripts Collection, Bodleian Library, Oxford University, Oxford, Oxfordshire.
Bodl. MSS. Carte	Carte Manuscript Collection, Bodleian Library.
Bodl. MSS. Eng. Lett.	English Letters Manuscript Collection, Bodleian Library.
Bodl. MSS. Montagu	Montagu Manuscript Collection, Bodleian Library.
Bodl. MSS. Rawl.	Rawlinson Manuscript Collection, Bodleian Library.
Buccleuch MSS.	Buccleuch and Queensberry Manuscripts, Montagu House, Whitehall (Report of Historical Manuscripts Commission).
C.A.	Correspondance Politique: Angleterre, Ministere des Affaires Etrangeres, Quai d'Orsay, Paris.
C.J.	Journal of the House of Commons, Vol IX-XVIII.
Debates of the House of Commons	An Exact Collection of the Debates of the House of Commons Held at Westminster. October 21, 1680 (12 Vols., London:

	Printed for R. Baldwin, 1689).
Finch <u>MSS</u>.	<u>Alan George Finch of Burley-On-The-Hill Rutland</u> (Report of Historical Manuscripts Commission).
Lords MSS.	Manuscripts of the House of Lords, Westminster Palace, Westminster, London
N.L.I.	National Library of Ireland, Dublin, Republic of Ireland.
North. Rec. Off.	Northamptonshire Record Office, Delapre Abbey, Northampton, Northamptonshire.
P.R.O./Adm.	Admiralty Papers, Public Record Office, London.
P.R.O./Ind.	Admiralty Index Manu-scripts Collection, Public Records Office, London.
P.R.O./S.P., Dom.	State Papers, Domestic, Public Records Office, London.
P.R.O./For.	State Papers, Foreign, Public Records Office, London.
P.R.O./P.C. Register	Public Record Office - Privy Council Register.
P.R.O./T.	Treasury Papers, Public Records Office, London.

S.R.C.	Scottish Records Office, Edinburgh, Scotland.
U. of L./I.H.R.	University of London, Institute of Historical Research, London.
Welbeck MSS.	Duke of Portland Preserved at Welbeck Abbey (Report of Historical Manuscripts Commission).
Airy, Osmund, ed.,	Burnet's History of My Own Time, Part I. - The Reign of Charles the Second. 2 vols. Oxford: Clarendon Press, 1897.
Browning, Andrew, ed.	Thomas Osborne: Earl of Danby and Duke of Leeds 1632-1712. 2 vols. Glasgow: Jackson, Son & Co., 1951.
Burnet	Bishop Burnet's History of His Own Time: With Notes by the Earls of Dartmouth and Hardwicke, Speaker Onslow, and Dean Swift. 6 vols. Oxford: University Press, 1883.
Christie, Sir Joseph Williamson	Christie, W.D., ed. Letters Addressed from London to Sir Joseph Williamson While Plenipotentiary at the Congress of Cologne in the

	Years 1673 and 1674. 2 vols. Westminster: Camden Society, 1874.
Cockayne	George Edward Cockayne. The Complete Peerage. Revised ed., eds. H.A. Doubleday and Lord Howard de Walden. London: St. Catherine Press, 1936.
The Court in Mourning	The Court in Mourning Being the Life and Worthy Actions of Ralph, Duke of Montague, Master of the Great Wardrobe to Queen Anne, Who Dyed at His House in Russell-street in Bloomsbury, on Wednesday the 9th of March 1708/9. Containing His Travels Abroad, His Marriages, Children and Other Actions at Home: With His Death, Sickness, and Character. Licensed According to the Order. London: Printed for J. Smith in Cornhill, 1709.
Curran, Despatches of William Perwich	Curran, M. Beryle, ed. The Despatches of William Perwich English Agent in Paris 1669-1677. London: Royal Historical Society, 1903.

Dalrymple	Dalrymple, John. Memoirs of Great Britain and Ireland: From the Dissolution of the Last Parliament of Charles II. Till the Capture of the French and Spanish Fleet at Vigo. 3 vols. London: Printed for A. Strahan, T. Cadell, et. al., 1790.
Ellis, Correspondence	Ellis, George Agar. The Ellis Correspondence. Letters Written During the Years, 1686, 1687, 1688, and Addressed to John Ellis, Esq., Secretary of His Majesty's Revenue in Ireland. Comprising Many Particulars of the Revolution, and Anecdotes Illustrative of the History and Manners of those Times. 2 vols., London: Henry Colburn, 1929.
Evelyn, Diary	Wheatley, Henry B., ed. Diary of John Evelyn, Esq. F.R.S. To Which Are Added a Selection From His Familiar Letters and the Private Correspondence Between King Charles I and Sir Edward Nicholas and Between Sir Edward Hyde (Afterwards Earl of Clarendon) and Sir Richard Browne. 4 vols., London: Bichers and Son, 1906.
Firth, "Montagu"	Firth, Charles H. "Montagu, Ralph, Duke of Montagu (1638?-1709)."

	Dictionary of National Biography, 8, 710-13.
Foxcroft, George Saville	Foxcroft, H.C. *The Life and Letters of Sir George Saville, Bart. First Marquis of Halifax & Co.* 2 vols. London: Longmans, Green and Co., 1898.
Foxcroft, H.C. ed.	*A Supplement to Burnet's History of My Own Time: Derived from His Original Memoirs, His Autobiography, His Letters to Admiral Herbert and His Private Meditation, All Hitherto Unpublished.* Oxford: Clarendon Press, 1902.
Letters	*Copies and Extracts of Some Letters Written to and From the Earl of Danby (now Duke of Leeds) in the Years 1676, 1677, 1678. With Particular Remarks Upon Some of Them.* London: Printed for John Nicholson, 1710.
Manchester	Montagu, William Drogo. *Court and Society from Elizabeth to Anne: Edited from the Papers at Kimbolton by the Duke of Manchester.* 2 vols. London: Hurst and Blackett, 1864.
Mignet	M. Mignet, *Negociations Relatives A La Succession D'Espagne Sous Louis XIV.* 4 vols. Paris: Imprimerie Royale, 1842.

Pepys, _Diary_

Wheatley, Henry B., ed.,
The _Diary_ of _Samuel_ _Pepys,_
_M.A.,_ _F.R.S.:_ _Clerk_ _of_ _the_
Acts _and_ _Secretary_ _to_ _the_
Admirality. 8 vols.
London: George Bell and
Sons, 1905.

Sidney, _Diary_

Blencowe, R.W., ed. _Diary_
_of_ _the_ _Times_ _of_ _Charles_
the _Second_ _by_ _the_
Honourable _Henry_ _Sidney,_
(Afterwards _Earl_ _of_
Romney) _Including_ _His_
Correspondence _with_ _the_
Countess _of_ _Sunderland,_
and _Other_ _Distinguished_
Persons _at_ _the_ _English_
Court _to_ _Which_ _are_ _Added_
Letters _Illustrative_ _of_
the _Times_ _of_ _James_ _II_ _and_
William _III._ 2 vols.
London: Henry Colburn,
Publisher, 1843.

Singer

Singer, Samuel Weller, ed.
The _Correspondence_ _of_
Henry _Hyde,_ _Earl_ _of_
Clarendon _and_ _Of_ _His_
Brother _Laurence_ _Hyde,_
Earl _of_ _Rochester:_ _With_
the _Diary_ _of_ _Lord_
Clarendon _from_ _1687_ _to_
_1690._ _Containing_ _Minute_
Particulars _of_ _the_ _Events_
Attending _the_ _Revolution:_
And _the_ _Diary_ _of_ _Lord_
Rochester _During_ _His_
Embassy _to_ _Poland_ _in_ _1676._
2 vols. London: Henry
Colburn, 1828.

PREFACE

The great house, so withdrawn, so quiet, keeps its secrets--mute witness to a proud, ambitious man who bestrode two cultures, and, though his name appears only in the footnotes of history, had in his contriving way some influence upon the European stage. Considering his ability, it is perhaps surprising he did not have more. But then his career, like the house, is chiefly remarkable for its grand facade and for its incompleteness.
(Peter Gorham Webb, <u>Portrait</u> <u>of</u> <u>Northamptonshire</u>, London: Robert Hale, 1977, p. 126).

The focus of this work is the public life-- diplomatic, political, cultural and social--of Ralph Montagu. In particular, his role as ambassador to the Court of Louis XIV during the reign of Charles II will be assessed, along with his activities related to the Treaty of Dover (1670), his motives in the impeachment of Danby, and his contribution to the formation of the Whig Party (1670s). Montagu was a prominent person in the highest rank of his society and court--his associa- tion with literary men (Congreve, St. Evremond, La Fontaine), artists (Kneller, Verrio, Monnoyer) and architects (Puget, Hooke) is recognized but has resulted only in an associative immortality. A man of question- able morals, infected with Gargantuan appetites for the things of this world--money, women, houses and painting--he always managed to scramble to the top. A traitor and a political prisoner under Charles II, he

survived to become a Duke under Queen Anne. A study of
Montagu, then, is basically a study in the art of survi-
vorship, political and economic, in a revolutionary era
when England's basic political ideals and institutions
were evolving toward ministerial responsibility and
popular sovereignty.

Interestingly enough, there is no modern biography
of Montagu. The information about him has not, hereto-
fore, been fully collected, analyzed or assessed; therefore, little insight exists into the character of the
man who so nearly caused the impeachment of the Lord
Treasurer Danby and directly caused the dissolution of
the 1678 Parliament. Other than these incidents, little
is known of Montagu's actual influence. He was
'reported' to be a major art collector, respected even
by the French painters as a man of taste; a builder of
fine houses at Bloomsbury and Boughton; and the owner of
a company which manufactured fine Mortlake tapestries.
This last suggests Montagu was not bound by the customary aristocratic aversion to engaging in trade and
manufacture.

While this work is not totally a political
biography as such, the importance of politics in
Montagu's life cannot be ignored, especially in its
early stages when he was ambassador to the Court of
Louis XIV. Yet it is important to remember that Montagu
was not exclusively a political man. He used politics
as a means to an end--his own personal advancement. A
man of varied tastes and interests, much of his life was
spent in the cultivation and enhancement of the arts.
His interest in painting and architecture was to become
a legend in his own time. His patronage of artists

such as Verrio, Monnoyer, and such architects as Puget and Hooke in the building of houses in Boughton and London, and his sponsorship of writers like Congreve, conferred on him in his lifetime the fame of an arbiter elegantiarum. His relationship with La Fontaine and Saint Evremond imparted to his taste an international flavor.

The materials used in this study of Montagu were located in the major libraries of Great Britain and Paris. The dispatches from the English envoys in Paris are in the published State Papers, Foreign of the Public Record Office, London, as well those of as the French envoys in the Baschet Transcripts. Montagu's letters, in the possession of the Duke of Buccleuch and Queensbury, have been printed by the Royal Commission on Historical Manuscripts as the Montagu House MSS. (known as the Buccleuch and Queensbury MSS.). Many of his unpublished letters remain in the manuscript collection of the Marquesss of Bath (Longleat MSS., Coventry Papers). Other sources were found in the Public Record Office's State Papers, Foreign: Venetian; State Papers, Foreign: France; State Papers, Domestic; Treasury Books and Papers; State Papers, Foreign Entry Books; Admiralty Index Manuscripts Collection; the British Museum Manuscripts Room include: Additional MSS., Harleian MSS., Egerton MSS., Stowe MSS., and Lansdowne MSS., sources in the Bodleian Library are the Clarendon MSS., Carte MSS., Ashmolean MSS., and Rawlinson MSS. The Royal Commission on Historical Manuscripts also published many of the Calendar of the Proceedings of the House of Lords, the Ormonde MSS., Finch MSS., Downshire MSS., Hastings MSS., and Lindsey MSS. The diplomatic instructions to the various French envoys have also been printed in two massive volumes by the French Government under the title Recueil des Instructions aux Ambassadeurs. Other important sources for diplomatic history are Mignet's Negociations Relatives a La D'Espagne Sous Louis XIV, and Correspondence Politique; Angleterre, Ministres des Affairs Estrangeres. This material has been supplemented by the Montagu family papers, documents and letters, etc. located at the family archives - Delapre Abbey, Northampton.

I would like to take this opportunity to render thanks to the many people who made this work possible and without whose help and encouragement it would not have been written. Thanks are due to Professors Orville T. Murphy and Charles L. Stinger of the State University of New York at Buffalo for their availability and willingness to help when called upon. I would also like to offer a special word of thanks to Professors Roger Lockyer and John Miller who gave me new insights while I attended a seminar they conducted on Seventeenth Century England at the Institute of Historical Research at University of London, and also to Mr. William Kellaway, Secretary and Librarian of this Institute, for his consideration and patience on my behalf. Further, I would be remiss if I did not acknowledge the invaluable aid of Manuel D. Lopez, Head of the Reference Department of Lockwood Memorial Library, State University of New York at Buffalo in the location of needed materials. Also, I must not overlook in my litany of thanks: Mr. P.I. King, Archivist at Delapre Abbey, Northampton, Mr. A.B. Bartlett, Archivist at Palace House, Beaulieu, Hampshire, Miss Jane Fowles, Archivist at Longleat House, Warminster, Wiltshire; the Keepers of Manuscripts at the Public Record Office, the House of Lords Record

Office, and the British Museum Manuscripts Room for their courteous help in the search for material. It is safe to say that without such kind and understanding people, who gave so much of themselves without question, that this work could not have been written. To each I offer my sincere thanks and appreciation. Anything that is of value in the work is to their credit, errors found herein are my own.

RALPH MONTAGU, FIRST DUKE OF MONTAGU

Ralph
FIRST DUKE OF MONTAGU
1638 - 1709

INTRODUCTION

To investigate the life of Ralph Montagu is to look at the age in which he lived--the political, social and cultural life of the last half of the seventeenth century, in particular, the Late Stuart Era. To study Montagu is to see England change--the transition from the absolute rule of Charles II to the limited constitutional monarchy of William III and Mary and future monarchs.

As a political figure, Montagu was basically a Whig. He might even be considered one of the major figures of the movement. An able and imaginative politician, at times given to what appeared to be radical thinking and acting, Montagu nevertheless was governed by the principle of total self interest, preservation and advancement.

> It lay between those members who, more or less disinterestingly opposed both the governmental principles and the persons of the ministers and those opportunists who attacked ministers in order first to supplant, and then to imitate, them.

> This group among the Whigs included some outstandingly able men, notably Ralph Montagu, William Harbord and Sir Francis Winnington. Apart from their greater unscrupulousness they were marked off

from the majority of the Whigs by the
fact that most of them had held office at
one time and were accustomed to the life
at Court. By vigorous denunciations of
ministers, by consistently advocating
the extreme measures, they tried to
efface these facts--with some success,
especially in 1680 when for a time they
dominated proceedings in the Commons, and
even tried to wrest leadership and the
direction of policy from Shaftesbury.
But it was impossible for them wholly to
overcome the justified suspicions felt by
many of the Whig rank and file, that
these men were thinking primarily of
themselves and would, if given
encouragement, desert to the Court.1

Montagu really never shared the ideology which fired the
imagination of the early Whig leaders. Somehow Montagu
was never driven by the excitement of creating a new
order out of the Civil Wars, the commonwealth and
Protectorate. The Whigs realized that the Restored
Monarchy did not fulfill their dreams. But their aims
were changed, and it was the Glorious Revolution that
was to offer the completion of the Whig dreams. A
member of the 'old guard,' yet a proponent of the
Revolution and the ensuing Bill of Rights, Montagu
disliked the unrestrained enthusiasm of the 'young
Whigs'. He resented the contentiousness in the ranks of
the Whigs which caused misunderstanding with the King,
William III, who was supposed to be the embodiment of
their noble experiment in the political life of England.
The resentment stemmed less from his devotion to the

Crown than from a sense of personal loss or affront to his dignity as a member of the landed gentry and nobility.

Montagu did not always occupy the forefront; he often preferred the background. Actually, he was careful not to involve himself personally in any of the great issues of the day other than supporting the Glorious Revolution; and on the basis of this support for the new monarchs, William and Mary, he petitioned an Earldom and Dukedom. Although present at the debates in the Commons (1678-81) and later as a member of the House of Lords (1685-1709), he allowed others to lead. Astute enough to let others be the moving forces, he desired to manipulate from blessed anonymity. By such means he achieved his ultimate goal of advancing in the ranks of nobility.

Born just twelve years before the execution of Charles I and the emergence of the Cromwellian Common-wealth, Ralph Montagu lived to see the Restoration of the Monarchy under Charles II, and, at approximately aged fifty he witnessed and took part in the event that was to affect profoundly the national destiny of England and its people: the Glorious Revolution and enthrone-ment of William and Mary. He lived and died during the reign of the last of the Stuart line, Queen Anne.

INTRODUCTION
Footnotes

[1]J. R. Jones, The First Whigs: The Politics of the
Exclusion Crisis, 1678-1683 (London: Oxford University
Press, 1961), p. 13.

CHAPTER I
The Formative Years: 1638?-1662

He was the Son of the <u>Lord</u> <u>Montague</u> of
<u>Boughton</u> in <u>Northamptonshire</u>, and I believe
Second Son for at the time of his appearing at
the Court of King Charles, the Second, we find
him in History only stiled <u>Mr.</u> <u>Ralph</u> <u>Montague</u>;
whether that was or not, it was not long
before he was dignifyed by another Title...[1]

In seventeenth century England, the education of
the landed class, which was directed to solidifying and
reinforcing the consciousness of class, was often
dictated by political ideologies and institutions, but
in particular by social position and religion. As a
result, education in England at the close of the Renaissance came to be one of the most highly stratified,
structured and elitist of all those in European
societies.

Classical studies were meant to preserve the
continuance of a "higher culture as the distinct
monopoly of the social elite,"[2] This prerogative of the
elite was maintained by the education of their children
in such institutions as Eton and Westminster, where,
through the curriculum, a sense of leadership was
instilled which would allow them "to command the
important positions in society and impose a sense...of
natural superiority."[3] Another task imposed on classical education was the preservation of religious
institutions - in particular those of established
Protestant structure. The pulpit directed all classes

of society toward peaceful submission and obedience to the government which God chose to give them through their King and State. The Bible, in Latin and Greek, was studied by the landed gentry as an integral part of their education; it was believed, Christian morality would be so deeply ingrained so as to become almost second nature and automatically lead to righteous living.[4] The child, hopefully, would become a moral, dutiful and loyal son and subject, through a classical education.

So have many fathers hoped.

The exact date of Ralph Montagu's birth is unknown. Church records of the Church of (St. Bartholomew-the-Less) indicate that he was born at the London house of his maternal grandmother, Lady Elizabeth Winwood, and was baptised on the 24th of December 1638.

Ralph, the second but first surviving son and heir of Edward (1616-1684), the second Baron Montagu of Boughton, had an older brother, Edward, and a younger sister, Elizabeth,[5] His great-great grandfather, Edward, chief justice to Henry VIII and Edward VI, had been sent to the Tower for his acquiescence in the attempt to put Lady Jane Grey upon the throne.[6] His grandfather, Edward, created First Baron Montagu of Boughton by James I in 1621, served as MP for Northamptonshire and Deputy Lieutenant of the shire. Ralph's grand uncles, Henry, Sydney, and James, were enobled and sat in the House of Lords: Henry, created Earl of Manchester in 1626, served as Treasurer, President of the Council and Lord Privy Seal under James I; Sydney was father to Edward, who later was created Earl of Sandwich; and James was elevated to the Bishopric of Winchester (1616) and exerted considerable influence at the Court of James.[7] Ralph's uncle, William (his father's brother), an able lawyer, became Attorney-General to Catherine of Braganza, and was appointed Lord Chief Baron of the Exchequer.[8] A cousin, Walter, son of Henry Montagu, first Earl of Manchester, converted to Catholicism and became Abbot of St. Martin's near Pontoise, France.[9]

Montagu's father, Edward, succeeded to the title in 1644. In 1646, along with the Earls of Denbigh and Pembroke, he was commissioned by the House of Lords to receive the King's (Charles I) person from the Scots and conduct him to Holmby Castle (1647). He opposed the trial of Charles and refused to sign the death warrant. Together with his sons, Edward and Ralph, he actively engaged in the Restoration of Charles II. Afterwards, unwilling to live in London, he spent most of his later life at his country home in Northamptonshire.[10]
To those who knew him he was:

> An honest, truthful and pious man, opposed to all changes in Church or State, a friend to the poorer clergy, and a patron to men of letters; a good landlord and a generous dealer.... "A man of plain and downright English spirit, viz. of a steady courage, of a devout heart, and a true son of the Church of England; yet so severe and regular in his life, that he was by most reckoned amongst the Puritans."[11]

> After the King's return he lived chiefly in Boughton, not caring to engage in the service of the Court, nor pleased that his sons bore part in it.[12]

Ralph's mother, Anne, was the daughter of Sir Ralph Winwood of Ditton Park, Buckinghamshire, and Elizabeth, daughter and coheiress of Sir Thomas Ball of Totnes, one of the wealthy gentry of the shire. Sir Ralph Winwood served as Secretary of State to James I from 1646 to his death in 1617.[13]

Ralph's grandfather, Edward, who died a prisoner of the Long Parliament in June 1644 for refusing to reside in London during its fall (1643) and spring (1644) sessions,[14] ruled over a household that was strict and regular, especially in its religious observance. Lord Edward was a devout supporter of the established Church, its ceremonies, and especially the Book of Common Prayer--even though he was thought to have Puritan leanings.[15] He was known to be a gracious and generous host and landlord who taught that service to the Crown, duty and honor were of supreme value. His household reflected the master's patriotism, charity and piety.[16] These virtues he taught his son, the Second Baron, Edward, who in time came to be known and respected for pious living, hospitality and abhorrence of the Restoration Court.[17]

Montagu's father, apparently practiced the admonitions that his father had given him, which are contained in Directions for my Sonne, written in January 1620/21, where he recorded the responsibilities which God and family imposed. He urged his son to be thrifty, avoid the borrowing of money, and practice moderation. Above all he urged his son, not to pursue material wealth, but to seek first the Kingdom of God. He warned his son to avoid excessive dependence on any one man and noted that success required personal sacrifice based on biblical principles.18

From such an environment and lineage young Ralph entered upon his formal education at about the age of eight or nine. The usual custom at that time was to send a young boy away from home for his education. No exception to the rule, Ralph Montagu, the future Third Baron Montagu of Boughton, went to London to be educated at Westminster School under the Headmaster Richard Busby, a noted educator of his time.[19]

The exact date when Montagu entered Westminster School, a "small" school with perhaps twenty or thirty pupils in all forms, in not known. Perhaps he was eight or nine, keeping in mind that Ralph was likely born in 1638. This estimate is based upon a letter from his maternal grandmother (Lady Elizebeth Winwood) to her son-in-law, the Lord Edward, Ralph's father, concerning Ralph's being ill. The letter is undated, but as the Dowager Lady Anne Montagu, Ralph's paternal grandmother referred to, died in July of 1648, it was probably written either in late 1647 or early the following year. The illness that Ralph contracted was that common to boys of his age--smallpox.20

Another letter from Lady Winwood, written about 1648, mentions young Ralph's illness.

> [1648?] You will see by Mr. Busby's letter that poor Ralphe has got the small-pox. As soon as it was suspected, Mr. Busby moved

him into a house in the stable yard, and sent for Dr. Wright, who, being ill, sent the apothecary instead, and would have sent a nurse, but Mr. Busby does not wish either of them to see him. As he has now been ill five days and is said to be doing well, I think we had better leave him in the hands of his master-- who, as you will see, expresses much love and care towards him-- and of the woman in whose charge he has been given. Edward, is quite well so far, but I advise that he should be sent to Lady Montagew's, and then if he falls sick, he can be nursed there. Meanwhile he can go to school, and he and his man can still diet at Mr. Busby's. I am of Mr. Busby's opinion that the boys have ridden too much in the heat, drinking beer when they were very hot, and eating too much also; and I believe Bettie will do the like as long as she is abroad.[21]

Ralph's grandmother went on to say that all these disorders were the result of an overheating of the blood which put it in very great distemper. An interesting observation concerning the overheating and the drinking of too much beer, and this at the age of nine or ten!

Montagu's education, in all probability, followed the classical concept of learning. This may be inferred from the fact that the school was under the direction of a Headmaster, Richard Busby, who was himself a renowned classicist, and reputed to be one of the greatest educators of his age. He retained his post as Head-

master for nearly fifty-seven years (1638-95), which
included the horrors of the Civil Wars, the establish-
ment of the Commonwealth and the Protectorate, the
return of the Monarchy and the Glorious Revolution   To
him is due the extraordinary success of the school,
having guided it through the years with a firm hand and
an unwavering determination. Testimony to this success
is a long list of successful students. He counted among
his pupils such personages as John Dryden, John Locke,
Sir Christoper Wren, Robert Spencer, Charles Montagu,
Earl of Halifax, Matthew Prior, and many other distinguished men.[22]

Richard Steele, another famous Westminster student,
and, in later years, the editor of The Spectator and The
Tatler, said of Busby:

I must confess (and I have often reflected
upon it) that I am of the Opinion Busby's
Genius for Education had as great an Effect
upon the age he lived in, as that of any
ancient Philosopher without excepting one, had
upon his Contemporaries.... I have known
great Numbers of his Scholars, and I am confident, I could discover a Stranger who had been
such, with very little Conversation: Those of
great Parts, who have passed through his
Instruction, have such a peculiar Readiness of
Fancy and delicacy of Taste, as is seldom
found in Men educated elsewhere, tho' of equal
Talents;... He had a Power of raising what
the Lad had in him to the utmost height in
what Nature designed him; and it was not his
Fault, but the effect of Nature there were no

indifferent People come out of his Hands; but
his Scholars were the finest Gentlemen, or
the greatest Pedants in the age. The Soil
which he manured always grew fertile, but it
is not in the Planter to make Flowers of
Weeds, but whatever it was under <u>Busby's</u> Eye,
it was sure to get forwards towards the Use
for which Nature designed it.[23]

One admirer of Busby, a Dr. Adam Clarke, claims:
"To Dr. Busby's plans, science, and discipline everything yielded; and no dunce or unlearned man was ever
turned out of Westminster School during his incum-
bency."[24]

Busby made little attempt to disguise his loyalty
to Crown and Church. Even during the Civil Wars, he
continued to educate the "King's Scholars", which
resulted in complaints that he educated men who were in
opposition to the Commonwealth and that it would never
be well with the nation until the school was suppressed,
since it was a natural breeding ground for counter-
revolution.[25]

Busby was a severe task-master, an approach both
admired and criticized by his contemporaries. He
commanded industry and learning on the part of his
pupils, at first by fear and then by `love', and thereby
was able to gain the veneration and affection of many of
his pupils. John Dryden held Busby in high respect
throughout his life, and Philip Henry, the Diarist,
referred to him in terms of gratitude.[26]

The religious training of Busby's pupils was carried out most conscientiously through word and example. Reported to be a man of unaffected piety and goodness, a man who held the Church in great respect and was most zealous for its welfare, he was on the best of terms with many of the leading churchmen of his day. From all reports, he was an agreeable mixture of `sweetness and light' with a touch of severity added thereto. Civil good nature and learned modesty were among his attributes, while it was noted his greatest virtue was charity.[27]

Under the guidance of such a man Ralph Montagu made the acquaintance of the writers and heroes of the Latin and Greek world--Terence, Ovid, Virgil, Horace, Euripides--since the curriculum centered around the Classics. Montagu learned his Greek grammar from a work written by Busby himself (<u>Graecae</u> <u>Grammatices</u> <u>Rudimenta</u> - 1647?), which aided his progress in reading the New Testament in Greek as well as the works of Homer.[28] It is also quite probable that Montagu learned Hebrew in order to read the Hebrew Psalter. However, Latin was the subject most necessary if one was to acquire an education and immediately fulfill the daily requirement of translating the Bible into this language, which was deemed as one of the most important duties of the pupils. Latin was not only studied in prose form, but also in the poetic form, and often the Latin work was required to be translated into Greek. The books prescribed reflected the Renaissance idea of the value of the classical authors, thus it is not inconceivable that Erasmian ideas of education were the principles which guided the system of education at Westminster.

The school day was indeed a hard day if we are to judge from contemporary literature. The school day began at the early hour of five in the morning with the call of the monitor (most likely an older student). At six the students met and recited their Latin prayers. The morning hours between six and eight were then spent with the Headmaster in the recitation of grammar lessons from Latin and Greek authors: Cicero, Livy, Homer, Xenophon. Between eight and nine the pupils partook of their `drink'--a kind of breakfast--and were then occupied in the preparation of future exercises. From nine to eleven the homework of the previous night was examined, which was either praised and rewarded or criticized and punished. Of course, Latin and Greek were the main staples of these exercises. Dinner was served around one in the afternoon, accompanied by the reading of Latin manuscripts at the common-table. The hours from one to three were devoted to expounding the lessons for the next day taken from Cicero, Virgil, Homer, Euripides, Socrates, Livy or Sallust. A short respite and refreshment was allowed between three and four, after which an hour (four to five) was given to the recitation of some rhetorical figure, proverb or sentence selected by the master for this purpose. This was followed by the translation of some <u>Dictamina</u> from Latin and Greek into English. Often times at the end of this exercise the assignment for the next day was given to the students. Then came suppertime, and after this evening meal the pupils were called to the Headmaster's chambers for lessons in cosmography (based upon Hunter's <u>Cosmographie</u>) and tested in their knowledge and ability to describe and locate cities and countries on the various maps.[29] Throughout the day the pupils were strictly required to speak in Latin, this injuncture being rigorously enforced by the appointed monitors.

Sunday mornings, before the recitation of Morning Prayers by the students, were spent in class where the students were required to construe some part of the Gospel in Greek or to recite some part of the catechism in Latin or Greek. The afternoon was spent in the construction of verses based upon the sermon heard in the morning religious service or upon some passage of the Gospels or Epistles.30

Each Friday the students gathered together for what might be termed a `discipline service'. At this gathering, punishments were meted out for any and all infractions of school discipline or any failure to do or complete their lessons. Scholastic tasks, such as the repeating of whole orations out of the authors studied, were considered as appropriate punishments. Also, as was custom and not connected with this `service,' every Friday was a day dedicated to the repetition of what was learned in the former part of the week. Every Saturday they proclaimed their `Declamations' in Greek and Latin in the presence of the Minister, who then gave them direction and encouragement.31

Such was the daily curriculum and routine of the young Ralph Montagu, student at Westminster School. It may be assumed that this routine was in vogue in the year 1642, as shown in the writings of Philip Henry, diarist and childhood playmate of Charles II and James II,32 and as late as 1680.33 Ralph was schooled in the classical tradition; he knew well the Latin and Greek authors, and had some knowledge of Hebrew. Further, we may well believe that he knew his Bible, Psalter,

Gospels and Epistles. The method used in teaching was based on memorization. Hence a student, such as Ralph, had to be able to recite from memory long and difficult passages from the works studied, and be able to render what the instructor had offered or recite from the Sunday sermon.

Ralph possessed the requisite abilities as far as his studies were concerned. He was accomplished in Latin and proficient in the composition of verse in that medium. He authored a Latin eulogy at the age of ten or eleven, on the occasion of the death of Henry, Lord of Hastings, perhaps a benefactor of the school, and it was incorporated in the school publication--Lachrymae Musarum (1649). (See Appendix). One of Dryden's poems is also included in this publication.34

Unfortunately, nothing is known of Ralph's attitude towards school, his conduct, or his academic achievements. No records remain to make any judgments in these areas. All that is known is that Ralph Montagu attended the school and authored a Latin poem while there. Had he been an outstanding scholar or a notable discipline problem, one can suppose some sort of record would have been kept of these items. Therefore, negatively, Ralph was not a serious discipline problem but rather a normal, playful boy. As far as his studies are concerned, he was probably, with the exception of his Latin poem, an average pupil.

Theoretically, such an education, with its specific emphasis upon Christian morality, was intended to have a lasting influence upon the student. It was intended to

train him to live the godly life once he left the institution and entered upon his life's vocation. However,
this type of education did not exert an enduring influence on Montagu's life--at least in the formation of a
moral character. His later actions in life seem to
assume the attitude prevalent at the time--that of
`going through the motions since that was what was
expected of him.' Ralph was shrewd enough to realize
that one did not please in the circles of the elite
unless one outwardly adhered to the espoused and
expected course of action, especially in religious
matters. Such an attitude caused Montagu to forego any
deep interest in things religious except when they might
be used as a means to an end; particularly where he
thought there was some profit to espouse some religious
principle.

Nor did Ralph distinguish himself in school in
intellectual matters. There is no record of his being
awarded any prize for scholarship or for diligence in
studies. Again, Montagu approached even this aspect of
life with a practical view--he apparently applied
himself only to the degree that would allow him to avoid
failure. Schooling gave him the veneer of intellect and
manners suitable for one of his station. While he
seemingly appreciated the intellectual content of his
studies, as far as one can tell, one might also infer
that there remained some intangible, invisible residue,
for Ralph in his advanced age turned to the conversation
of such intellectuals as La Fontaine and St. Evermond,
as well as becoming a celebrated builder and an impressive and respected collector of art. For the moment,
however, his education gave him, in a practical sense,
access to a career at Court and supplied him with the

necessary background for making his way in the world of
men and their affairs.

The exact date of young Ralph's departure or
graduation from Westminster School is unknown. There
are no school records extant relating to either the
listings of his enrollment in, or leaving of the school.
Nor is there any evidence of Ralph's having `gone up' to
either Cambridge or Oxford. How old the lad was when he
departed the school is also a question; however, it is
reasonable to assume that he was probably sixteen or
seventeen years of age when he quitted Busby's guidance.

Montagu's early adult life is shrouded in mystery.
Exactly how he spent the next years (seven or eight) of
his life is not known. Perhaps he made the customary
`European Tour,' but there is no supporting evidence for
such a conjecture. Certainly, his largely classical
education eminently fitted him for such travel. His
later service to Charles II in France proved that he
knew French as well as Latin and Greek. Where he
learned this language is also something of a mystery--it
probably was the result of the care and concern of his
maternal grandmother, Lady Elizabeth Winwood, who saw to
it that he learned the amenities of life at her London
home in Smithfield, near St. Bartholomew-the-less Church
and hospital. Being a Winwood and possessing wealth--
her husband was once Secretary of State (1614-17)--it is
reasonable to suppose that she was involved in the
social and cultural whirl of the city. Hence, young
Ralph must have come into contact with the 'beautiful
people' of his generation and been, in some manner,
influenced towards cultivating a taste for the finer
things which was so characteristic of his later life.

He did not learn French at St. Peter's College
(Westminster School), for no 'modern' languages were
taught there -- Latin, Greek and Hebrew being the
curriculum. Then too, it was simply expected that one
would learn another language, especially French, on
one's own, since it was the unofficial language of the
educated person who wanted to make his way to Court.
What ensued from the time of his leaving Westminster to
the first documented event of his adulthood (1661) is
simply not known.

In 1661, the twenty-three year old Ralph became
joint keeper of Harleton Lodge in Richmond Park, along
with Sir Daniel Harvey, his future brother-in-law, for
the annual (shared?) fee of fifty pounds.[35] The next
year he came to Court and was appointed as Master of the
Horse to Anne, the Duchess of York.[36] In all probability, Montagu entered upon his career at Court through
the aegis of his older brother, Edward, who was already
at Court at this time serving as the Master of the Horse
to the Queen Consort, Catherine of Braganza.[37]

At the Court, Ralph soon acquired a reputation for
gallantry, and his rise in Court society owed much
apparently to the influence of the ladies. Ralph could
claim some recognition and preference at the Court by
reason of the service rendered to the Crown by his
relatives. His father had refused to participate in the
execution of Charles I. Together, father, brother
Edward, and indeed Ralph had enthusiastically endorsed
the restoration of Charles II. To aid him in his quest
for royal preferment, Ralph could also rely on his
wealthy grandmother, Lady Winwood. However, Ralph
relied, on himself and his personalily attributes: a

nimble wit, a suave manner, charm, and personal to
promote himself. Comte Philibert Gramont, a French
courtier, says of Montagu:

> It was Montagu, a person not at all formidable
> as far as his face was concerned, but very
> much to be feared on account of his assiduity,
> the agility of his wit, and certain other
> talents by no means despicable when once a
> suitor has received permission to bring them
> into play.[38]

In fact, Montagu could not depend on his father to
further his career at Court. Lord Montagu considered
the Restoration Court corrupt and ungodly, a cesspool of
immorality and the cause of the kingdom's evils--
attitudes that were widely known and noted in court
circles. Still, Charles II, upon his restoration,
endeavored to honor those who rendered him service and
aided his coming to the Throne; it was probably out of
this sense of loyalty that he accepted Edward and Ralph
in an official capacity at his Court.

Edward, an agreeable person and of an accomplished
nature, was dismissed from Court for squeezing the hand
of Queen Catherine, and went as a volunteer on board the
Earl of Sandwich's ship, and was killed in the Battle of
Bergen in August 1665. While at Court there was a
scandal directed towards him and his brother.

> There was some scandal at court directed
> against Edward and his brother Ralph, which
> seems to have troubled Pepys, as they were

"persons of honour." He notices a dispute
between the queen's Lord Chamberlain, Chesterfield, and Edward Montagu, her Master of the
Horse, as to "who should have the precedence
in taking the queen's upper hand abroad, out
of the house, which Mr. Montagu challenges.
It was given to my Lord Chesterfield; so that
I perceive," adds the diarist, "he goes down
the wind in honour as well as in everything
else, every day." Pepys was at feud with
Edward Montagu, and loses no opportunity of
speaking ill of him, though he was warned by
Lord Sandwich to be on his guard against doing
so publicly, lest he should suffer by the
other's passion. Montagu's alleged ingrati-
tude to his cousin Sandwich is said to have
excited the wrath of Pepys, who thus joyously
narrates the details of Edward Montagu's disgrace at court: "20th May, 1664. Mr. Edward
Montagu is turned out of the court, not to
return again. His fault, I perceive, was his
pride, and most of all, his affecting to be
great with the queen; and it seems, indeed, he
made more of her care than everybody else, and
would be with her talking alone, two or three
hours together, insomuch that the lords about
the king, when he would be jesting with them
about their wives, would tell the king that he
must have a care of his wife, too, for she
hath now the gallant; and they say the king
himself did once ask Montagu how his mistress,
meaning the queen, did. He grew so proud, and
despised everybody, besides suffering nobody,
he or she, to get and do anything about the

queen, that they all laboured to do him a good turn. . . Strange it is that this man should, from the greatest negligence in the world, come to be the miracle of attendance, so as to take all offices from everybody, either men or women, about the queen. So he is gone, nobody pitying, but laughing at him; and he pretends only that he is gone to his father, who is sick in the country." There is evidently prejudice in all this. The Comte de Comminges, French ambassador in London, writing on this subject to Louis XIV., says, "M. de Montagu, Master of the Horse to the Queen of England, as well made and as witty a gentleman as any at this court, has received orders to retire to the country. His disgrace is privately discussed; but people are agreed that this new Tantalus has not been discreet in his views, but has pushed these so far that they took light in the source of light itself." The Frenchman thought none the worse of Edward Montagu for a gallant homage rendered to the queen. If there was fault, it was effaced by his death in action at the sea-fight off Bergen, a death which opened the barony of Montagu to the second son of the first lord, Ralph, who was subsequently created Duke of Montagu.[39]

Pepys relates the story of a duel between Edward Montagu and one Mr. Chomley, first gentleman-usher to the Queen. Mr. Chomley supposedly received:

...many affronts from Mr. Montagu.... He proved too hard for Montagu, and drove him so far backward that he fell into a ditch, and dropt his sword, but with honour would take no advantage over him; but did give him his life; and the world says Mr. Montagu did carry himself very poorly in the business, and hath lost honour for ever with all people in it, of which I am very glad, in hopes that it will humble him.[40]

In 1662 Charles decided that an alliance with France would be of great benefit to him and so desired for a closer friendship with the French King, Louis XIV. Charles, of course, was astute enough to realize that such an alliance would not be readily accepted by his people and that he must act warily in this matter. The mood of the people necessitated caution. Any alliance with France was automatically suspect; it smacked of Popery. Charles had to take into account the very real and very strong anti-French and anti-Catholic sentiments of his people. Any misjudgment on his part could easily inflame his nation and lead to an open rebellion. Eventually, Charles arrived at the idea of a treaty of commerce between the nations--this would be a most effective way of screening his motives and a most satis-factory means of preparing his people for such an alliance. Under cover of commercial negotiations Charles proposed to discuss with Louis XIV in a secret manner ways and means of securing closer cooperation between the two sovereign states. Charles also decided that no better agent for these negotiations could be found than his sister, Henriette Anne, sister-in-law to Louis XIV. Secrecy was of absolute necessity if an alliance was to be formed. Whom could he send on a mission of such delicacy--one that involved the sending of highly secret and sensitive information to his sister?[41] Charles finally decided on a young courtier named Ralph Montagu.

Montagu had not been long at court before he was noticed by Charles. Impressed with Montagu's qualities, Charles decided to make use of his talents by employing him in the royal service.[42] The King chose him as his representative in this delicate mission and his choice was to be a decisive factor in the young courtier's life. It gave him an inflated sense of self-worth and dignity. This mission, although not of a long duration-- perhaps six months - - Oct. 1662-Feb. 1663--was to give Montagu his first real taste of court intrigues and of foreign diplomacy. It gave him the giddying sensation of the exercise of power, although on a limited basis, which was to have a lasting impact upon his choice of a life style and of the means to obtain it. This surprise choice of an obscure courtier by Charles was to have far-reaching effects upon King, nation and the agent himself.

Accordingly, Montagu, at age 24, was sent as envoy to France to conduct the necessary negotiations. He carried two letters from Charles to Henriette Anne: one a letter of credence which introduced him to Louis as Charles' representative, the other introduced him to her "as one well instructed as he will inform of all that passes here."[43]

Madame (Henriette Anne) was quite thrilled to meet this urbane and well mannered messenger from London who was the bearer of all the latest news of the English

Court. Montagu, as Charles' representative, apparently received every courtesy and even a most cordial welcome by Louis himself. He returned to England in February 1663 much impressed with things French, an impression that was to remain with him all his life and which influenced his taste in art and architecture. His admiration for the French Court, with its gaiety and splendor, was to be the standard by which he judged life. Having been the guest of the French King and Madame at lavish entertainments--masques and balls--he could not but be impressed by the opulence and magnificence of those galas with their beauty of jewels and costumes.[44]

Upon Montagu's return, Charles, in a playful mood, wrote his sister (Feb. 9, 1663) a letter in which he ridiculed Montagu. Henriette Anne was Charles' favorite sister, and as such, she was the recipient of his confidences, pleasantries and caprices.

> Mr. Montagu is arrived heere, and I wonder Monsieur (Phillippe, Duc d'Orleans) would lett him stay with you so long, for he is undoubtedly in love with you, but I ought not to complaine, haveing given me a very fine sword and belt which I do not believe was out of pure liberality but because I am your brother.[45]

With the completion of his mission, Montagu receded from the limelight. He now had to be content with the relatively minor position of Master of the Horse to Anne (Hyde), the Duchess of York. However, it was not to be too long before Ralph received advancement at Court.

Later that year Ralph was appointed to take his brother's place, as Master of the House but it was not an automatic promotion. Perhaps Charles feared that Montagu might have the same failings as his brother and looked upon him with a jaundiced eye. It was only through the insistance of the Duchess of York, to make place for Henry Sidney, one of her favorites, with James, the Duke of York, Charles's brother, that Montagu was made Master of the Horse to Queen Catherine.46

For the next three years (1665-68) Montagu remained at Court in his capacity as Master of the Horse awaiting an opportunity that could be turned to his advantage. To remain in such a minor position for the rest of his life was not to his liking. He aspired to greater things. Montagu felt his qualities and talents deserved much more than a minor place--hence, his thoughts turned to diplomacy as the means of advancement at Court. Why not an ambassadorship? Why not sue for the post at Paris? Having been there already he had an advantage; he still had contacts there. The memory of Paris still lingered and it lured him back.

Not one to let any advantage slip by, Montagu entreated his sister, Elizabeth, Lady Harvey, Ralph's ardent supporter and intimate in all things and a close friend of Mary Fairfax, the Duchess of Buckingham, to use her influence with Mary to win her husband, the Duke (George Villiers), to his designs. Montagu and his sister felt deep affection and admiration for each other; they were very close as children and as adults. Their actions in this incident and later on show that they apparently shared the same attitude about Court life and its adornments of power and honor. They seemingly had a mutual liking for intrigue and delighted in the sense of power and importance that the shaping of events in secret gave. Further, Elizabeth, as a close friend of the Duchess of Buckingham, well knew the importance of patronage in the attainment of high office.[47] Practically any office was obtainable for the right price provided one had a powerful patron at Court who lent his or her voice on the suppliant's behalf. Elizabeth did not hesitate to use her friendship with the Duchess to influence the Duke to become her brother's patron. She was not averse to using any means that would aid Montagu in his quest for `royal' employment and advancement.

The Duke agreed to help. Perhaps he viewed Montagu as a future ally, one whom he could manipulate to his advantage. Twice Buckingham appealed to the King on Montagu's behalf, and twice the King refused. Charles insisted that Montagu was too young and inexperienced. He preferred to send the 2nd Earl of Sunderland, Robert Spencer, as Ambassador. Montagu, realizing that Buckingham's intervention proved fruitless, turned to the Secretary of State, Lord Arlington (Henry Bennet), and enlisted his help in his petition to the King.

In a letter to Arlington, Montagu openly revealed both his ambition and frustration:

> 1688, [July 20], Monday noon, London. -- Since your Lordship went out of town, my Lord Buching[h]am spoke twice to the King about declaring me his Embassadour to France. The first time the King asked him whether he did not think I was too young; the second time he

asked him what he thought of my Lord
Sunderland's going; whereupon my Lord Duke
says he gave him some reasons in favour of me,
which made him not insist upon my Lord
Sunderland, but yet [he] did not at that time
resolve anything. Now, my Lord, since the
King has of himself taken away his own
objection by naming a younger man than myself
to the same employment he thought me too young
for, I hope your Loordship will be so kind to
me as in your next letter to the Treasurer to
say something that may move the king to
determine this in my favour.[48]

With Arlington's aid, Montagu finally secured his
appointment as ambassador to France (1668). Arlington
saw Montagu as an ambitious young man, but he was also a
man of intelligence and shrewdness, a man who could be a
most useful ally.[49]

Montagu, Ambassador to the Court of Louis XIV, was
instructed to act merely as the King's representative.
He was not to be admitted to any of the secret negotiations that eventually would lead to the Treaty of Dover.
This is really not so surprising when the extremely
delicate and volatile nature of the negotiations is
recalled. Charles could simply not take the chance of
the possibility of a mishap through an inadvertant act
or word on the part of his ambassador. Also, Louis
allowed the French ambassador to England to remain
ignorant of the ongoing negotiations. Neither King was
willing to allow any more people to be privy to the
Treaty than was absolutely necessary. Although Montagu

was appointed ambassador in the summer of 1668, he did not take up his post till the following Spring. His instructions and letter of credence are dated February 1669.[50]

Montagu returned to France in the official capacity of ambassador, a position he had been most desirous to obtain. He now devoted his time and talents to fostering his career as a means to a life of wealth and power.

A man of reasonable intelligence and of real determination, Montagu had the capacity to succeed. He was educated, urbane, suave, talented and ambitious. Furthermore, he had the proper background and family connections so necessary to achieving success in court politics.

CHAPTER I
Footnotes

[1]The Court in Mourning, p. 2.

[2]Stone, Lawrence, "Literacy and Education in England 1640-1900," Past and Present. 42. February 1969, 71.

[3]Ibid., p. 73.

[4]Ibid., p. 90.

[5]Charles Firth, "Montagu, Ralph, duke of Montagu (1638?-1709)," Dictionary of National Biography. 13, 710-713; George Edward Cockayne, The Complete Peerage, Revised ed., eds., H. A. Doubleday and Lord Howard de Walden (London: St. Catherine Press, 1936) IX, 106.

[6]Ester S. Cope. The Life of a Public Man. Edward, First Baron Montagu of Boughton, 1562-1644 (Philadelphia: The American Philosophical Society, 1981), p. 7.

[7]William Hunt, "Montagu or Mountague, James (1568?-1618)," Dictionary of National Biography. 13, 698-99; Gerald Patrick Moriarty, "Montagu, or more properly Mountague, Edward, first Earl of Sandwich (1625-1672)." Dictionary of National Biography. 13, 679-684; Bertha Porter, "Edward Montagu, first Baron of Boughton (1562-1644), Dictionary of National Biography. 13, 672-673; James McMullen Rigg, "Montagu, Sir Henry, first Earl of Manchester (1563?-1642)," Dictionary of National Biography. 13, 696-697; Cockayne, IX, 104, notes a and b; Cope, p. 3, p. 81, p. 90, p. 186.

[8]William Drago Montagu, Court and Society from Elizabeth to Anne Edited from the Papers at Kimbolton, by the Duke of Manchester (London: Hurst and Blackett, 1864), I, 272.

[9]Thompson Cooper, "Montagu, Walter (1603?-1677)," Dictionary of National Biography. 13, 171-719.

[10]Bertha Porter, "Edward Montagu, second Baron Montagu of Boughton (1616-1684)," Dictionary of National Biography. 13, 673; Cockayne, IX, 105.

11Cockayne, IX, 105, footnote a.

[12]Charles Wise, The Montagus of Boughton and Their Northamptonshire Homes (Kettering: W. F. & J. Goss, 1888), p. 36; Cockayne, IX, 106.

13Sidney Lee, "Winwood, Sir Ralph (1563?-1617)," Dictionary of National Biography. 21, 704-707; Cockayne, IX, 105-106.

[14]Porter, "Edward Montagu, second Baron Montagu of Boughton," p. 673; Cope, pp. 194-197.

[15]Porter, "Edward Montagu, second Baron Montagu of Boughton," p. 673; Cope, p. 3.

[16]Cope, p. 3.

[17]Porter, "Edward Montagu, second Baron Montagu of Boughton," p. 673.

[18]Cope, pp. 86-89.

[19]G. F. Russell Barker and Alan H. Stenning, The Records of Old Westminster (London: Cheswich Press, 1928), II, 656; Cockayne, IX, 106.

[20]G. F. Russell Barker, Memoir of Richard Busby, D.D. (1606-1695) With Some Account of Westminster School in the Seventeenth Century (London: Lawrence and Bullen, 1895), p. 85.

[21]Great Britain, Historical Manuscripts Commission, Report on the Manuscripts of Lord Montagu of Beaulieu (London: Edw. Eyre and Wm. Spottiswoode, 1990), I. 164. See also letters of July 5 and July 25, 1648, p. 111 and p. 162.

[22]Barker, pp. 24-26.

[23]Richard Steele, The Lover, 27th April 1714, No. 27; Barker, pp. 26-27.

[24]Barker, p. 27, footnote 1.

[25]Ibid., p. 15-16.

[26]Ibid., p. 27.

[27]Ibid., pp. 27-29.

[28]C. W. J. Higson, Supplement to Sources for the History of Education (London: The Library Association, 1976), p.5.

[29]Barker, pp. 77-81.

[30]Ibid., pp. 80-81.

[31]Barker, Memoir of Richard Busby p. 82.

[32]Mathew Henry Lee, ed., Diaries and Letters of Philip Henry (London: Kegan Paul & Co., 1882), pp. 9-11; Barker, pp. 83-85; Nicholas Carlisle, A Concise Description of the Endowed Grammar Schools in England and Wales (London: W. Blumer and Co., 1818), pp. 107-113; John Sergeant 1542-55. A handwritten exposition of eight pages dealing with the horarium [daily schedule] of the school. Marked D4 AE1 as found in the Library of the school Westminster.

[33]Dulwich MSS. Collection. 2nd Series, XXIX. Register of Accounts 1680-1714/5 - The Third Book, under Letter W. (Westminster School).

[34]_____, Lachrymae Musarum: The Tears of the Muses; Written by divers persons of Nobility and Worth, Upon the deathe of the most hopefull, Henry Lord Hastings, Collected and set forth by R.B. (London: Printed by T.N,, 1650), p. 98; Mark Noble, A Biographical History of England from the Revolution to the End of the George I's Reign (London: W. Richardson, 1806), II, 36.

[35]William A. Shaw, ed. Calendar of Treasury Books, 1660-1677 (London: Mackie and Co., Ltd., 1904) I, 612; Cockayne, IX, 106.

[36]Barker, Records of Old Westminster, p. 656; Julia Cartwright, Madame: A Life of Henrietta, Daughter of Charles I and Duchessof Orleans (New York: E.P. Dutton and Co., 1901), p. 123; Cyril Hughes Hartman, The King My Brother (London: Wm. Heinmann, 1954), pp. 52-53; Firth, p. 710.

[37]Firth, p. 710; Burke, p. 374; Cockayne, IX, 106.

[38]Peter Quennell, trans. Memoirs of the Court of Charles II by Comte de Gramont. (London: George Routledge and Sons, Ltd., 1930), p. 115; - Bishop Burnet, History of His Own Time: With Notes by the Earls of Dartmouth and Hardwicke, Speaker Onslow, and Dean Swift (Oxford: University Press, 1833), I, 616; Firth, p. 710.

[39]Montagu, I, 273-75.

[40]Henry B. Wheatley, ed., The Diary of Samuel Pepys (London: George Bell and Sons, 1904), II, 280-281.

[41]Hartmann, pp. 52-53.

[42]The Court in Mourning, p. 1.

[43]Cyril Hughes Hartmann, Charles II and Madame (London: Wm. Heinneman, Ltd., 1943), p. 58.

[44]Ibid., pp. 67-68.

[45]Ibid., p. 68

[46]Montagu, I, 273; Cockayne, IX, 106; Firth, p. 710.

[47]Bernard Falk, The Way of the Montagues: A Gallery of Family Portraits (London: Hutchinson and Co., Ltd., 1947), p. 77

[48]Buccleuch MSS. I, 420.

[49]Falk, pp. 77-79.

[50]Rawlinson MSS. A. 225. ff. 79-82. Calendar of Treasury Books, 1667-68, p. 644; S.P. Dom. Entry Book, 30, f. 107b.

CHAPTER II
Montagu, Envoy to Henriette Anne

...he was in the Year 1669, chosen by the
Prince to be his Ambassador Extraordinary to
the Court of France; for which Embassy he
prepared a very splendid Train, with which he
sail'd for France about the beginning of
April, in the Year afore-said, where he was
receiv'd with great Magnificence, and a vast
Equipage was preparing for him to make his
Publick Entry, which he did on the 25th of
April, in most splendid manner, that the like
had never been seen in France before....1

Montagu arrived in Paris in April of 1669 as
Ambassador to the Court of Louis XIV. His mission,
ostensibly, was to represent Charles II's government in
the diplomatic relations between the two countries, but
in reality, and unknown to Montagu, he was again to be
only a liaison between Charles and his sister, Henriette
Anne, for the purpose of negotiating the secret treaty
between England and France. Charles, at first, did not
allow Montagu to participate directly in the actual
negotiations of the secret treaty (Treaty of Dover,
1670). He restricted Montagu's role to that of a
messenger or courtier.

When he ascended the English throne, Charles
followed a duplicitous policy. While he openly

proclaimed his intention to preserve England's anti-French and anti-Catholic policies, [Charles] secretly sought to unite his fortune with those of [Louis XIV], whom he came to know and admire greatly during his exile in France. He felt an affection and admiration for the French monarch and fashioned many of his ideas of government on concepts learned from the Sun King. Charles desired to rival Louis and extend England's influence beyond the Channel. In imitation of Louis, Charles wanted to further his own _gloire_, i.e. to use the talents given him by God in behalf of his kingdom.2 It was a duty that could not be evaded. Such thinking led Charles to believe, as Louis did, that the nation and its people were his property and that it was his duty to rule in place of God. Any increase in the renown of the land was, in actuality, an increase in the personal renown of the King. The King and the land were one. Yet Charles realized that, however much he envied Louis his personal rule, this was impossible in England. He had to take into account the desires of his subjects as they were reflected in the Parliament.

Charles recognized the limitations that such a body placed on his rule both at home (he remembered the object lesson of his father's death by Parliamentarian order) and abroad and hoped to neutralize it. However, to do so demanded that he free himself of Parliament. But such freedom required financial independence. This was difficult since Parliament, in 1665, assumed to itself the power to appropriate funds for the Crown and then specify the use of such funds. In 1667, Commons complicated matters further by establishing a committee to oversee and audit the use of public monies.[3]

Charles came to believe that any hope for fiscal independence and personal rule depended on France. He began to make secret overtures to Louis for the purpose of forming a binding alliance between themselves. However, Charles, conscious of the distrust and hatred of the French so alive in his country and of the need to placate his subjects, entered into an alliance in 1668 with Holland, England's former enemy in the commercial wars of 1652 and 1665, and with Sweden. Charles decided to use the Triple Alliance's anti-French policy to lull the Commons into a false sense of security. The League sought to contain French expansionism in Flanders and force an agreement for the restoration of peace in Europe. As an anti-French policy, it was received enthusiastically by the English. Ironically, its popularity gave Charles the freedom he so desired to continue his secret negotiations with France. Charles thought that his boldness in forming such an alliance in the face of Louis' possible disfavor would impress Louis with his diplomatic ability. He intended to pass a signal to Louis that England was a power to be reckoned with and that an alliance with England had real value. Negotiations were then conducted in secret. So secret were the negotiations that neither ambassador, (French or English), knew anything about their true nature. Nor did the King's councillors, including the Duke of Buckingham, know of them. Meanwhile, Arlington was ordered to carry on diplomatic negotiation with the Dutch so as to deceive them concerning Charles' real intentions.[4]

However, before actual negotiations began, Charles prepared the way by employing Henriette Anne, whom he had affectionately nicknamed `Minette,' or `little puss,' in the negotiations. Catholic and married to

Louis' brother, the Duc d'Orleans, in 1661, she was the second most powerful woman in France. Full of life, witty and physically charming--of a rosy complexion, with chestnut hair and blue eyes, she possessed a full rich figure--she was able to influence the men whom she met.[5] "All France was at her doors, the men thought of nothing but to pay their court to her, and all women strove to please her."[6] Using these attributes, she overcame any objections on the part of either monarch to the Treaty. Moreover, she was, in all probability, primarily responsible for the inclusion of the famous article concerning Charles' open declaration of Catholicism. Charles informed her that he would first begin with a treaty of commerce in order to make any dealings with the French acceptable at home. On March 7, 1669, he sent Lord Arundell of Wardour, Roman Catholic and Master of Horse to Henrietta Maria, Charles' mother, as negotiator for a commercial treaty. Charles believed that Arundell would not be suspected of opening secret negotiations. Arundell received instructions from Charles to emphasize the Catholic policy and to request the suspension of the construction of French warships for one year.[7] Charles viewed a strong French navy as a real threat to his own navy.

Early in 1669, James, Charles' brother and Duke of York, announced his conversion to the Catholic faith. With this announcement, Charles made known his intentions to Louis of promoting Catholicism in England.[8] However, in order to translate this intention into reality, he needed help. To obtain this assistance Charles made known his ready desire to enter into secret negotiations with France which eventually led to the signing of the Secret Treaty of Dover (1670). By Treaty Charles bound himself to assist Louis in a war with

Holland in return for a large subsidy. However, the payment of this subsidy depended upon Charles' conversion to the Catholic faith.

Charles was to make public his conversion to Roman Catholicism and to reconcile England with Rome at the most propitious moment--the moment was left to Charles' judgment. Charles could then ask for the sum of two million livres--half to be paid three months after the ratification of the treaty, the other half due some three months thereafter. Should Charles need troops to make good his commitment, Louis would send, at his own expense, some six thousand troops to help quell any opposition that might arise. Charles indicated his readiness to Louis to declare his conversion, but he felt he must delay this announcement inasmuch as Louis demanded Holland be dealt with first.

Charles' desperation for money played an important part in determining his actions in this matter of the treaty. Charles, in all probability, probably used his proposed declaration for Catholicism as a ploy to dupe Louis into granting him subsidies. The sums ordered by Commons amounted to over a million and a half pounds, while Louis's subsidy was to total only one hundred seventy thousand pounds. Under these circumstances, the subsidy promised by Louis seemed hardly a sum worth risking his crown for. Why should Charles venture into such folly? Was it Henriette Anne, a devout Catholic, who influenced Charles so strongly in this direction? Possibly. Charles adored her and could refuse her nothing. However, all evidence points to the contrary. In all his dealings with women, Charles never allowed any woman to shape his political judgment. The deciding factor may have been an ever increasingly hostile Parliament. Charles regarded this body as one which would never allow him to solve his financial problems independently and which wanted to keep him tied to it by the purse strings. Charles sought ways to free himself from any obligation to or dependence upon it. In Charles' eyes, Louis with his offer of money was heaven sent.[9]

Charles used the intervention of his sister for the actual negotiations of the treaty, while using Montagu and his diplomatic pouch as his liaison with her. Montagu acted as courier--receiving and delivering Charles' messages, and, in turn, sending on Henriette's replies. Montagu was therefore part of the negotiations, but at no time was he privy to the actual terms of the treaty. He was trusted, but only so far.[10] Nevertheless, his appointment seemed at last to start him on his way to fame and fortune, or so he thought. As he stated to William Temple three years later:

> ... told sir William Temple, he designed to go
> ambassador to France. Sir William asked how
> that could be; for he knew the King did not
> love him, and the duke hated him. "That's
> true," said he, "but they shall do, as if they
> loved me." Which, sir William told, he soon
> brought about, as he supposed, by means of the
> ladies, who were always his best friends, for
> some secret perfections, that were hid from
> the rest of the world.[11]

Montagu, just appointed Ambassador Extraordinary to France, was preparing for his departure from England when his name became linked to a scandal caused by his sister, Elizabeth. Five years previous he had to endure the humiliation of his brother's (Edward) "scandalous" behavior with Queen Catherine. However sad this incident may have been, it was fortuitous for Montagu since it led to his advancement in the King's service. Montagu must now certainly have been aware of the possible damage to his good name that a scandal could bring and of the potential danger to his mission that this incident of his sister with a page could cause him. Elizabeth killed one of her pages with a sword, claiming he attacked her. Fortunately, for him, however, little was made of it and Montagu was allowed to enter upon his embassy.

Leaving England in the Spring of 1669, his instructions and letter of credence dated February 6, 1669, Montagu traveled to Paris. He was accompanied on his journey by Queen Catherine's Almoner, Fr. Patrick Maginn, a Catholic Priest whom Charles held in high regard, who was on his way to France for reasons of health. Montagu wrote Arlington (March 8/18/1669) upon his landing from Calais that Fr. Patrick was recovering from his illness and that by the time they reached Paris the priest would be fit to return home.[12]

Once in his post as ambassador at Paris, Montagu set to work to ingratiate himself with his master with a view to advancing himself. Being an ambitious man, he resolved to be a worthy ambassador and as such he took his duties seriously. From the first moment of his reception and his initial address as representative of his King to the final ciphering and transmission of intelligence gathered, by official and unofficial means, which any ambassador of the age considered it his duty to collect as a resident agent of his sovereign, Montagu acted as the King's man. In early letters Montagu indicates how he undertook to carry out the ceremonial courtesies so important a part of the embassy and restricted himself to such matters of particular negotiation as were formally stated in his introduction. As yet, unaware of Charles' aims, he played no part in the execution of the shaping of high policy outside the limits of his appointment.[13]

Montagu was chosen ambassador not for any outstanding merit of his own, but after long deliberation by Charles and then only through the intercession of Arlington. He was to go to Paris merely as the King's official representative and was not to be privy to even the less secret parts of the treaty negotiations. Above all, Madame was to be careful of what she said to him; Montagu was to know nothing of the projected alliance.[14]

Established in Paris, Montagu's letters immediately reveal his not too happy adjustment to mundane affairs such as his place of residence. He did not conceal his pique at being forced to take housing, found for him by his secretary, De Moulin, which he termed "ill lodgings not fit for a dog to lie in."[15] Shortly after his arrival in Paris Montagu began to prepare for his public entry into the capitol and his first public address to Louis on behalf of Charles. The public entry of an ambassador was of vast importance. The more magnificent the entry of the agent the greater and more powerful was his sovereign. In other words, the display of the envoy was the gauge of the glory and power of the monarch.

Montagu entered Paris on the 25th of April, 1669 with a magnificence never before seen in France:

His Excellency, accompanied by several of the English Nobility and Gentry, attended by a Gentleman of the Horse, and twelve pages; fifty-six footmen, twelve Led Horses; four Coaches with eight Horses, and two Chariots with six Horses, was received by several of the French Nobility and conducted to the Hotel, reserv'd in Paris for the Entertainment of Foreign Ambassadors....16

On the 27th of April Montagu had his first public audience with Louis XIV, "...which for a distinguishing Mark of Honour he had in his Most Christian Majesty's Bed Chamber and within the Rails round the Bed, where the King stood to receive him."17 Montagu thereupon presented his credentials as ambassador and delivered his first address. Following this ceremony, he was presented to the Dauphin and the rest of the Royal Family, and was, by Louis's express order, shown the most singular marks of honor and respect.18 Montagu then went to Versailles for several days and was once again entertained in a magnificent manner. "Here it was his Grace [Montagu] formed his idea of building and gardening, erecting his Seat at Boughton, in Northamptonshire, after the pattern and as his dimensions would allow, after the model of Versailles."19

As ambassador, Montagu knew that he was expected to

spend money freely. This free use of money was consistent with the philosophy that the magnificence of the ambassador reflected the power and glory of the sovereign. Shows of splendor and the lavish bestowal of gifts by the envoy were both expected and necessary. Should this be neglected, the ambassador was likely to have difficulty in finding entry to the Court or access to information necessary to keep his monarch well informed. What was worse, the reputation and honor of his sovereign would suffer diminution. Hence Montagu's very lavish display of pomp and magnificence upon his public entry.

Montagu almost immediately became known in Paris for his largesse and ostentation. However, all this pageantry, entertainment and the giving of gifts was expensive. Montagu was given one thousand five hundred pounds for his equipage and one hundred pounds a week (1676-77) for maintenance, entertainment, intelligence money and such sums as were allowed by the Secretary of State.[20] This was not that large an amount since the ambassador was expected to conduct his everyday business from this sum and at the same time to be able to distribute his gifts in order to produce the desired results.

Even though promised a regular salary and an allowance for expenses, Montagu often received only part of the promised salary or of the allowance for his expenses as ambassador. Presumably, his lodgings in Paris, employment of servants, the giving of dinner parties, masques or balls that he as ambassador was expected to give, travel and lodging on official business, any information purchased for his government was often paid in part with his own monies. Frequently the cost of ambassadorship exceeded the income from the Crown. The amount of money Montagu spent as ambassador is unknown, but it must have been a considerable amount. He later (1683) petitioned for the amount of twenty-two thousand pounds as back salary; hence, it can be assumed that the amount he spent equaled this amount or exceeded it. He claimed he was never paid his full salary and later petitioned for money with which to cover ambassadorial expenses.

As one who rendered no service without a price, he naturally expected to be reimbursed. His letters to Arlington and Coventry constantly complain that he is short of funds caused by the delay in being paid while at the same time being forced to meet expenses out of his own pocket, e.g. the expenses he incurred for his `mourning' for the death of the Queen Mother (one thousand three hundred and eighty-two pounds).[21]

Montagu's public entry posed diplomatic difficult- ies with the envoys of other countries and the royal family itself as to the question of precedence. Just where was he to ride in the royal procession? Due to the intercession of Madame, a compromise was reached, who as Montagu said, "understands all these things extreamly well, and is in all points that concerne the king's Honor equally concerned with himselfe."[22]

Montagu revealed in a letter to Arlington, dated April 20th, to what childish lengths the questions of precedence could go.

My two coaches are to goe immediately after the kings in which I am to be and just before

the queens coach, this ranke that I take is
judged by every body as the most Honourable,
for if I should put my coaches before the
kings in which I am it would be improper to
have them goe before my selfe, and they would
be in noe Rank at all, as it was when Lord St.
Albans was Ambassador and had the Queene
mothers armes on his coaches, they made him
goe a mile before as if they did not belong to
the traine. I have desired Madame to give his
Majestye this account too, who is convinced
that there cannot be more Honour done to the
queene of Englands coach then this way that I
have taken.[23]

Technically, had Montagu insisted, his coach, by reason
of precedence, could have preceded even that of a King
of France. However, Montagu carefully avoided making a
`diplomatic scene' and all went well with the entry.

Montagu's entry was, above all, colorful: it was a
most splendid equipage. Accompanied by seventy-four
pages and footmen in magnificent attire and twenty-four
gentlemen on horseback, the ambassador made his entry.[24]

Eventually, Montagu came to believe that something
was going on behind his back. He felt that he was being
ill-used, and began to think that it was on account of
his friendship with Arlington that he was being kept in
the dark. In a letter dated 23rd of April he observed:

This court is much like ours in England, full
of cabals and stories, of which I have a great
many brought to me. How true they are your

Lordship may best judge. The hearing of some
of them has made me forbear saying much to
Madame about your Lordship, for though I
believe she would be very glad of having a
good understanding with you, yet she acts so
contrary to what should make it, that I think
it would not yet be safe to put yourself at
all into her hands. I heard from a very good
author that she told the King of France there
was no good to be expected from me, for I was
sent hither to do just as you pleased and
directed, which here they do not think is
likely to be much to their satisfaction, but
that for my Lord Buckingham she durst almost
answer for; and I see plainly that they design
here as they did [in] England to make you and
my Lord Duke fall out, and everybody is very
inquisitive of me about it; but I assure them
they will never see any such thing.25

Lord Arlington (Henry Bennett), Secretary of State
to Charles, was a man of stately bearing and ever the
minister of his king. He was easily recognized by a
strip of black plaster which he constantly wore across
his nose covering a wound received in a skirmish at
Andover in the Civil Wars. The French viewed him as an
enemy of their interests because of his avowed anti-
French policy. As such he was held in distrust by
Henriette Anne. Undaunted by her attitude, Montagu, who
regarded Arlington at this time as his friend and
mentor, attempted to convince her that Arlington was not
the enemy of France she imagined him to be. When asked
why she did not care for him, and what caused her
dissatisfaction with him, Madame replied that she

thought Arlington slighted her and her friendship--he never answered her letters whenever she wrote him. In reply to this criticism, Montagu tried to soothe her injured feelings by urging upon her the need for the Secretary to be at his cautious best at all times lest he present opportunities to his enemies for reprisal. Montagu then intimated to Arlington the real necessity for him to be on good terms with her and the advantages that would accrue from such a friendship.

Montagu soon came to know how much Charles II trusted and confided in Madame. Madame was privy to much diplomatic maneuvering. She showed Montagu the King's letters, letters in which Montagu noted that Charles freely opened his mind to her and spoke of very private matters. Montagu then urged Arlington to write her a letter of a soothing tone in which he assured her of his `devotion' to her. He warned Arlington that he had enemies in France who would like nothing better than to nurture her prejudice against him. The French ambassador, Colbert de Croissy, brother of Louis XIV's minister of finance, in England helped foster this prejudice by reporting to her that if it were not for Arlington France and England would have formed an alliance before this, but as long as Arlington remained in power there would be no union.26

Montagu lost no opportunity to put Madame's mind at rest concerning Arlington and attempted to influence others to a good opinion about him. He informed Lionne, Louis XIV's Secretary of State, that it was a tragic mistake to regard Arlington as being in the Spanish camp. Lionne replied that nobody but a Spaniard would have helped form the Triple Alliance. Montagu wrote

Arlington (May 8, 1669):

> I told him I thought it was rather a mark of
> your being a Frenchman, for that by the ligue
> you had put the King your master upon equal
> terms with the King his master, which is the
> only way to make a proud nation and stout
> people, as the English are, ever to agree with
> the French; and whilst we were upon unequal
> terms, there never could be any Alliance nor
> friendship thought of. After this he had not
> much to say against you, but rallying thanked
> me for the good news I told him.27

In another letter of the same date, Montagu
complained of his cousin, the Abbe Walter Montagu, whom
he found to be useless to him in the field of diplomacy
since he was, as Montagu stated, rather ignorant and
"out of fashion."28 Walter Montagu converted to
Catholicism in 1635 and was made Abbot of the
Benedictine Monastery of St. Martin's at Pontoise in
1649. He later became Chief Almoner to Queen Catherine,
Henrietta Maria, Charles' mother, and Henriette Anne,
and in this trust he was consulted in matters of state.
His relationship to the two eventually brought him into
the negotiations for the Treaty of Dover as official
translator of documents from French to English and vice
versa.

Arlington found an enemy in the French ambassador
to the English Court. He disliked de Croissy and found
him to be heavy handed and arrogant. Accordingly, he

urged Montagu to do his best to have him recalled by Louis.[29] When Madame indicated to Montagu that Buckingham's letters were constantly alluding to de Croissy in a derogatory fashion, Montagu seized the initiative:

> ...so I took up the discourse and told her that I wondered, being that France has such a mind to gain England of their side, that they did not send a man of more address and better understanding and quality, who, by his credit and the good opinion we should have of him, might incline us to comply with what they desire. She told me that here they thought to have made us a great compliment in sending the chief Minister's brother, who would see everything performed that his brother should engage for in England. Upon conclusion, I found Madame would be very glad there could be another man sent, but that by reason of Mr. Colbert's great credit here she was not willing to meddle in the recalling of him, for fear of displeasing the French king. I told her what I said was only a fancy of my own, and that out of my good wishes to both the Crowns I was sorry to see a man employed in a business of that consequence, of whom all the Ministers that he must have to do with have so ill an opinion. (May 24)[30]

In addition to the ill feeling and distrust at the ministerial level, Charles began to be piqued at how matters were progressing. He resented that Louis had now seen fit to allow de Croissy full participation in the secret negotiations. Charles was of the opinion that it was not yet time to let either de Croissy or Montagu participate. Also, de Croissy's arrogance and condescending manner alienated him at the English Court and he was becoming a liability to the French. De Croissy was losing credibility and his abilities were no longer highly regarded by Charles and his ministers. Louis did his best to honor Charles' wishes and de Croissy was `kept at arm's length.' He was deliberately kept in the dark as to the actual goings on.

Charles and Arlington managed to keep the negotiations so secret that even Buckingham (as handsome as his father and equally as foolish), who prided himself on being `in the know' of things diplomatic, and ever eager to be in the limelight, was kept in ignorance of the treaty. However, Buckingham became suspicious of Montagu's and Madame's activities. As a person who could easily imagine that he was being snubbed, Buckingham complained to Madame, that he was being ignored by her. She then hastened to reassure him and easily calmed his anxieties.[31] In the meantime, Charles anxiously awaited word from Paris about the treaty. He was anxious to know what France would do, Triple Alliance or no Triple Alliance.[32]

Montagu continued to plead Arlington's loyalty and suitability with Madame. He praised Arlington at every turn. Madame eventually informed Charles that Arlington's integrity was beginning to impress her. Montagu wrote Arlington: "You are the most obliged to the King that can be, for she showed me the kindest letter that could be that the King writ to her about you--too kind for her ever to be unkind to you again."[33] Montagu's persuasive manner and his persistance were beginning to win the Lady over.

Montagu then conceived a plan which he hoped would succeed in finally putting all fears of Arlington to rest. Writing to his sister, he proposed that Arlington "suggest" to Charles that he make his sister a present of a considerable sum of money, five thousand pounds. Montagu even suggested where the money was to come from; the money was to be taken from the dowry of Catherine of Braganza. Sir Robert Southwell, ambassador to Portugal recently had had a measure of success in obtaining the remainder of Catherine's dowry. Out of this windfall some five thousand pounds could surely be spared for Madame. She was in need of money since she was only receiving three thousand from Monsieur per annum for her household. The twenty thousand crowns that Louis used to give her as a present he gave no longer. Montagu then suggested, should the King approve of this plan, that Lord Arlington should be the first to inform her of the gift and thereby show his good faith and devotion to her.34

The idea was quickly accepted and Montagu was soon able to show Madame a letter from Arlington indicating to her that the King intended to give her a present out of the money from Portugal. Madame, of course, was delighted, surprised, and very pleased. She now considered Arlington a friend. Montagu wrote to his sister: "She says that my Lord Arlington is such a kind man that it is impossible not to be his friend: she has given me a thousand thanks for the true character I gave of him...."35 But with her joy came fear, fear that if her husband or her mother should hear of the gift they would demand a portion of it. Again Montagu came to the rescue! He suggested that if nothing was said about the gift no one would be the wiser. Madame now became enthralled with Arlington. He appeared to her as her benefactor. Montagu noted her changed perception of Arlington and gleefully chortled that Henriette Anne had "perkt up" and she was certain that she would never have received the money had it not been for Arlington. Montagu wrote his sister (Aug. 26, 1669): "You never saw anybody perkt up as she is since this money, and it makes her so sure to my Lord Arlington that he had better have given it out of his own pocket than not a-got it her."[36]

While Montagu was reconciling Madame and Arlington, Charles' efforts for an alliance went forward. Lord Arundell of Wardown returned from France with an answer from Louis. Louis had agreed to an alliance with England; an alliance which would provide the needed monies to make Charles independent of Parliament, give him control of the army, and would allow him to announce publicly his conversion to Roman Catholicism. The items of the Treaty concerning the subsidies and religion were the most delicate and the most difficult part of the negotiations, and as such, the most dangerous if revealed. Charles was sure of his sister, and of Walter Montagu (Abbe Montagu), and at this point had no reason to suspect the loyalty of his Ambassador Extraordinary-- Ralph Montagu.

Madame, in her capacity as mediator between Charles and Louis, was naturally anxious for the treaty to be concluded. She was eager for her brother's interests, perhaps a little too eager. Her enthusiasm for her brother's cause was not lost upon Louis. It soon became a source of irritation to him and resulted in an increasing coolness in his affection. Montagu noticed this gradual cooling in Louis' regard for Madame but he did not know the exact reason for the estrangement. In a letter to Arlington (July 26) he commented:

> I have so much respect for her and wish her so well that I have done all I can do disabuse her for her own sake as well as for your Lordship's. She is the most that can be beloved in this country by everybody but the King and her husband, and you cannot imagine how much short of what she deserves is used by both of them. She has too great a spirit I believe ever to complain, or to let the King her brother know of it, but I tell your Lordship of it, that you may take all the occasions wherein the King can, of putting his Majesty upon supporting her, both as his sister, and as a sister that deserves it from him by her real concern in everything that relates either to his honor or interest.[37]

Charles sent Louis his answer sometime in the middle of August 1669. He expressed his intention to do everything possible to bolster his position militarily and financially, but definite action would have to wait for the next session of Parliament, which would not begin until the coming October. Consequently, he would be unable to make his declaration of conversion until the following summer. Charles expected stiff opposition from his subjects, but hoped that, in publicly announcing his conversion, the Pope would make some concessions

to his people to aid the reconciliation between England
and Rome.

From the foregoing, it is evident that Charles used
the declaration of Catholicism as a lever to pry subsidies from Louis. Charles complained that his delay of
conversion was due to his lack of the necessary monies
needed to make the declaration. At long last, Charles
and Louis reached agreement on the two major points of
disagreement: Charles' declaration of his conversion
and Charles' aid to Louis in a war with Holland before
this declaration. However, he insisted that as he left
the time of Charles' declaration to his own discretion,
he must have the right to choose the time of the declaration of war on Holland.[38] With these points settled,
ratification could take place at once--no time was to be
lost in choosing the place, time and plenipotentiaries.
Louis left the choice of the place up to Charles.

Negotiations were interrupted temporarily due to
the death of the Queen Mother, Henrietta Maria.
Charles' mother died on September 10, 1669, apparently
from an overdose of laudanum or some other narcotic
which her physician administered. As she left no will,
Louis immediately sent his officers to seal her house
and impound everything in her possession. This he did,
he claimed, in the interest of the King of England since
everything she had fell to his Majesty, King Charles.
For some reason, Henry Jermyn, the Earl of St. Albans,
Queen Henrietta Maria's major-domo and member of the
Commission sent to France by Charles for the disposal of
the Queen Mother's goods, became indignant at Louis'
action and called upon Montagu to do his duty and lodge
a protest on Charles' behalf against these measures of

the French King. Evidently he thought that Louis was merely using the French law in order to obtain the personal belongings of the Queen as his own. What he did not know was that Louis' actions were undertaken at the secret urgings of Montagu. Montagu intended, so he informed Charles (September 11): "...to hinder everybody, as is usual on those occasions, from running away with everything they can lay their hands on, so that everything there is safe till your Majesty gives orders what you will have done."[39] In another letter also dated September 11, Montagu stated:

> I told him the King's intentions to the King my master were so good, that I could not tell how to take it ill. I am sure without this my Lord St. Albans would not have left a silver spoon in the house, and now all she had is safe for whoever it belongs to. I would not have any but his Majesty know I did this, because it makes one have enemies to no purpose.[40]

Montagu claimed that, in the case of the Queen Mother's belongings, Charles was not bound by the laws of France since he was the ruler of a sovereign nation. He was bound only to the custom of his own kingdom. In this supposition, Madame supported Montagu. She openly opposed her husband, Monsieur, the Duc d' Orleans, who wanted to claim all the Queen's property as his wife's property, she being the Queen's heir, and, in turn, use it as his own. Montagu wrote Arlington (Oct. 26th): "The King [Charles II] ought to take some notice of this to Madame, whose proceedings towards him have been very generous and obliging on this occasion."[41]

Taking Montagu's advice, Charles acted generously towards his sister. She received the house at Colombe and most of the furniture; the Queen's jewels, plates and valuable paintings being sent to England.[42] Montagu was further instructed to turn over to Madame a set of pearls of great value that she had often seen her mother wear and had admired greatly.[43]

In the meantime the relations between Louis and Madame progressed to the breaking point. Louis began to suspect that she preferred her brother's interests to his own, and, although she acted as intermediary ir the negotiations between the two sovereigns, Louis demanded that she place the interests of France above all other considerations. Montagu confirmed Louis' suspicion in a letter to Arlington dated September 6th:

> Madame told me that you would do well to advise the King to look narrowly to the French Ambassador, for that she knows certainly he has orders to distract the Parliament, and give the King as much trouble that way as he can; and for your own particular, that your ruin is intended and aimed above all things. I have been told the same from several other people, but you may give credit to Madam's intelligence; for some of the most understanding people of France apply themselves to Madame, having a great opinion of her discretion and judgment, and tell her all they know; and it is not without reason they have that opinion of her, for she has them both in great perfection; besides in England you ought not

to slight any advices that come from her,
because she is so truly and passionately concerned for the King her brother.44

At this time the news of the falling-out of
the Duke of Buckingham and the Lord Arlington over the
basic anti-French-pro-Dutch foreign policy reached
Paris and was received with much pleasure. Montagu, who
had once attached himself to both ministers and hoped to
use them to forward his own career, now gave his
complete support to Arlington. Accordingly, he successfully persuaded Madame to pledge her support of
Arlington. On September 6th he wrote to Arlington:
"There is a great noise of the Duke of Buckingham and
you being fallen out, which the French are not dissatis-
fied with, for you are the man they think hinders
everybody from coming into their interest."[45]

In proof of the effectiveness of Montagu's efforts
to win Madame to Arlington's support, Madame wrote
Arlington (September 24th, 1669) to thank him for his
letter concerning the birth of her daughter. In this
letter she reassured him that in all things she had the
interests of her brother at heart.

> I will confess to you that if I had known that
> a promise would be made to undertake to assist
> France in the just pretentions she may have
> against Spain, I would have begged the King my
> brother not to do it so soon but to wait till
> something has happened to procure more advant-
> ages from it than the thanks he has been
> given....But you must see that even in the
> smallest thing, I think of furthering the

interests of my King my brother.

. . .

The King informed that he loves me dearly, and
though I am persuaded of it, this confirmation
has not failed to be very agreeable to me. He
will be very glad to see so good an
understanding between us, you and me. For
this was one of the things he seemd to hope
for the most. I can answer that it will
endure; at least I will contribute to it by
all the sincerity and regularity that a friend
should have.[46]

This letter showed the understanding she possessed
of the political reality of her day. It also indicated
the important role she played in bringing about an
alliance between Charles and Louis and clearly dispelled
any ideas that she acted solely in the interest of the
French. Louis suspected that Madame was not always as
loyal to him as she ought to have been and probably
felt that he had grounds to doubt her sincerity now and
then.

Eventually the interrupted treaty negotiations were
resumed. On October 3rd, 1669, Arundell returned to
France to continue the negotiations. The reason given
for his journey was his representation of Charles at the
funeral of Henrietta Maria and the settlement of her
estate. He was assisted by St. Albans, the Abbe Walter
Montagu, Dr. Leoline Jenkins, Mr. Howard and the English
ambassador, Montagu--appointed by Charles as Commissioners for this purpose.[47] Arundell carried a letter from
Charles to Louis declaring his intention to carry out
the negotiations at Dover rather than in France.

Charles indicated that he did not want to run the risk of the consequences of the long stay of an envoy in France. To reassure Louis about his intention, he delayed an answer to Holland, Spain and Sweden in their demands to bolster the Treaty of Aix-la-Chapelle (1668) by means of a union of forces against France. Charles again demanded secrecy in any future negotiations for the treaty. Further, Charles requested Louis to inform him if he felt that the French ambassador could be trusted. Charles may have hoped to bring him into the business of the negotiations and thus speed up the process. In late October de Croissy was given permission by his sovereign to take part in the making of the treaty. His counterpart, Montagu, across the Channel was specifically excluded.48

In the meantime, Montagu became involved in a domestic quarrel concerning Madame. Louis had dismissed Madame de St. Chaumont, governess to Madame's children, at the instigation of Madame de Montespan, who was no friend to Madame. Madame, extremely distraught, entreated Louis for the reinstatement of her favorite, but in vain. Her sorrow and pain actually delighted her husband, Monsieur, who continued to treat her with contempt and lost no opportunity to humiliate her in private as well as in public. Montagu took a very dim view of such treatment of his master's sister. He wrote Arlington a letter (December 12th 1669) stating that everyone was waiting to see what the King of England would do to show his displeasure at such treatment of his sister.

Montagu discussed the situation in a long letter to the King himself. It is illustrative of Montagu's

ability to seize upon a situation and use it to his
advantage.

1669, Dec. 12, Paris---I suppose your Majesty
has, by Madame's own letter, as well as by
what I write to my Lord Arlington, had an
account of the disgrace of Madame de Chaumont,
which had been done with so many unkind
circumstances, and so little consideration of
whose daughter and whose sister she is, that I
do not see how your Majesty can avoid doing
something that may show the world that you
both intend to own her and right her when
occasion shall serve, which will make them
here for the future use her at another rate,
when they see that your Majesty lays her concerns and interests to heart. By all the
observation that I have made since I have been
in this country, nobody can live with more
discretion than Madame does, both towards the
King and Monsieur, and all the rest of the
world; but she is so greatly esteemed by
everybody that I look upon that as partly the
occasion of her being so ill used both by the
King and her husband. To remedy this, I would
humbly propose to your Majesty what Madame has
already discoursed to me of, which is, that
your Majesty would tell the French ambassador
in England, that you know the Chevalier de
Lorraine [the favorite of Madame's husband,
Philippe, Duke of Orleans] is the occasion of
all the ill that your sister suffers, and that
she is one that you are so tender of that you
cannot think the French King your friend,

whilst he suffers such a man about his brother, by whose counsels he doth every day so many things to Madame's dissatisfaction.

. . .

Your Majesty may perhaps think me very impertinent for writing of this, but I assure, Sir, not only all the French, but the Dutch, the Swedish, and Spanish Ministers are in expectation of what your Majesty will do in this business, for they all know Madame is the thing in the world that is dearest to you; and they whose interest it is to have your Majesty and the King here be upon ill terms, are very glad that he has done a thing which they think will anger you. I believe the King is now sorry that he has done this, though he be of a humour not to own it. This is a conjuncture of that consequence for the quiet and happiness of the rest of Madame's life, that I thought I should be wanting both in the duty I owe your Majesty and the zeal I have for her service, if I did not give you the best account I could of what concerns her, which I hope you will pardon.[49]

This letter proved unnecessary. Charles sent for the French ambassador and protested vigorously against the treatment of his sister. The ambassador protested that this was in no way meant to be an insult to the Sovereign of England or to his sister. Charles was not convinced, he demanded more positive proof. Arlington then took the occasion to point out to Croissy that Madame's cooperation was essential to the success of the coming negotiations. Informed of Charles' indignation,

Louis underwent a change of heart and reinstated Madame de St. Chaumont, banished his brother from the Court and sent his brother's favorite, off to prison.50

The negotiations for the treaty now went forward in earnest. Louis felt that it was time for Madame to travel to England to meet her brother and procure his signature. Actually, he hoped to use her influence over her brother. This influence just might obtain him more positive and favorable results in a shorter time than many weeks of diplomatic maneuvering. Over the objections of his brother, Louis ordered Madame to prepare to travel to Dover. Monsieur had at first absolutely refused to allow his wife to travel. When Louis insisted that her journey was in the interest of France, he consented to let her go. However, Monsieur stipulated that she was to go no farther than Dover and under no circumstances was she to go to London. Nor was she to remain with Charles more than three days.[51]

Monsieur was so utterly opposed to the journey that he was willing to use any means to prevent it.

...but that he is altogether opposed to this journey and that he has slept with Madame every day since he has known about this business in order that she may become pregnant, which condition would prevent her from exposing herself to so long and dangerous a journey.52

Montagu wrote Arlington (Jan. 19, 1669/70) that Monsieur was so jealous of his wife that there was nothing he would not do to destroy her.

Madame had discoursed with me about her coming into England, when the King shall be at Callice. I believe the King our master will like the proposition very well, and I believe the King here will be inclinable enough to it, out of the hopes that he may have of the good offices that she may do between the two Crowns, but I believe M[onsieu]r will never consent to it; he is so jealous, I mean, of her credit and her interest both in England and here, that there is nothing he would not do to diminish it both places. She will write to the King and you at large upon this subject, so I will say no more of it.[53]

In the face of Monieur's obstinacy and peevishness, Madame sailed for Dover. On April 29, 1670, Montagu accompanied the Court to Lille at the request of Madame. Here, Montagu felt constrained, for some reason, to write a letter to Arlington protesting his personal loyalty to him. Evidently some problem arose that caused Arlington to question Montagu's service to him and Montagu felt he had to justify Arlington's continued trust.

1670, May 23, Lisle---I was extreme glad to meet with Father Patricke here. I hope he will be able to satisfy you as to some particulars that concern myself, which perhaps I should never have been able to have done with all the letters that I could have writ. I am not very flattering, nor changing in my nature. Your Lordship therefore may the

better believe me when I assure you that you
have no man living that than is truer to your
interests than I am, and have always been
since I have been acquainted with you; and
till you have more evident proofs to the
contrary than any I have given yet, I beg of
you not to suspect me, but to believe this
bearer as to the account he will give you of
me.54

Returning to Paris he felt the need once again to
reaffirm his devotion to Arlington and thus wrote him on
June 21, 1670:

I flatter myself that it can be in nobody's
power to indispose you so to me as that you
will not believe me one of the first of all
your friends and servants to rejoice at any
good fortune that befalls you; especially
because, ever since I had the honour to know
you, I have always looked upon my own fortune
in a manner linked to yours; so I look upon
myself to share in any good that happens to
you.55

Madame traveled to Dover. The treaty was signed
and she returned to Paris in triumph, but also a very
tired and ill woman. Montagu met her at Calais and
accompanied her on her journey back to St. Germain on
the 17th of June.56 He reported (June 21st) that all at
the Court were well satisfied with her success and were
very pleased with all the civilities and courtesies
shown her at the English Court. Louis was delighted
with what she had accomplished at Dover. However,

Montagu added a note of caution: "I find all the foreign Ministers here extremely alarmed at this interview of the King and Madame, and extremely impatient to know the result of the negotiation."[57]

The Protestants among Charles's closest advisors, commonly known as the CABAL (Clifford, Arlington, Buckingham, Ashley Cooper and Lauderdale) knew nothing of the secret treaty or of the second clause of the treaty dealing with Charles's conversion to Catholicism. Accordingly, with the convivance of Louis XIV, these men were eventually to be duped into accepting the negotiation of a second treaty which was almost indentical to the treaty of Dover. The new treaty was not to contain the clause dealing with the Catholic faith in deference to their Protestant susceptibilities. This treaty came to be known as the bogus treaty or the treaty simule, to which all the members of the CABAL put their signature.

Charles, to disguise his true dealings with Louis, presented Commons an agreement with France for a joint war against Holland. Originally, Parliament knew nothing of either treaty, secret or open, since foreign policy was the sole preserve of the monarch. Parliament, therefore, in its sitting of 1670, laboured under the assumption that the Triple Alliance, with its underlying protection of Protestantism, was alive and well and that it remained the keystone of Charles' actions and thereupon voted subsidies of eight hundred thousand pounds for the war. Charles' success in keeping Parliament tied to his interests was due in large measure to Arlington, who had organized the King's men in the Commons.[58]

On June 26th Madame traveled to Versailles to pay a

visit to Louis. There she became quite ill and returned to St. Cloud complaining of stomach pains. On the 28th she received a visit from Ralph Montagu, and, with Charles' blessing, she told him of the secret alliance just negotiated between Charles and Louis and of the coming war on Holland to be waged jointly by France and England. Over the years, Madame had often found Montagu to be a good listener and a good friend (perhaps Montagu had come genuinely to like Madame), had tended to confide in him and tell of her troubles.

Madame's condition steadily deteriorated forcing her to take to her bed. When she was thought to be _in extremis_, Madame de Meckelbourg, presumably a Lady-in-Waiting at Court, notified the English ambassador. Montagu rushed to her bedside to be with her in her last hours. Madame reminded Montagu of what she had told him about the war against Holland and declared that she had persuaded Charles to it for his own interests and not for hers or for those of France. She asked him to tell her brother that her only real regret in leaving this world was "the leaving of him whom she loved the most." She repeated this and enjoined Montagu not to forget her words. Montagu, suspicious, asked her if she thought she was poisoned; he asked this question several times to be sure that she understood his meaning. Madame shrugged her shoulders, but gave no answer. She is then supposed to have begged Montagu to say nothing of the sort to the King (Charles); he must be spared the grief, and, above all, he must not think of taking vengeance. Louis was not guilty; she begged Charles not to blame Louis.[59] She then sent loving messages to her brother, James, Duke of York and drew a ring off her finger and asked Montagu to send it to her brother, Charles, when she was dead.60

Madame died at the early age of twenty-six, after she had made her peace with God and received the Sacrament of Extreme Unction of her Church, in the presence of Louis XIV, her husband, Monsieur, Montagu, Bishop Bossuet and a large number of the French Court. Never very robust in health, she suffered continually from indispositions. Further, she lived under tremendous pressures: she observed two loyalties to two Kings (Louis XIV, her brother-in-law and Charles, her brother) neither hesitating to place her in the taxing position of taking part in Court politics and intrigue; she suffered a marriage to a homosexual, who paraded this tendency at every opportunity in her presence and greatly delighted in insulting and humiliating her in public; and the sorrow and pain of a miscarriage, the death of a son at age twenty-eight months and the birth of a stillborn daughter. Given these pressures, the lack of sympathy and understanding such a woman needed, and the state of the medical profession at the time, there is little wonder that this once vivacious lady developed acute peritonitis and a duodenal ulcer which led to her death.

In the course of their last conversation at St. Cloud, Montagu reminded Madame that she had certain letters from Charles in her possession which were highly compromising to Charles. Madame asked Madame des Bordes, probably also a Lady-in-Waiting, to see that the letters were turned over to Montagu after her death. Unfortunately, the lady failed to do as asked. It was impossible, under the circumstances, to demand the letters from Monsieur, and so, Montagu was forced to

drop the matter till another time. He hurried back to
Paris and wrote a hurried letter to Arlington apprising
him of the situation. Montagu then gave this letter to
Sir Thomas Armstrong and sent him off to England to
deliver it.61

Learning of his sister's death and of her possible
poisoning, Charles took the news very badly. Grief
forced him to his bed for several days. Rumors of the
possible poisoning spread throughout London and the
nation. This disquiet for the nation gave those who
advocated closer ties with Holland and Spain what they
needed to arouse resentment against France and any
French sympathizers at the English Court. Had it not
been for the calmness of Arlington and Charles in
dealing with the situation, the crisis might have become
very dangerous, especially, if the secret negotiations
were exposed.62

The rumor of the poisoning did not die so easily in
France. Madame's death was attributed to the malevol-
ence of the Chevalier de Lorraine. Louis, agitated by
such rumors, instructed Montagu to inform the King of
England that: "...if there could be the least imagination that Madams' death should have happened by poyson
that noe severity should be wanting either towards the
discovering or punishing of soe horrid & infamous a
fact." (July 12, 1670).63 Louis ordered a post-mortem
performed on June 30th, Montagu, Lord Salisbury and the
Abbe Montagu being present. The autopsy proved that she
died from natural causes: cholera morbus, that is, peritonitis resulting from a perforated duodenal ulcer.64
Montagu, however, still believed that Madame was
poisoned.65

With the news of Madame's death, Arlington was now constrained to obtain Charles' letters to her. Monsieur, had seized all Madame's possessions, including her letters, after her death and refused to surrender them. Montagu, upon Arlington's instructions, lodged a complaint with Lionne, Louis' Secretary of State, and with Louis himself. Louis saw to it that the letters were returned and assured Montagu that no one other than Abbe Montagu had seen or read any of the letters.[66]

A second treaty of Dover (the treaty simule) was negotiated later that year in December with Buckingham as its chief architect. Buckingham, high in self-esteem and imagined popularity, was played the fool by the English king. Montagu, sensing Buckingham's disfavor, now detached himself totally from Buckingham's circle. Exhilirated by the first real taste of secret diplomacy carried out by the Crown, he now attached himself to Arlington and confidently promised himself the diplomat's life.

Montagu learned early and well the art of diplomacy. The young ambassador showed his ability as a diplomatist in the clever handling of Arlington and Madame; thus causing Madame to come eventually to regard her enemy as her friend and a friend of France. Montagu's further manipulation of Arlington exhibited a definite willingness to employ duplicitous conduct. He allowed Arlington to think that he was serving Charles without realizing that he was serving Montagu at the same time. Such feats were remarkable in one so young and without long diplomatic experience.

CHAPTER II

Footnotes

[1] The Court in Mourning, p. 2.

[2] John B. Wolf, Louis XIV (New York: W. W. Norton and Company, Inc., 1968), p. 71.

[3] Roger Lockyer, Tudor and Stuart Britain 1417-1714 (London: Longman Group Limited, 1946), p. 339.

[4] Maurice Ashley, Charles II: The Man and the Statesman (Forgmore, St. Albans: Panther Books, 1971), p. 173.

[5] Carola Oman, Henrietta Maria (London, Sydney and Toronto: White Lion Publishers Limited, 1936) p. 296.

[6] Ibid., p. 296.

[7] Ashley, pp. 173-74.

[8] Lockyer, p. 340.

[9] Ibid., pp. 339-41.

[10] Rawlinson MSS. A. 225, ff. 79-82; Instructions for Ralph Montagu as Ambassador; H.M.C. 5th Report; p. 316; Thomas Bebinton, The Rt. Honourable the Earl of Arlington's Letters to Sir. W. Temple, Bar. From July 1665 (London: Printed by W.N., 1701), p. 393; Firth, p. 710.

[11]Burnet, I, 616, footnote d.

[13]Rawlinson MSS. A. 225 - Instructions for Ralph Montagu as Ambassador; A. Boyer, The History of the Reign of Queen Anne, Digested into Annals. Year the Eighth (London: Printed for T. Ward, 1710), VIII, 366; M. Mignet, Negociations Relatives A La Succession d'Espagne Sous Louis XIV (Paris: Imprimerie royale, 1842), III, 88, 91; Bebington, p. 440; Firth, p. 710; Hartmann, Charles II and Madame, p. 243.

[12]State Papers, Foreign: France/78/126/f. 53; Hartmann, Charles II and Madame, p. 243. An account of the incident involving Elizabeth (Montagu) is related in a letter from L indenov, the Danish envoy to London, dated March 16, 1669. (Waldemar Westerguard, The First Triple Alliancce: The Letters of Christopher Lindenov, Danish Envoy to London, 1668-1672. (New Haven: Yale University Press, 1948), p. 111.)

[14]C.A. 93. Lionee to Colbert de Croissy, March 9, 1669; Hartmann, Charles II and Madame, p. 243.

[15]State Papers, Foreign: France/78/126/f. 36.

[16]The Court in Mourning, p. 3.

[17]Ibid., p. 3.

[18]Ibid., p. 4.

[19]Wise, p. 37.

[20]Cal. Treas. Bks. 1667-68, p. 644; Cal. S. P. Dom. 1668-9, p. 124; 1676-77, p. 208.

[21]Cal. S. P. Dom. 1683, p. 24; 1668-69, p. 533.

[22]State Paper, Foreign: France/78/126/f. 71.

[23]Ibid., f. 139; Boyer, Annals VII, 366-67.

[24]Maurice Petherick, Restoration Rogues (London: Hollis and Carter, 1951), p. 113; Boyer, Annals VIII, 366-67; State Papers, Foreign: France/78/126/ff. 158-19.

[25]Buccleuch MSS. I, 421.

[26]Ibid., p. 422.

[27]Ibid., p. 424.

[28]Ibid., p. 423.
[29]Ibid., p. 423.

[30]Ibid., p. 426.

[31]Hartmann, Charles II and Madame, pp. 258-59.

[32]C.A. 95, f. 31; Hartmann, Charles II and Madame, pp. 255-259.

[33]Buccleuch MSS. I, 426.

[34] Ibid., p. 431, p. 434.

[35] Ibid., p. 435.

[36] Ibid., p. 435.

[37] Ibid., p. 431.

[38] Hartmann, Charles II and Madame, p. 270.

[39] Buccleuch MSS. U, 439; London Gazette, Sept. 13-16, 1669, Numb. 400; Hartmann, Charles II and Madame, p. 272.

[40] Buccleuch MSS. I, 440; Bebington, pp. 438-447; Firth, p. 710.

[41] Ibid., p. 445.

[42] Ibid., pp. 448-49, p. 455.

[43] Ibid., p. 445.

[44] Ibid., p. 437.

[45] Ibid., p. 438.

[46] Hartmann, Charles II and Madame, pp. 276-77. C.A. 95, f. 33.

[47]Cal. S.P. Dom. 1668, p. 503, p. 514; Buccleuch MSS. I, 442, p. 444.

[48]Hartmann, Charles II and Madame, pp. 282-83.

[49]Buccleuch MSS. I, 453-54.

[50]Hartmann, Charles II and Madame, pp. 288-89.

[51]State Papers, France/129/f. 184; C.A. 99. Lionne to Colbert de Croissy, April 2/12. 1670; Hartmann, Charles II and Madame, p. 303.

[52]Hartmann, Charles II and Madame, p. 304.

[53]Buccleuch MSS. I, 460; Montagu Memorandum Book (1669-1671), p. 32; Boyer, Annals, VIII, 367.

[54]Buccleuch MSS. I, 474.

[55]Ibid., p. 474.

[56]Montagu Memorandum Book (1669-1671), p. 35, p. 36.

[57]Buccleuch MSS. I, 474.

[58]Lockyer, p. 341.

[59]M.M. Shelmerdine, trans. The Secret History of Madame Henrietta of England by Marie M. Motier, Madame de la

Fayette (London: George Routledge, 1929), pp. 106-107, pp. 119-121; Hartmann;, Charles II and Madame, p. 237.

[60]Portland MSS. XXI, ff. 213-14; Shelmerdine, p. 121.

[61]Shelmerdine, pp. 119-121.

[62]Hartmann, Charles II and Madame, p. 329-30.

[63]State Papers, Foreign: France/78/129/f. 204; Shelmerdine, pp. 121-22; Hartmann, Charles II and Madame, p. 330.

[64]State Papers, Foreign: France/78/129/f. 269, f. 278, f. 280, ff. 283-84, f. 285, f. 292; Cartwright, p. 371; Hartmann, Charles II and Madame, pp. 330-31.

[65]Hartmann, Charles II and Madame, p. 331; Shelmerdine, pp. 121-123 (Letter of Montagu to Charles II, July 15, 1670), pp. 123-124 (Letter of Montagu to Arlington); Cartwright, p. 360.

[66]Buccleuch MSS. I, 477; Hartmann, Charles II and Madame, pp. 333-34.

CHAPTER III
A Man of High Aspirations (1670-73)

> And now being to return Home, he had
> his publick Audience and Leave of
> the French King, and all the Royal
> Family; after which he staid some
> time at the Court of Versailles to
> enjoy the Diversions of the Season,
> where at length he had a private
> Audience, and took his final leave
> of his Majesty and the whole
> Court;...[1]

The magnificence and elegance of the Restoration Court, so ably represented by Ambassador Montagu in Paris by the splendor of his public entry, was due directly to the tastes and standards of Charles II. Charles, tall in stature with dark brown eyes and hair, of a swarthy complexion, was arresting rather than attractive and possessed of an easy charm and manner.[2] He set and maintained the distinct standard of elegance in dress, food and entertainment which all at the Court were expected to `live up to.' Life at the Court, for those fortunate enough to have place there, was an experience in sensuality--"profuse gaming, luxurious dallying and prophaneness."[3] The King's morality, or lack of it, especially where women and the truth were concerned, was accepted as normal. Coarseness of manner and speech was held in high disfavor.[4] The King set the tone of court life--a gracious manner and a sparkling wit.[5] Charles's court was the scene of the greatest liberality of conduct, a source of pleasure and, of course, scandal. It was also the center for patronage of the arts, learning and politics. Those eager for recognition or preferment came to the Court hoping for gain, position or honor--more times than not they were sadly disappointed.[5]

It was at Court where the government of the realm and the royal house were wedded. Behind the trappings and display of Court life lay the grim actualities of rule, war and peace; the Court at Whitehall was the true scene of English governance. At the center was the King and his ministers--for where the King was there was the State and its justice in his person.[6]

The Court with all its glitter and pomp was carefully established to cover the true political activities of the government. It became the subtle shield for the making of secret foreign policy. Here Charles was able to speak on one level and act on another; the Court was a means by which he presented himself as a monarch desirous of the good of his Protestant nation, while at the same time he furthered his schemes for a French subsidy and promotion of Catholicism. He was very careful to present the image of an indolent, luxury-loving, sensuous King whose only concern was the enjoyment of the blessings of his throne. His mask of insouciance kept his critics, at Court and in Commons, at a distance and deceived them as to his real intentions and activities. Charles may have honestly believed that this was the only moral way to carry out his policy and subscribed to the maxim-- the end justified the means. To keep his power, Charles may well have regarded it as justifiable to pledge his word while intending to act otherwise: e.g., promising to love his Parliaments all the while intending to rule without them.[7]

Charles sent Montagu to France to represent him in his negotiations for the desired alliance with France, but he did not allow him to be privy to his real intentions. The conduct of this duplicitous ruler, the king of a nation composed of five and one half million people,[8] was not lost on Montagu. He determined to put into practice all the lessons learned in a royal service that had begun in 1661.

Montagu was representative of the diplomatic corps of the times. He was typical of those who wished to serve at Court and thereby assure themselves future position and power. A number of the lower degree--the gentry--entered the diplomatic service, with no intention of making diplomacy their life's career or of accepting the `rewards' offered by a diplomatic career as sufficient for services rendered. Few had any intention of remaining in the service any longer than absolutely necessary.[9] Often special inducements had to be offered to a person to remain. A possible reward might be a 'place' at home--"...[Robert Spencer, 2nd Earl of] Sunderland on his return from a foreign mission was called to the Privy Council."[10] Candidates often expected a peerage or at least the promise of one as a necessary condition for going or returning to a foreign court--Henry St. John, Bolingbroke, desired an earldom for his service but had to be satisfied with the rank of a Viscount.[11] Some even hoped for the Order of the Bath or of the Garter (Montagu himself asked for this honor) while others sought more tangible rewards for their service in the form of monetary reward.[12] Further, service to the King in the diplomatic corps was often a costly business for the diplomat. Many times the salary and expense money promised the representative was never paid. The ambassador was then forced to meet the necessary expenses of his mission out of his own pocket with little hope of ever obtaining the monies spent in the national interest. In 1683, for example, Montagu petitioned for twenty-two thousand pounds back salary from 1669. This request may have included an item for one thousand three hundred and eighty-two pounds for expenses incurred at the Queen Mother's funeral.[13]

Many men seemed to drift into diplomatic service rather than choose it as a definite career.[14] Montagu's apparently accidental choice by Charles II indicated a random choice of career. However glittering the promised rewards of position and honor were for diplomatic service to the King most had to be cajoled into accepting it. Perhaps the candidates saw the many obvious drawbacks to such service: the small chance of promotion, the competition from noblemen, royal favorites, and politicians with no experience whatever in diplomatic service.[15] To further complicate matters, the time of service was at royal pleasure--there was often no definite length of time for a mission.[16] In other words, the diplomatic service had many built-in frustrations: it lacked security,one might be recalled in order to please a royal favorite; the system was not built on merit, there was no surety of promotion for service well done;and it was often a drain on the ambassador's personal fortunes.

Montagu regarded tenure as ambassador to be a sign of royal favor. He sought after and indeed welcomed the rank of Ambassador and the honor it conferred. He viewed the service in the diplomatic body as a necessary step in obtaining preferment and recognition from the King, and was quick to accept the post when given.

As ambassador to Louis XIV, Montagu felt right at home in Paris. Paris was the city of pleasure! Pleasure was a way of life in this city and was almost a duty. He anticipated the festivities and the celebrations of Louis' Court: the plays of Moliere (perhaps--<u>Le</u> <u>Misanthrope</u>, <u>Le</u> <u>Bourgeois</u> <u>Gentilhomme</u>), the musical entertainments of Lully, the opera and the young ballet (born in France around 1581). Attractive were the prospects of invitations to the banquets, balls and masques that were offered not only at Versailles but also at the homes of the nobility (Madame, Marquis de Louvois, Jean Baptiste Colbert) that he, as ambassador, was to enjoy. Paris beckoned him with its endless opportunities for enjoyment in its cultural and social activities. Rather, Montagu was anxious to enter into the world of political activity which Versailles as the real capital of France came to represent. The mission gave him entry into the world of diplomacy and intrigue which attracted him and offered him promise of advancement into the Peerage.

Montagu took care not to place his future career as diplomat in jeopardy by acquiring the reputation of a wastrel. Nevertheless a certain regard for his own worth directed him to plan his entry into Paris as Ambassador Extraordinary so as to impress all who viewed it with the great trust reposed in him by his sovereign. Some years later (1698), Montagu's cousin, Charles Montagu, the First Duke of Manchester, when departing his embassy in Venice, attempted by his display of pomp to show that he was upholding the standard of magnificence expected from the Montagus.17

Montagu soon realized early in his dealings at Court that France viewed an alliance with England as important. He tried to convey this idea to Arlington, Secretary of State and his superior, when in July of 1669 he wrote: "As long as the King keeps form to the Triple Alliance, they will not know what to do here...." (July 3, 1669).18 A union of France with England would certainly destroy this Alliance and render the Dutch defenseless to Louis' designs. However, Arlington desired to adhere to this Alliance, thinking it would keep France off balance and force her to sue for Charles's good will. Montagu agreed with Arlington and in the same letter wrote: "It is not to be imagined how the King my master's credit increases every day here and how well everybody speaks of him and the Government...."19

Operating in the atmosphere of the French Court where intrigue was a way of life, Montagu knew the value of the art of manipulation through subtle ingratiation. This enabled him on his former mission to accomplish his objective (Treaty of Dover) and at the same time prove his `loyalty' to Arlington. It was then that Montagu boasted of his tireless efforts to win a good opinion of him from Madame: "...and therefore I labour as much as I can to make her have a good opinion of you and be your friend really and truly; and I must think her the falsest creature in the world if she is not so." (Sept. 6, 1669).20 Montagu took a real risk in making such a statement. If Charles had known that he dared to call his sister false, Montagu would, in all probability, have faced dismissal and disgrace. He was conscious of the penalty for his free speech: (May 8, 1669) "I venture to speak very freely at times of people in my letter to your Lordship, which perhaps the King [Charles II] would not like if he sees my letter."[21]

Like many of his age, Montagu was not above making a judgment of a person not on the basis of that person's abilities or talents but based on his personal like or dislike. He had little liking or regard for some of the French Ministers; he disliked Colbert de Croissy and Lionne considering them inept and unknowledgeable, especially about England. On July 26, 1669, he had written to Arlington: "I swear the ministers here, with all their great abilities and understanding, know no more of England than they do of Persia; and I do not wonder at it, considering the dexterity of their Ambassador, that he gives them so good intelligence; and lest you should think me like him, I will say no more."[22] Neither did he care for Charles' mother, Henrietta Maria. His critical appraisal of the Queen Mother was rather unflattering. He disliked her showiness and her needless household. He believed she kept the Stuart family in France in constant need of funds. In the same letter Montagu commented:

Here is a great clamour at the Queen Mother's about the King's stopping her money. There is a project on foot now among them to get the King to pay her, which is, they say she must be forced to go into a monastery if the King does not pay her, and they think the King will be ashamed to let his mother be driven to that necessity. I told Madame what I heard; she said it was a shame that her mother could not live upon what she had, for she had more, notwithstanding all the King stopped, than she had for her family, and yet hers was as big again; she disputed this with the Queen Mother, who, she told me, was extreme angry with her about it; therefore this is under the rose; the King may do what he pleases, but the Queen, though he does not pay her, will not suffer much.

. . .

All the French think it ridiculous, at a time when we are thought so poor in England, to have so much money spent abroad.23

Further, his opinion of Louis was not charitable.

The King [Louis XIV] here is the least beloved and esteemed by all his servants, even the nearest about him, that ever king in the world was, because of his ill-natured and proud usage of them upon all occasions. They have no way of complaining of it, as a very witty man told me the other day, but by extolling the King of England's using of people, which they say angers and vexes the French King more than anything they can say. He is the same to the women, except to one, as he is to the men, and a little while ago some ladies were commending the King of England before him. He appeared nettled at it, and said "Les dames ayment toujours les aventuriers, mais je ne

croy pas moins, honeste homme pour n'avoir pas
este chasse de mon royaume.[24]

Montagu considered Louis to be proud, vain, lacking in
grace and charm, prone to anger and a user of people.
Evidently Montagu believed that Louis' treatment of
women was no better than his treatment of his household
servants.

Montagu also believed that it was his duty not
merely to observe but also to inform his superior. On
Again, in the same, letter he penned:

> I know not how the King my master stands
> affected to this country, or how he may think
> it in his interest to enter into a stricter
> league with them here. My business is not to
> be so politic as to give my opinion of what is
> best. I leave that to wiser and more
> experienced men. The part of an Ambassador is
> to be a spy and tell-tale; I must, therefore,
> contrary to my inclinations and practice, tell
> you all I hear and learn in this country.[25]

Although Montagu was limited officially by his instructions to give only observations of climes and times, he
was not remiss in following the accepted duty, as he saw
it, as ambassador of being a good 'spy and tell-tale.'
He believed it the duty of a good ambassador to be the
eyes and ears of his sovereign and report what he
thought of significance. No bit of information should
ever be overlooked--no matter how small, for it might be
of great service to furthering the cause of his master,
and, it would, of course, help his own.

He also considered it the proper duty of an envoy to dissimulate--to conceal the real interests of his master and to deceive his enemies. Through cunning and deceit he often accomplished his objectives. His pretended friendship with the Dutch ambassador (perhaps M. van Benningen) at Paris completely kept him off guard against the impending war.26

He further proved himself to be a master of the art of intrigue when he wrote to Arlington on January 17, 1670/71, about the method of paying Louis' subsidy to Charles.

> ...and if I may venture to advise it, it were much safer and would be much more secret if the money that is paid in February were put into Spanish pistoles, which should be weight (sic), and then put into some ballot of merchandise, and conveyed from hence all the way by water into England. ... You will excuse the liberty I take to propose this, but I am sure, as Mr. de Lionne was telling me that they proposed to have it sent by bills of exchange, it will be impossible that so great a sum can be returned and the Dutch not find out about it,....27

Montagu evidently reasoned that if the money were sent in some form of bill of exchange, the Dutch would most certainly find out about it since they too had their spies.

Montagu took his role of intelligence agent seriously. He was indeed more conscientious in this role than perhaps was to be expected. He believed that the observation and report of even the smallest detail to Charles and Arlington would certainly earn their respect and grateful gratitude in a very material manner. He singled out de Louvois (Francois M. Le Tellier, Secretary of War to Louis XIV) as a source of valuable information for his master, and got to de Louvois through his mistress, Madame de Fresnoy. Actually he did not directly approach the mistress but rather her sister and offered to bribe Louvois' mistress through her. He proposed to make them both a considerable present for their assistance.

> I told her I had a business of importance with Mr. de Louvoy that concerned the King my master; that if she would dispose him to help me in it, I would acknowledge her favour in the manner as I had told her sister.
>
> . . .
>
> I told her, as soon as I could hear out of England, I durst be responsible to her for a jewel of two thousand crowns, and to her sister one of the six thousand, or, if they would the money, to please themselves. I have not money enough to do it here, but I can borrow it if you let me know the King approves of it,.... I hope the King will not think it money flung away, and I ventured nothing except the business were done;....[28]

Nor was Montagu above employing the services of his sister in the game of intrique.

Lady Hervey is described by St. Evremond [Charles de Marquetel de Saint-Denis de Saint-Evremond, a French essayist] as being largely gifted with wit, and being endowed with a genius for the most refined politics. She had a great hand in several changes in the ministry, and contributed more than any one to the bringing over of the Duchess of Mazarin (1675) with whom she afterwards contracted a very large intimacy. She went to Paris, where M. de la Fontaine had frequently the honour of seeing her at her brother Ralph's house, he being the English Ambassador in Paris.

...

Lady Hervey was a woman of so much mark that Mrs. Corey, acting Sempronia, in Jonson's play `Catiline's Conspiracy,' imitated her voice and manner. Mrs. Corey was celebrated for the ability with which she played Doll Common, in the `Alchymist,' and was popularly known by that name. It was thought a great impertinence in Doll to mimic a lady who was akin to "my Lord Chamberlain" (a probable reference to her friendship with Arlington who became Lord Chamberlain in Sept. 1674); and that official moved by the angry lady put Doll Common into <u>durance</u> <u>vile</u>. Thence arose a storm at Court. Doll had a patroness in Lady Castelmaine, which imperious mistress of the King not only obtained an order from Charles II, for the prisoner's liberation, but a command for the repetition of the play. The king attended the performance, which the offensive limitations were repeated with much aggravation, and accompaniedly by loud hisses and flinging of oranges on the part of persons hired by the offended Lady Harvey.[29]

She was a talented, witty and gifted woman with a unique insight into the workings of politics. As a friend of Arlington, she was in touch with happenings at English Court, The role of spy fascinated her and she readily threw herself into the world of espionage. It was only natural that she became Montagu's eyes and ears; keeping him abreast of happenings in England and allowing him to take advantage of events with a view to using them to further his career.

Montagu's cynical attempt to use Arlington's friendship for his own ends was tempered by an almost boundless admiration for him. He was convinced that Arlington's star was on the rise and he could do no better than make sure that his star rose in concert. The letters he wrote Arlington during the period of 1669 to 1673 show how determined he was to take every advantage of Arlington's patronage to further his career at the English Court. (September 15, 1670), Montagu wrote of his devotion and friendship in an effort to continue Arlington's patronage:

> As for all the obligations I have to your Lordship, I am sure I never was failing towards you in the least, either in acknowledging them publicly, or doing and contriving privately with all persons that I have ever had to do with everything that might be for your service or advantage. As for myself, I have always flattered myself with the opinion

that you were still kind to me, so much that
in all my concerns I have never desired anybody's help or favour but yours,.... This I
assure you, my Lord has always been my conduct
towards your Lordship; perhaps I have had very
ill offices done me towards you, but if you
will give yourself the trouble of examining
all my actions, you will find you have not in
the world a truer servant than myself; and
whenever I am so unfortunate as to lose your
kindness, you shall never see me value
anybody's else.[30]

What he probably admired about Arlington was the
clever and competent management of friends and affairs,
but especially the style in which he lived. Montagu
resolved to live in such splendor. He too wanted to
possess a London town-house with the elegance of
Arlington's Goring House (later Buckingham Palace), and
to own a country estate as magnificent as Arlington's
Euston. But such plans never come to fruition without
the means to carry them out. Montagu realized that
power and prestige equal to that of the Secretary's
required great wealth. He may have believed that without wealth one went nowhere. Montagu now began to put
forth some legitimate claims for various sums of money
owed him from the King and his ministers on the grounds
that his duties as ambassador were a constant drain on
his personal funds. He also took to complaining that
the salary owed him was constantly in arrears.

In a letter dated September 6, 1670, he stated that
he had been put to great expense by his service to the
King:

The Duke of Buckingham intending in a day or two to set out for England, and there being occasion of much greater expense than the money he brought over will furnish to, I thought myself obliged both for the Kings's honor as well as his, to serve him in the helping him to what money was necessary to bring him off clear here.[31]

On February 24, 1671, Montagu complained about the money owed him:

I have sent my servant into England, hoping by this time money will be a little more current than it has been all this year. ... I would therefore be in a condition of clearing all my troublesome or clamorous debts against the journey of Flanders, that I may find no stop when your Lordship shall send me to come into England....[32]

Another letter (March 26, 1672) illustrated how hard-up financially he felt himself to be.

I took the liberty to trouble your Lordship in one of my former letters concerning an order of mine from the Treasurer for my entertainment from Midsummer last to Michaelmas, which is stopped and of no effect to me, by has Majesty's late resuming all those things into his own hands. My servant, that his solicited Mr. Treasurer in it, gives me little hopes, unless your Lordship does me the favour to move the King in it. ... but I can no ways in the world make shift without it. I had spent the money here long before his Majesty stopped my assignments.

I must be taking my leave here in a month, about which time the King will be going into the field, and I shall make but an ill figure, both for my master and myself, to be left in pawn; for though I may a shift to come away without paying all my debts here, yet there are some that will be clamorous and dishonour- able that it will be impossible for me to stir till they are satisfied (March 26, 1672).33

Although Montagu complained of the constant need of money due to his duties as ambassador or the failure to be paid, he never really stated the amounts due him. Perhaps he thought that by being evasive he could inflate his requests.

Although no figures are available as to the amount of the Montagu family fortune, it is reasonable to assume that it was substantial. His father possessed considerable properties in Northamptonshire (Boughton, Warkton, Kettering and the surrounding area) and enjoyed substantial income from these lands and their rents. The family fortune was certainly no less than that of the Wriothesley family, whose annual income was eight to nine thousand pounds per annum in 1668.34 With this to rely on to carry out his ambassadorial duties, regular and otherwise, Montagu found that this post involved a greater expenditure of funds than had been expected. If his salary (one thousand five hundred pounds for equipage and one hundred pounds a month salary in 1668-

69) was not enough, he was expected to maintain the honor and prestige of his monarch by the use of his own funds.[35] It was for this reason that Montagu felt, since he was forced to use his own monies in the service of his country, there was no immorality in his frequent requests for the sums he considered his due; sums over and above his salary which he constantly complained was totally inadequate for the post of Ambassador. Therefore, he saw no impropriety in seeking as compensation a position either as a Commissioner of the Treasury, or membership of the Commissionaries of the Prizes. (Arlington - April 13, 1672).

On February 5, 1669/70, Montagu wrote Arlington:

Madame [Henriette Anne] did me the favour to recommend me in her last letters to the King for the Commissionaire's place in the Treasury, void by my Lord General's death. Sir William Coventry's is not yet filled, though I hear Mr. Grey has the other; so she has now recommended me to that. I do not doubt but you will stand my friend in the business. It will be very seasonable to help me in the expense I am at here, which I swear is double of what the King allows me, and it will be a good retreat for me when the King shall have no more occasion of my service here. It costs the King nothing, for I share only with the other four Commissionaires, who will do the business better in my absence than, may be, if I were upon the place. ... This thing will be an absolute settling of my

fortune, which you know, with my brother's
debts, my father's liberality, and what I am
forced to spend here, is in no good condition.
To conclude, my Lord, I assure you, upon my
word and honour, I have spent already, and I
have been here but ten months, above nine
thousand pistoles, not reckoning my equipage,
towards which the King gave me fifteen hundred
pounds, and afterwards out of the Prizes a
thousand, which did not near serve.[36]

A Commissionaire's position was a lucrative one, for it
brought with it a percentage of the booty of captured
shipping and this was one way to amass a fortune to
enable him to secure his own future, pay his brother's
debts, reimburse his father for his largesse and help
to pay his own debts.

Montagu did not have long to wait. On January 2,
1671 he received the first of the honors he thought were
due him. He was admitted to the King's Privy Council,[37]
and was to be a member of this body until his disgrace
in 1679. Nevertheless, he thought himself worthy of
more and greater honors, even that of the Garter, as a
result of his services. In his letters there are constant reminders of his exceptional devotion to the King
and many hints that there should be some reward for his
services which Arlington brought to Charles's notice.[38]
Still, despite the constant pleas, Charles evidently
felt that a place on the Privy Council and the permit-
ting of Montagu to purchase the title of Master of the
Great Wardrobe from his cousin, Earl of Sandwich, for
fourteen thousand pounds (August 12, 1671) with an
annual yield of three thousand pounds, were rewards

enough for services rendered to the Crown.39 It would seem that the refusal on Charles' part of the Garter should have indicated to Montagu that Charles had given all he intended to give. Perhaps he had tired of Montagu's constant importunities for favors. But Montagu missed this possibility. He complained of his master's treatment (April 12, 1672):

> In all things that concerns my person or my fortune the King has showed me so little favour or good will, and yet I know not why, for I never displeased him, that I am obliged to take hold of a favourable conjuncture, or somebody's recommendation that he considers, for upon my own account I can never expect his Majesty will think I deserve anything.40

The next day he again petitioned for a place on the Commission of Prizes. This too was refused him.41 This time Arlington was unable to help him; Buckingham continually undermined Arlington's position at Court and Arlington found himself growing more and more ineffective in his dealings with the King. The quarrel between Buckingham and Arlington had been growing for some time. They disagreed intensely over Charles' pro-French-anti-Dutch foreign policy; Buckingham supported the pro-French policy and Charles inclined to favor Buckingham. Observing the growing coolness between the two, Montagu warned Arlington some years before of Buckingham's growing animosity towards him (September 15, 1670):

> Upon all discourses I have had with him [Buckingham] concerning your Lordship, I find

he pretends to be very fair, but I cannot but
let you know that he has a great opinion of my
Lord Ashley, Orery, and Sir Thomas Osburne.
Your best way with him, if I may advise you,
is to let him see you do not want him much;
for I am confident you are much the stronger
of the two, and whilst he knows that, there is
no danger of him.[42]

This animosity between Buckingham and Arlington would
eventually touch Montagu and he would find himself in
open opposition to Buckingham.

Meanwhile, Montagu hinted that he could not
continue on as ambassador because of the expenses he
incurred as a result of his office and on account of the
slowness of the King in releasing the owed funds. Even
his office of the Wardrobe was no help; it did not
fatten his empty purse--for no payment was made.
Charles, badly in need of funds to prepare for the war
with the Dutch, stopped all government payments, the so-
called Stop of the Exchequer of January 1, 1672.

The government was heavily in debt to the
bankers because it had borrowed from them at
an exorbitant rate of interest on the security
of forthcoming taxes, the money being
automatically repaid as the revenues flowed
through into the Exchequer by what were known
as 'orders in course', a system which began
when it had been decided in 1665 that revenues
were to be appropriated to specific purposes
("the Downing proviso"). If these orders were
stopped, the money would become available for

current expenditure. The government was not
thereby declaring its bankruptcy, but postpon-
ing for the time being the repayment of its
debts with interest to the bankers.[43]

Montagu was suffering from the `disease' common to
all who tried to fulfill diplomatic obligations: the
constant lack of money. In a letter dated April 2, 1672
he stated:

> I have, since my employment here, lived at
> much a greater rate than formerly the English
> Ambassadors used to do. ... I have never
> troubled his Majesty for anything, nor in my
> three years' time had any extraordinary paid
> me, only for the mourning of the Queen Mother
> [died Sept. 10, 1669] and something for my
> journey into Flanders. I know how precious a
> thing ready money is now in England, and
> therefore in this conjuncture I would like to
> be as little pressing upon his Majesty as I
> possibly can be. All I desire is that he
> would be pleased to order my ordinary allow-
> ance to be paid me, of which one quarter's
> allowance is stopped by the last resuming of
> the assignments.[44]

Montagu now had to look elsewhere for a source of ready
funds. He hit upon the idea that the quickest way to
attain money was by a good marriage; that is, by a
wealthy marriage! But who was available for marriage
and who possessed at the same time a vast fortune?
After "surveying the field," Montagu settled upon the
charming and very wealthy Elizabeth Wriothesley,

daughter of the Earl of Southampton, Charles II's first Lord Treasurer, and the widow of Joceline Percy, 11th Earl of Northumberland.

Elizabeth was 24 years of age at this time. She was beautiful, fascinating and (this was of extreme importance to Montagu) she possessed vast property in her own right and received an income of over six thousand pounds a year, her inheritance from her maternal grandfather, the Earl of Chichester. Elizabeth married Lord Joceline Percy in 1662 and bore three children: Lady Elizabeth, later Duchess of Somerset; Lord Henry, died in 1669; and Lady Henrietta, who died in infancy. In 1669, Elizabeth and her husband traveled abroad for their health. It was in Paris that Montagu met the couple and was able to be of service to them: finding them available lodgings at the Hotel de Basionere, which was at one time the residence of the Queen Mother.[45] Montagu was again of aid, when, in his capacity as ambassador, he was able to save them considerable trouble with some over-zealous customs agents. "My Lord Northumberland has been extremely ill used here by the officers of the Customhouse, about some Spanish horses that they have seized; and if they do not give him all satisfaction, I shall be obliged to make a public complaint" (January 11, 1669/70).[46] The Countess Northumberland became ill and the Earl placed her in the care of the physician and philosopher, John Locke, who was the medical consultant to the Northumberland family[47] Lord Northumberland then traveled on to Italy, where he died on the 21st of May 1670. Young Lady Northumberland (about 23 years of age), returned to England to oversee the management of her vast inheritance and to oppose the spiteful conduct of her mother-in-law, the Dowager Lady of Northumberland, regarding the custody of her daughter, Lady Betty,[48] aged five or six.

[Elizabeth] was on good terms with [Charles II]. It had been earlier rumored that Charles would have liked to draw her into a closer and more intimate relationship. However, she had no wish to become either Charles' mistress, sister-in-law, (wife of the widowed Duke of York) or the mother-in-law of Charles' illegitimate sons should one of them marry one of her daughters, the Lady fled to France.[49]

Elizabeth returned to France in 1672 and remained there to avoid the "designs" of Charles and of her shrewish mother-in-law. She had no sooner arrived in Paris than Montagu made his first move to win her hand. Freed from ambassadorial duties by Robert Spencer, Second Earl of Sunderland, appointed successor to Montagu as Ambassador to the French Court, 1672, Montagu became her sympathetic and understanding friend; at all times he was most solicitous in tendering his polite attentions. Montagu did not rush the courtship, he knew enough to take his time, and so he conducted a slow and gradual 'assault' for her affections. He knew that he must gradually win her regard for Montagu was neither good looking nor greatly wealthy.

Montagu was by no means an Adonis, being not very tall, inclining to fat, and the owner of a coarse and rather swarthy countenance. But what he lacked in looks he made up for by polish and courtliness and still more by an extreme assiduity in business....[50]

He was, as Philbert Comte de Grammont, French anecdotist, says in his Memoirs: "...no very dangerous rival on account of his person, but very much to be feared for his assiduity, the acuteness of his wit, and some other talents which are of importance, when a man is once permitted to display them."[51]

Montagu, man of the world, knew that if he was to win the Lady it would take patience and persistence on his part. Little by little he succeeded in gaining her confidence and affection. He soon recognized, however, that the greatest obstacle to his courtship was the need to reconcile the lady to the possibility that should she marry she would lose the guardianship of her young daughter. According to her late husband's will this was the penalty she would be forced to suffer for remarriage; the child would become the ward of her ill-tempered mother-in-law.[52] This proviso discouraged any idea of remarriage; it left her with the hard choice of either marrying and turning over her child to her detested mother-in-law or remaining a widow the rest of her life.[53] In order to protect the child, the father had penalized the mother. Faced with such distasteful alternatives, the mother had determined upon widowhood. But she had not reckoned on a man of Montagu's determination. With the coolness and the self-confidence of a commander beseiging a fortification which he knew would fall in time, he set about to weaken her resolution and induce her to sacrifice her maternal instincts.[54]

Montagu made sure he was with her constantly, rendering every possible assistance.[55]

Montagu, the spoilt darling of society, long
continued her most humble and devoted slave,
gratifying all her caprices, resenting no
coldness or rebuffs, and refusing as much as
to look upon other beauties for fear of giving
her offence, and in the end his constancy and
perseverence met with their reward.[56]

Once he even followed her to Aix (Aachen) for the
winter of 1672, using as his excuse the breaking of his
journey to Italy where he intended to take a long
contemplated holiday.[57] In a letter to Arlington dated
January 6, 1673, he said he put off his proposed trip
using as his excuse that he did not want to go to Rome
"...lest people think I go on business."[58] Montagu did
not want anyone to think that he, like his cousin,
Walter, converted to Catholicism.

Montagu would hardly have converted to Catholicism!
Religion did not apparently play an important role in
his life. He was not conspicuous for his worship in or
advocacy of the Established Church of England. Religion
simply presented the necessary facade for respectability
and one's acceptance in society. If he did not take his
professed religion seriously, it is hardly possible that
he would embrace a religion the profession of which was
a political liability. Had Montagu converted or had
there been even a rumor of his conversion to
Catholicism, his career as a diplomat would end and his
place at Court be taken away. Even though Charles
favored the Catholic religion personally, he could not
openly espouse it and had great difficulty protecting
anyone who embraced it. The political climate of
England in the seventeenth century was extremely hostile

to those who professed any form of the "Papist" doctrine. They could only expect harrassment, persecution and possibly death. Such a future had no appeal to Montagu; he aspired to a life of honor and wealth.

In April of 1673 Montagu returned to Paris. At this time he reportedly began to offer his attentions to a former "object" of his affections--the Duchess of de Brissac (probably the widow of the Duke de Brissac). Lady Northumberland took a dim view of the attentions her 'suitor' offered to the Duchess, more to him than a mere acquaintance, and it was rumored, according to Madame de la Fayette, Montagu now had little or no chance of winning the Lady Northumberland.[59] However, Montagu suffered only a temporary setback in his pursuit[60].

Meanwhile, Elizabeth returned from Aix and was once again enjoying the Montagu wit and charm. Although a source of amusement and of witty conversation for her, he could not quite solve her dilemma: to marry and lose her child or not to marry and remain a widow for the rest of her life. Montagu accordingly wrote to Arlington about the Earldom promised his father by Charles in gratitude for his loyalty.[61] The letter about the promised Earldom was a calculated move on Montagu's part. If his father were so honored, Montagu could then pursue his suit all the more strongly because of this indication of a royal favor. Having an Earl as a father would then allow him to approach his lady as a potential equal. His father, however, never received the Earldom.

Eventually, however, Montagu, at 35 years of age, won the day and the match was made; a rich and charming bride of 28 was won. Once when Charles met Elizabeth at

Court, probably shortly after her marriage, he asked her what she saw in Montagu that caused her to love him. She wittily answered that she was more interested in his mind than in his body. Charles apparently accepted a loyal wife's appraisal of Montagu, and he was returned to Royal favor.

However, some secret Whispers have made it current that besides the publick, one his Grace [Montagu] had another Instruction, which was to solicit the King's Interest to a very fine English Lady then in France, whom King Charles had entertain'd during his abode there, a very great Opinion of, and as some say, sought her in an Honourable way: be that as it will, his Ambassador like'd of the Lady extremely well, himself, and judg'd as she was a match hardly suitable (tho' very well deserving) of a King, he did not, nor was he able to judge of his Majesty's Intentions; and if the King design'd no more than an Amour, he thought it likewise that the Lady's deserts, as well in Beauty and Wit, as in Fortune, put her something above an Affair of that kind; for which reason his Grace wittily try'd his own Interest, and for one Word he spoke for the King, spoke two for himself, till at length receiving some Encouragement to his Proceedings, he enforc'd his suit so far, that the Lady wholly gave up the Possession of the Person, being one of the greatest Fortunes than any English nobleman could boast of. And as it has often been said, when King Charles afterwards saw the Lady at his own Court, he

asked her what she could see in Montagu's Face
to love him? To which the Lady wittily
answer'd That indeed she did not see much in
his Person; but she saw a great deal in his
Mind and Accomplishments. This very well
satisfied the King, and restor'd his then
Lordship at least seemingly to his Favour
again.[62]

Through this marriage Montagu would establish close
ties with such distinguished families as the Percys
(Northumberlands), the Wriothesleys (Southamptons),
Leights (Chichesters) and the Russells.[63] Such a
marriage was also most fortunate for Montagu from the
standpoint of wealth. Elizabeth brought as her dowry
vast wealth in family lands and the amount of six
thousand pounds per annum. Further, in case there were
no children from the union, she settled the entire
estate upon Ralph during his life in preference to any
other claimant. Montagu's father was so pleased with
the impending marriage that he settled his estate upon
his son and granted him the gift of two thousand pounds
per annum.[64] This sum plus the revenue from the office
of the Great Wardrobe (3,000 pounds per annum) meant
that Ralph, at age thirty-five, was to begin married
life with a sum of five thousand pounds a year on his
own. This sum along with the six thousand pounds by
reason of his marriage truly made them one of the
richest couples in all of England.

On the 24th of August 1673, at the ancestral home
of the Wriothesley family at Tichfield (about forty
miles southwest of London), Ralph Montagu and Elizabeth,

Countess of Northumberland were wed.65 True to her promise, as soon as the marriage took place, the Dowager Countess of Northumberland, now in her sixties, declared her right to take custody of the infant heiress, Lady Betty Percy, according to the will of her late son.66

The match was not the success hoped for. Within a year a separation was contemplated. Their marital difficulties soon became known. The troubles are recounted in the Letters of Sir Joseph Williamson. "My Lady of Northumberland and her new husband, Mr. Montague, have already begun to differ upon a report risen from him, as she says, that he bought her of her mayd for 500=per annum, and the Towne talks of parting them."67 "Mr. Montague and his Lady begin already to live like man and wife, neither caring a rush for the other, which makes her marrying of him more and more to be wondered at, and that for him she should refuse not only Mr. Savill but Mr. Gray too; ...."68 "Your friend Ralph Montague hath managed his matter soe that he and his Countess lye in two beds, the reason sayd to be strong jealousy of the old mistress" [probably the Duchess de Brissac].69 However, there must have been some rapproachment between them, since for she bore him four children, three sons: Ralph, Winwood and John; and one daughter, Anne.

Montagu may not have been `lucky in love,' but this did not stop him from devoting himself to fulfilling a promise he made to himself while ambassador: to live in the style he became accustomed to while in Paris. He devoted his time and energies to the planning and building of a great town house worthy of the rank to which he felt sure he would rise in the not too distant future. The site for this mansion was in The Bloomsbury section of London, on land purchased in June of 1675 for the sum of two thousand six hundred and ten pounds and a farm fee of five pounds a year for the seven acre plot.70 This was the first Montagu house and was destroyed by fire in January 1685/6; the second was readily rebuilt out of the remaining shell.

The year 1673 was not the happiest for Montagu; his life was somewhat complicated by a quarrel with Buckingham. Because Buckingham characteristically over-estimated his self-worth, he tended to look upon any kindness done him as naturally his due. "As for my Lord Buckingham, I have done all [probable reference to any aid or assistance given Buckingham when Montagu was ambassador in Paris] that a man can do to send him away well satisfied with me; if I have succeeded I shall think I have done no small matter."71 Buckingham was in Paris in 1670 negotiating trade agreements (September 3, 1670).70 Montagu came to view this usage by one whom he used to count amongst his friends with a jaundiced eye. He once wrote Arlington concerning his friendship for Buckingham (May 8, 1669): "I am more nearly concerned for the King my master, without being formal or politic, and afterwards for you and my Lord of Buckingham, who are both my friends."73

It never occurred to Montagu that the reason for Buckingham's hostility was that he blamed him for the loss of the honor and glory of being the commander of the six thousand troops to be raised against the Dutch, at Charles' expense, as stated in the Secret Treaty of Dover. Buckingham complained to Charles of this. He knew that Montagu had by this time thrown in his lot with

Arlington and opposed him for both his pro-French sympathies and his part in promoting the Anglo-French Alliance. Charles answered that it mattered not if Montagu had acted out of spite, or even of hatred for Buckingham. To his credit, Charles declared that he could not help approving of Montagu's conduct if only from the good he had done his nation. He then added, in anger, that on such occasions when great interests are at stake he would consider him, Buckingham, a dog fit only to serve his master.[74] Buckingham was never to forget this stinging rebuke from his monarch nor was he ever to forgive Montagu.

In December of 1673 Buckingham openly quarreled with Montagu, whom he made the scapegoat for the injuries he suffered: his loss of command, and the King's reprimand. One day at Whitehall, Buckingham, on his way to see the King, noticed Montagu in the circle of Courtiers around the King and deliberately tried to jostle Montagu out of his way.[75] Montagu then supposedly then challenged Buckingham to a duel with the words "Follow me!" But Buckingham preferred to wait till the next day for this meeting. Directly upon learning what had happened, Charles took Buckingham's part in the quarrel and sent Montagu to the Tower (December 3, 1672).[76] Montagu then asked Arlington (who equally disliked Buckingham) to intercede for him.

Hester W. Chapman in her work <u>Great</u> <u>Villiers,</u> <u>A</u> <u>study</u> <u>of</u> <u>George</u> <u>Villiers,</u> <u>Second</u> <u>Duke</u> <u>of</u> <u>Buckingham</u> says that Arlington put Montagu up to the quarrel.

It is quite possible that Arlington, not caring to reply to Buckingham's attack at the Council board, had instructed Montagu to pick a quarrel with him. No one, not even Charles himself, would be able to protect the Duke if he became involved in another duel. Unfortunately for Arlington, Montagu was arrested for challenging a peer in the King's presence and sent to the Tower. Montagu denied that he had ever made the challenge. What probably happened was this: Montagu, primed by Arlington and relying on Buckingham's irritable and hostile humour, brought on the quarrel in the hope that the Duke would take the initiative. When they left the withdrawing room, he must have been certain of success; but by the time he was angry with Buckingham, and the giving and taking of the challenge was no doubt confused and simultaneous; they had barely interchanged a few words before the King, aware of the trap, had Montagu arrested.77

Being sentenced to the Tower held fear for anyone so sentenced. It meant separation from family and friends, confinement in a cell that was rather bleak and usually cold (especially during the winter), subsistence on food of very poor quality and the added penalty of being a financial burden to the family of the prisoner. Added to this, there was always the matter of the length of stay. This was of especial concern since it often depended upon the 'pleasure' of the King or Parliament, and often this 'pleasure' was not expressed; the prisoner was left to wonder about the duration of his imprisonment. It is little wonder then that the very name of the Tower struck fright in the hearts of the people and caused a deep fear of both King and Parliament. Montagu with his taste for the finer things of life had very little desire to spend even one day in the precincts of this prison. He feared for his life and his family. Writing to Arlington he complained (c.1673):

> Just now the Sergeant-at-Arms was with me with
> an order to go to the Tower. I am very
> willing to obey the King's commands, but the
> words of the order are drawn up, I suppose,
> with an intention of further inconvenience to
> me, for it is expressed, `for challenging the
> Duke Buckingham in the King's presence'; which
> interpretation to the word[s] `Follow me", was
> made by the Duke of Buck[ingham's] friends,
> whereas I meant nothing but the avoiding a
> noise in the presence. Therefore I desire, if
> it be possible, that the King be moved to have
> the order altered, for you know the Duke of
> Buck[ingham's] <u>chicon</u> (?) enough, that if it
> be taken for granted I challenged in the
> King's presence, he may pursue it farther, and
> I do absolutely protest against any such
> thing.[78]

Montagu was willing to obey the order for his imprison-ment but he objected to the wording of this order. He claimed it did not really tell the facts as they were. Montagu was released from the Tower three days later and put under house arrest to satisfy Buckingham.[79]

Arlington was slow to help Montagu in his plight. Even though Arlington had been made a Knight of the Garter (June 15, 1672) and an Earl (April 2, 1672), and

could have used these new honors to be of aid, Montagu
was passed over for the office of Secretary of the
Treasury, one of the most important official posts the
King could confer upon a servant of the Crown.   Lord
Thomas Clifford, Arlington's choice, was given the post,
but shortly resigned and Thomas Osborne, Buckingham's
protege and the future Earl of Danby, was appointed Lord
Treasurer.[80]   Arlington was beginning to lose ground.
Assailed as a promoter of popery and an embezzler, he
was impeached on January 15, 1674, by the House of
Commons.   As a result of this, he sold his post as
Secretary of State to Sir Joseph Williamson and content-
ed himself with the ornamental post of Lord Chamberlain
(September 11, 1674).   Montagu now began to think that
he best shift loyalty.   He recalled what he had written
some time previously (October 19, 1669):

> ...it is a custom in England that when the
> King is angry with anybody, that he makes them
> be acted, and that my Lord Buckingham and Bab
> May had acted you to the King, and endeavoured
> to turn you en ridicule. The expression is
> not very civil from me to you, but in a story
> one must leave out nothing. ...who said he
> heard it at the French Ambassador's in
> England, from one who was present when the
> King was entertained with your comedy. Who-
> ever did it, it could not make you more
> ridiculous in England than the thing appears
> ridiculous here.   ... Pray God in heaven
> keep you from the Court's falling on you in
> jest, and the Parliament in earnest, when the
> King does not take your part.[81]

Arlington was out of favor and could do no more for Montagu. Montagu now pondered how he could retain favor at Court. Should he take up with Osborne, the new Lord Treasurer? Montagu did not like him nor did he trust this man since he was a friend of Buckingham and Buckingham was definitely his enemy. After much thought, he came upon the idea of a compromise. He would attempt to retain Arlington and seek Osborne in a position of patronage. To give up on Arlington was to give up on a known quantity; besides, he liked him. Arlington was a man of an affable and pleasant nature. Montagu's correspondence shows he was able to communicate with him in an easy manner; his wry humor and tendency towards newsiness easily comes through as one reads his letters to the Secretary. Osborne was not of this temperament. He was careful in speech sanguine in temper, stiff and business-like in his deportment with those who had dealings with him.82 Noting these differences between his former master and his possible new supporter, Montagu may well have then decided that it would be best to deal with Osborne in a business-like manner.

Looking back at the ambassadorial year it becomes evident that Montagu's need for money to maintain his embassy in Paris forced him into the position of constantly requesting funds from his sovereign. This was not out of the ordinary, it was the constant complaint of those on envoy. There was never enough money to cover ordinary expenses, much less those of extraordinary nature. To recoup his losses as ambassador Montagu was forced into petitioning the King for money on all sorts of pretexts. When no money was forthcoming, he had to seek other means.

Montagu's desire to live well and nobly fed his need for wealth. But his ambassadorial situation never yielded enough money. This illustrates a weakness of the patronage system. Office gained on the basis of family ties and personal wealth and not upon ability meant that it was not always the most able who represented the monarch. A further weakness of this system was that it offered mainly to the wealthy the opportunity of entering the diplomatic body and closing it to the less fortunate. In this respect, Montagu was representative of the standards of his age. He was wealthy enough to enter the diplomatic service, and he could support himself and at the same time manifest the glory of the monarch. However, expenses over and above the normal representation were at his own personal risk. As such, then, any opportunity which presented itself that could enlarge his fortune without, however, being prejudiced to the monarch, was his own. Accordingly, then, Montagu, as did many others, accepted as justifiable a standard of conduct for activities in the political, social and economic spheres which accepted the use of duplicity and expediency. It was simply put in the axiom: "The end justifies the means."

When the needed funds were not forthcoming, Montagu turned to the next best expedient. He sought, found, wooed and married one of the wealthiest hieresses in the land. This marriage was most fortunate for him, not only in the size of the fortune which came to him, but because of the social status it brought him. The Countess of Northumberland was both rich and prominent. She was well received at Court and was on inimate terms with Charles II. While Montagu could not have made a better choice and his future should have been bright. However, such was not the case. Montagu gained enormously in wealth, he did not thereby improve his place in society. He remained plain Mr. Montagu and his wife necessarily accepted a reduction in title to that of Lady Montagu. Whether his marriage brought him often to Court and into contact with the King is not known--however, it is probable, since Montagu was extremely anxious for royal favor, and his wife was a royal favorite, that he and his wife were frequently in attendance. Montagu knew the value of the rank of his wife and no doubt intended to make the best use of it for his own personal gain. His marriage was, like everything for Montagu, a means to an end.

If he thought that his marriage raised him in social estimation and thereby gained him the favor of the King, Montagu was mistaken. In fact, he almost lost everything by his own imprudence. His quarrel with Buckingham almost cost him his fortune and future; it earned him the displeasure of the King and a term in the Tower. This turn of events might have been catastrophic to one of lesser aspirations. It did seem to pose a major setback to his political career and his rise at Court, but Montagu was not a man to take defeat lightly. He prudently retired from Court and coolly assessed the situation. He intended to return.

CHAPTER III
Footnotes

1The Court in Mourning, p. 3.

2J. P. Kenyon, The Stuarts (London: Fontana/Collins, 1958), pp. 102-103.

3Sue Bradbury, A Few Royal Occasions (London: The Folio Press, 1977), p. 47; E. S. de Beer, ed., Diary of John Evelyn (Oxford: Clarendon Press, 1955), IV, 403.

4Ralph Dutton, English Court Life - From Henry VII to George II (London: B. T. Batsford, 1963), p. 137.

5George Maculay Trevelyan, English Social History - A Survey of Six Centuries from Chaucer to Queen Victoria (London and New York: Longman Group Limited, 1978), p. 295.

6Mary Coate, Social Life in Stuart England (London: Methuen and Co. Ltd., 1924), p. 73, p. 75.

7Maurice Ashley, Charles II (Frogmore: Panther Books Ltd., 1973), pp. 328-29.

8Coate, p. 1.

9D. B. Horn, The British Diplomatic Service, 1689-1789 (Oxford: Clarendon Press, 1961), pp. 93-94.

[10]Ibid., p. 92.

[11]Ibid., p. 90.

[12]Ibid., pp. 90-92.

[13]Ibid., p. 92; Cal. S.P. Dom., 1683, p. 24; 1668-9, p. 533.

[14]Horn, p. 94.

[15]Ibid., p. 95.

[16]Phyllis Gene Blazer, "The Life of Sir Thomas Chaloner; Tudor Soldier, Courtier, Poet and Diplomat, 1521-1565," Diss. State University of New York at Buffalo 1978, pp. 335-36.

[17]Falk, p. 78.

[18]Buccleuch MSS. I, 428.

[19]Ibid., p. 428.

[20]Ibid., p. 436.

[21]Ibid., p. 423.

[22]Ibid., p. 432.

[23]Ibid., p. 432.

[24]Ibid., p. 432.

[25]Ibid., pp. 431-32.

[26]Ibid., pp. 491 (Dec. 17, 1670), 492 (Dec. 24, 1670), 493 (January 10, 1670/71).

[27]Ibid., pp. 494-95.

[28]Ibid., p. 504.

[29]Montagu, I, 275-76; Henry B. Wheatley, The Diary of Samuel Pepys, (London: George Bell and Sons, 1904, II, 188.

[30]Buccleuch MSS. I, 484.

[31]Ibid., p. 483.

[32]Ibid., p. 497.

[33]Ibid., p. 517.

[34]Lawrence Stone, Family and Fortune: Studies in Aristocratic Finance in the Sixteenth and Seventeenth Centuries (Oxford: Clarendon Press, 1973), p. 240.

[35]Buccleuch MSS. I, 520: Cal. Treas. Bks. 1667-68, p. 644; Cal. S.P. Dom. 1668-9, p. 124; 1676-77, p. 208.

[36]Buccleuch MSS. I. 465.

[37]P.R.O. Privy Council/2/63; John Dalrymple, Memoirs of Great Britain and Ireland: From the Dissolution of the last Parliament of Charles II, till the Capture of the French and Spanish Fleets at Vito (London: Printed for A. Strahan and T. Cadell, et al., 1790), I, 127; Boyer, Annals, VIII, 369; Cockayne, p. 106; Firth, p. 710.

[38]Buccleuch MSS. I, 468-69 (March 12, 1670). 483 (Sept. 6, 1670). 594-96 (Jan. 28, 1671). 512 (Feb. 15, 1672). 518-19 (Apr. 2, 1672).

[39]Firth, p. 710; Falk, p. 82.

[40]Buccleuch MSS. I, 519.

[41]Ibid., p. 520.

[42]Ibid., p. 484.

[43]Ashley, pp. 181-82.
[44]Buccleuch MSS. I, 518.

[45]Falk, p. 85.

[46]Buccleuch MSS. I, 459.

[47]John Lough, Locke's Travels in France; 1675-1679: As Related in His Journals, Correspondence and Other Papers (Cambridge: At The University Press, 1952), p. VIII; Edward Barrington de Fonblanque, Annals of the House of Percy: From the Conquest to the Opening of the

Nineteenth Century (London: Richard Clay and Sons, 1887), pp. 484-85; Lewis Melville, The Windsor Beauties (Boston: Houghton Mifflin Co., 1928), p. 211; Falk, p. 85; Firth, p. 710.

[48]Montagu Memorandum Book, p. 36; Melville, pp. 488-89.

[49]Melville, p. 489; The Court in Mourning, p. 5; Boyer, Annals, VIII, 368-89; Firth, p. 710.

[50]Petherick, p. 112.

[51]Bohn's Extra Volume. Count Grammont's Memoirs of the Court of Charles the Second and the Boscobel Narratives: (Henry Bohn 1846) p. 121; Melville, p. 212.

[52]Falk, p. 87.

[53]W. D. Christie, Letters Addressed from London to Sir Joseph Williamson While Plenipotentiary at the Congress of Cologne in the Years 1673 and 1674 (London: Camden Society, 1874), I, 180; Melville, p. 212.

[54]Melville, p. 212, p. 213.

[55]de Fontblanque, p. 490.

[56]Ibid., p. 521.

[57]Buccleuch MSS. I, 521; Melville, p. 512.

[58]Ibid., p. 521.

[59]Melville, p. 213. "Montagus' en va, on dit que ses esperances seront renversees; je crois qu'il y a quelque chose de travers dans l'esprit de la nymphe."

[60]Ibid., p. 213.

[61]Buccleuch MSS. i, 521 (April 15, 1673).

[62]The Court in Mourning, pp. 4-5.

[63]Cockayne, IX, 107; Melville, p. 215.

[64]Edward Maunde Thompson, ed., Correspondence of the Family of Hatton: Being Chiefly Letters Addressed to Christopher First viscount Hatton, A.D. 1601-1704 (WestminsterL: Camden Society, 1871) I, 68; William Durrant-Cooper, Saville Correspondence: Letters to And From Henry Saville, Esq., Envoy at Paris, and Vice-Chamberlain to Charles II. and James II. Including Letters From His Brother George Marquess of Halifax (Westminster: Camden Society, 1878), p. 32 and p. 38; Christie, I, 179-80; Firth, p. 710.

[65]Marriage Register - Hampshire Record Office; Firth, p. 710.

[66]Melville, p. 213-214.

[67]Christie, II, 35; Firth, p. 710.

[68]Christie, II, 63; Firth, p. 710.

[69]Christie, II, 71; Firth, p. 710.

[70]Gladys Scott Thompson, The Russell's in Bloomsbury: 1669-1771 (London: Jonathan Cape, 1940), pp. 64-65.

[71]Buccleuch MSS. I, 484.

72Ibid., p. 482; Falk, p. 92.

[73]Ibid., p. 424.

[74]Dalrymaple, I, App. 127-128; Falk, pp. 93-94.

75Christie, II, 89-90; Firth, p. 710.

[76]P.R.O. Privy Council/2/64/f. 138; State Papers, Domestic/29/338/ff. 66-67, 69-70; 1673-5, ff. 43-6; Hester W. Chapman, Great Villiers, Second Duke of Buckingham, 1628-87 9London: Secker and Warburg, 1949), p. 204.

[77]Chapman, p. 204.

78Buccleuch MSS. I, 522.

[79]Falk, p. 93.
Imprisonment in the Tower was a definite expense in those days. In the Tower Warrants (WO 94/4) at Kew Gardens Public Record Office there is found a record of the cost of the housing and feeding of the prisoners. For example: The Earl of Danby's imprisonment (a) June 25,1680-Sept, 29, 1680 (13 weeks, 6 days) at 10 shillings per day - total 30 pounds, 15 shillings and 5-1/2 pence; (b) March 26,1681 to June 24, 1681 (13 weeks)

at 10 shillings a day - total 28 pounds, 17 shillings
and 5 pence. There is no record of Montagu's imprisonment being recorded in the Prisoners Roll Book, nor is
there any record of his expenses incurred while being
imprisoned there.

[80]Osmond Airy, "Bennet, Henry, Earel of Arlington,"
Dictionary of National Biography I., 232--233.

[81]Buccleuch MSS. I, 442.

[82]Sidney Lee, "Osborne, Sir Thomas, Earl of Danby and
Duke of Leeds (1631-1712)," Dictionary of National
Biography XIV, 1189-90; Lockeyer, pp. 345-6.

CHAPTER IV
Montagu, The Thwarted Schemer

Few men knew better than Montagu the
advantages which England might derive from
intrigue with France, and had it not been for
the attendant dangers he would have entered
into direct relations with Charles II and
organized such an intrigue himself. As it
was, he considered it more prudent to induce
or even compel Danby to take up the matter,
confident that if all went well he would
profit by the Treasurer's gratitude, while if
anything went ill he would be able to shelter
behind him.[1]

Momentarily forced out of government by royal
displeasure, Montagu did not give up hope for future
advancement. He quietly bided his time. Occupying himself with domestic affairs such as building his palace
in Bloomsbury, he quietly awaited that opportunity
which came in August of 1676 to become once again a
royal servant- Ambassador to the Court of Louis XIV.
Whether or not the lesson of the Tower had been lost on
Montagu the reader will discover in the following pages,
but first a discussion of his building.

Selecting a piece of land in Bloomsbury
called Baber's Field which, in turn, enclosed another
field called the Long Field, Montagu purchased seven
acres for his new home. He planned a home worthy of a

nobleman and, therefore, he determined to spare no expense in its building. He had not forgotten the lessons of magnificence learned in France.

> Every care was taken in drawing up the agreement that the new house should be worthy of Southampton House, which was so close at hand. Just as it had been stipulated in the Earl of Southampton's building license that their intended mansion was to be suitable for a nobleman of his rank, so the Earl's successors made the same kind of stipulation in the agreement with Lord Montagu. Any building erected by the latter was to be specifically a fair and large dwelling, fit for the noble family, designed in a uniform style, with offices suitable to such a mansion house.[2]

The architect chosen for designing the house was Robert Hooke, of the Royal Society, while the artist chosen for its decoration was the famous Italian painter Antonio Verrio (1675).[3] The house took some time to complete, but must have been finished by the late Spring of 1676 since John Evelyn mentions his going to view it (Diary, May 7, 1676): "I dined with Mr. Charleton, and went to see Mr. Montague's new palace neere Bloomsbury, built by Mr. Hooke of our Society, after the French manner."[4]

Although occupied with domestic items, Montagu did not give up his hope of obtaining some future important post in government. Accordingly, he was not above the use of flattery, liberally dispensed, as an integral part of his strategy in dealing with his superiors.

However, he reasoned, and rightly so, it would take more than flattery if he was to obtain the good will of Osborne, new Lord Treasurer and Chief Minister of Government, and ensure his help in securing some Court appointment.

But luckily for Montagu, Charles began to take a renewed interest in him. Montagu, husband to one of the richest women in the land and stepfather to an hieress of the vast Percy estates, was not a person to be ignored. Charles began to show favorable signs of recognition to the Montagus. Ralph's uncle, William Montagu, was appointed Lord Chief Baron of the Exchequer, an office he held till the second year of James II's reign.5 Perhaps in some way Charles felt that small signs of favor would make up for his failure to truly honor Montagu's father, Edward, Second Baron of Montagu, for his help in his restoration to the Throne. Possibly he thought that by these gifts he might receive favorable compliance from that family should he decide to invoke the Royal prerogative of Wardship, and unite Ralph's step-daughter, the Lady Betty Percy, now eight or nine years of age, to one of his illegitimate sons. Such a union would definitely be of financial benefit to him, not to mention the ties of loyalty to the Crown such a union would insure. At any rate, in August (September 1) of 1676,6 Charles appointed Montagu Ambassador to the Court of Louis XIV, and again on December 4, 1677.7

With his appointment as ambassador, Montagu now had to deal directly with Charles' Lord Treasurer, Thomas Osborne, created Earl of Danby in 1674. Danby's

priority upon assuming his office of Lord Treasurer,
was to achieve a balance between income and expenditure.
Danby favored a Protestant foreign policy (anti-French
and anti-Catholic) which would remove the enmity of the
House of Commons and turn it into a corperation conduc-
ive to a Parliamentary solution to the Royal financial
problems. Peace with Holland (Treaty of Westminster,
1674) had helped ease the flow of cash out of the
treasury and Danby concentrated on domestic affairs.

Danby was not a member of the CABAL. He did not
have the confidence of the King to the degree once
possessed by its members. A Tory Squire, turned politician, as a member and supporter of the Church of England
he was a staunch opponent of Catholicism. He opposed
the corruption of the Court and his great hope was to
see the real strength of England residing in a harmony
between a Protestant King and an Anglican Parliament.
With these political objectives, he early decided to
steer Charles on an anti-French, pro-Protestant course
in his foreign policy. Committing the King to such a
policy, he felt, would win the King the confidence and
support of the Commons, and thereby insure the steady
flow of subsidies allowing Charles his desired financial
independence of the same House.

Danby thought his plan would win favor with the
Commons, but he failed to reckon with Louis XIV and
Charles' desire to emulate him. Louis regarded the rise
of a Protestant England as a possible check to his
expansionist aspirations and did not hesitate to see to
it that his ministers in England were supplied with
funds to be used to bribe members of Parliament to

break openly with the King. Had he been more observant, Louis could have saved himself some money; opinion in the Commons at this time ran counter to Charles' policy. Anti-French feelings in the House were alive and well and any vote for money for Charles was viewed as a vote for France and Catholicism.

Charles' aim in life was to keep his Throne and at the same time live in a luxurious style. His years of poverty before the Restoration made the retention of his throne of vital importance to him. He did not wish to `go on his travels' again, hence he was most cautious that this desire be fulfilled without antagonizing the Protestant faction. As a result of this caution, Charles was rather slow to declare for Catholicism as agreed upon in the secret Treaty of Dover. Perhaps, on the one hand, Louis sensed the change of heart on Charles' part, and was, therefore, willing to spend thousands of pounds to thwart Danby's desired rapprochement between Charles and Commons. Charles was not willing, on the other hand, to commit himself to a war with France at the behest of Commons and then find that he had no means with which to extricate himself. Therefore, Charles desired that a secret link be kept open with France in the event that Danby's hope for rapprochement failed. Charles was constantly aware of the mistrust and suspicion on the part of Parliament when it came to the question of armies and subsidies and he lived in continual fear of the stopping of Parliamentary grants. This deep and almost constant distrust of Charles and his pro-French tendencies, on the part of Parliament, coupled with the fear that he would some day return England to the arms of Rome, forged a wedge between sovereign and Parliament that was to be an almost continual source of conflict.[8]

Montagu was no fool! He knew the King needed money. What better way of `serving the King' than by obtaining this much needed commodity for his master? If he could help to obtain the needed funds by means of a large subsidy there was no telling what personal advantages could come his way! With knowledge of how Louis operated, from his previous appointment, Montagu knew that Louis would be willing to part with gold in order to keep England from interferring on the Continent; he also knew of Danby's anti-French policy and his unsuccessful attempt to persuade Charles to adopt his plan. Montagu, reading Danby's dispatches `between the lines,' became aware of Danby's hope to counteract the effects which Charles' friendship with France might have on England.

With the advent of the Restoration, the office of the Lord Treasurer gradually came to dominate the various departments of the English government, even to the overshadowing of the office of Secretary of State. In reality the Lord Treasurer, since he controlled the expenditure of the public monies allotted the King, came to be the most important of the governmental functionaries and was viewed as the King's First Minister. As such, he was next in importance to the King in the formation of policy and issued the directives that ensured its being carried out. It was in this capacity that Danby came into direct contact with Montagu and directed his activities for the furtherance of the Crown's policy. That Danby acted as coordinator of Montagu's ambassadorial duties in relation to the French Crown is shown by the phrase "by your instructions" so often found in Montagu's official correspondence with Danby. However, this phrase in reality reflects nothing more than Montagu's stratagem. In letters dated January 3, January 18, August 12, December 29, 1678, for example, Montagu used such phrases as "I suggest", "I humbly advise", to convey his subtle hints to the Lord Treasurer as to the direction the King's policy should take in dealing with the French. Thus by means of subtle convincing, Montagu hoped to cause Danby to commit himself to the subsidy scheme and to hold out for the best offer--a subsidy of two hundred thousand pounds sterling. From Fountain-bleu, Montagu wrote to the King: "My Lord Treasurer having sent me new orders from your Majesty to insist still upon a supply of two hundred thousand pounds sterling till the peace were made and your letter commanding me to observe what orders he should give me.... (September 25, 1677)."[9] Montagu was, by all appearances, attempting to manipulate the Lord Treasurer and ingratiate himself all the more with the King and his First Minister in order to insure his further advancement.

Danby (about forty-seven years of age at this time) had taken office when Parliament was not sitting and labored under the supposition that there was to be a subsidy from Louis of two hundred thousand pounds sterling with which to operate the government. Montagu urged Danby, in another letter dated September 25, 1677:

I would have you doe that which none of the King's ministers have yet had the adresse to doe, which is to take an ascendent over France, which is next to what you have a mind

to doe, that is to cudgell them into a better
behavior and more respect towards our master.
And this is the time of doing it, for by
this we shall judge of our strength, which as
yet we are ignorant of.10

Meanwhile, Danby persuaded Charles to agree to the
marriage (first proposed in 1675) of William to Mary,
Charles' niece, daughter of James, Duke of York, by his
first wife, Anne, only insisted on this before any
agreement between England and Holland could be made by
which both nations agreed to force a peace treaty upon
Louis. The marriage took place in October 1679. By
January 1678 Danby also convinced Charles to sanction
the terms of the peace.11 Charles then sent Louis
Duras, Earl of Feversham, a Frenchman in the service of
England, to Paris with the authority to obtain an uncon-
ditional acceptance of this peace. Feversham was back
in England in early December with Louis's rejection of
the terms.12 As Montagu was in England for a short
visit, he was sent back to Paris with a request from
Charles to accept the demands. He returned to Paris
accompanied by the young Lord Dumblane, Danby's son,
Peregrine, who was to be Montagu's pupil in diplomacy,
but more probably to keep an eye on Montagu and report
back to Danby (December 29, 1677).13 Apparently, Danby
was still not too sure of his minister in Paris.

Montagu now found himself immersed in official
activities. Although involved in an almost endless
round of negotiations bargaining for English neutrality,
Montagu was ever careful to report to Coventry,
Secretary of State, about Louis' war in Flanders. These
almost daily reports were Montagu's way of impressing

upon his superiors that, even with all his duties, he was attentive to details and was indeed a reliable source of information so necessary in the formulation of Anglo-French policy. Montagu reported about Louis' troop movements, recruitments, the strengthening of the navy and fortifications of the various centers of conflict; he became a regular fountain of information as to the strengths and weaknesses of the French forces.[14]

Louis XIV's ambitions dominated the European political situation. For quite some time he desired to enhance his gloire through the extension of France's boundary beyond the Rhine barrier. But to do so meant the taking of the Spanish Netherlands (Flanders) and such a move imperiled the independence of the Dutch States. Still, Louis invaded the Dutch Provinces in March of 1672 and by the year 1673 the war became a European conflict. France was then placed in a very precarious position, for England, a secret ally of France against the Dutch, abandoned France and negotiated a separate peace with the United Provinces by the Treaty of Westminster in February of 1674.

Louis continued his struggle, but was forced by the year 1677 to sue for peace. After a number of successes as well as a number of defeats, the final campaign at Cassel, with the defeat of the Dutch, sealed the fate of Valenciennes, St. Omer and Cambrai. With this campaign, Louis at least 'straightened out' the line of his northern frontier into a a defensible perimeter. However, by 1677, the expansionist dreams of the Sun King faded; the Dutch put up too costly a resistance. Louis came to believe that France would not control the outlet of the Scheldt or of Antwerp and Louis accepted the political and military realities of the day. He had taken about all of the Spanish Netherlands that France needed to `round' out her frontiers. Further, political and military realities forced Louis to be satisfied with any peace which gave him even limited success in the Spanish Netherlands. Besides, Louis had to contend with difficulties at home: a bad harvest, near famine, and the unrest of the people made peace an imperative. France deserved and needed peace. The problem was how to obtain it. A general truce and cessation of arms for a year to fourteen months was proposed. This produced vigorous negotiations.

Naturally, and most importantly for Charles, financial arrangements were not forgotten in these negotiations. Louis was most anxious that England remain neutral. To ensure this neutrality large sums of money would be made available to Charles if only he could prevent Parliament from drawing England into a war with France. Montagu wrote Danby on December 29, 1677 that if Charles was able to preserve English neutrality the money would soon be forthcoming. Montagu assured Charles that:

> ...Monsieur de Louvoy [Louis's Secretary of War] told me that if the calling of the Parlament soe soone was an effect of your Majesty's greate want of money, there was noe summe you could desire that he did not believe his master, even to the engaging of his jewells, which are to soe vast a value, would not furnish you with, provided you would not let the Parlament draw you into a warr against France, that you could stop theire mouths with a generall truce for a year....15

The Dutch need never be the wiser about this money. "...such a summe of money as this would be hard to returne. But it should be put into wedges of gold; and soe put into Bales of silk and sent over in a Yatch...."16 Louis would not forget Charles, nor would Louis forget the Lord Treasurer:" ...as for my Lord Treasurer whome they looked upon as a greate adviser in this affaire, if I could but doe them the kindnesse heere as to sound him, there is nothing they would not give him to make him his fortune, it should be given him in diamonds and pearles that noe body could ever know it and I my self should not be forgott if I would propose it to him."17 To gain such treasures all Danby need to was to repudiate his anti-French attitude and policy.

While Charles was anxious about favorable financial arrangements with Louis as the price of English neutrality, he could not forget the need for of an advantageous trade agreement with France so necessary for England's economy. Charles remembered only too well the past trade relations of the English with the Dutch.

The Dutch were England's greatest commercial rival in the seventeenth century. England had suffered from this rivalry and had warred as a result of it. Charles intended to see to it that the Dutch never recovered from the blows inflected upon them by the English in the War of 1652-54 under Cromwell and the War of 1665-67. With this in mind, he entered into the Third Dutch War (1672-74) and hoped for the total elimination of the Dutch Republic. However, as the war was unpopular in England, Charles withdrew from the conflict and concluded the Treaty of Westminster in 1674. Dutch superiority in trade eventually evaporated and London became the world's market and banking center.

France had also come to rival England in the world of commerce. France controlled the Mediterranean and engaged in the colonization of Canada; the United Netherlands concentrated its energies in the Americas and the Far East. Products such a linen, wrought silk and wine were the most important imports from France and the heavy duties imposed on these goods by England in the 1660's generated a long and bitter tariff war which occupied much of Charles' reign. To offset the French duties on English goods, notably wool, England imposed a tariff on imported grain in order to protect its agriculture. This constant shifting of the type and rates of the customs on imported goods aggravated the trade situation and caused Charles to set in motion serious negotiations with France for a Marine Treaty that would, naturally, heavily favor England.

Although concerned with peace negotiations, Montagu's primary duty now was to obtain from France a trade agreement favorable to England. His letters have much to say about the French favoring an imbalance of trade (France exported more than she imported from England and taxed the imports heavily), the French privateers' harrassment of English merchant men, and the complaints of the London merchants over the seizures of their ships and goods. Montagu apparently spent a good deal of his time pleading with Louis seeking the redress of their grievances; his letters indicate the difficulty of achieving redress by Treaty. A number of articles of the Treaty were often examined and argued due to their lack of clarity:

Article 9 - that free ships should make free goods - this Charles did not accept as having no benefit or security for trade (Dec. 12, 1676); Louis objected: "...french goodes would be free if they were found upon a English ship and therefore did not think it reasonable that his enemies goodes should be secure and free upon ships where his owne subjects should not be alsoe." (Dec. 15, 1676); "...as for that article which he insisted upon of not allowing enemies goodes to be free on Board English Ships except his owne subjects might be soe too he hoped it would not be taken ill...." (Dec. 23, 1676); Article 4 - "...he makes an Exception to that part of the article which mentions pitch ropes anchors Masts plankes Boardes Beames and all other materialls requisite for the repairing or building of ships.... That the afore mentioned goodes might be reported (?) counterband." (Jan. 13, 1677); "...I shall not signe it but in token (?) and will desire Mr. Brisban to see before hand all the other formes you have recommended to be offered and if I Gaine the 14 article I will. But will rather signe the Treaty without it then they for new directions for the time of the sessions of parlement drawing so neere." (Feb. 3, 1677); finally the Treaty was signed. "Everything else is agreed upon and I return again this afternoone by appointment to signe the Treaty soe that Before the receipt of his you may conclude it as done." (Feb. 24, 1677).[18]

While Montagu was busy with his mission in France, Danby directed his efforts towards his goals of a Protestant policy along with fiscal solvency for Charles. However, domestic affairs diverted his attention and he became entangled in an enterprise not of his choosing: the disbanding of the army Parliament had forced Charles to raise to fight the French. In the beginning his desire to maintain an anti-French posture to please the Commons necessitated the raising of an army, now not needed since peace had been declared. This army proved an obstacle: Charles had not then the means either to maintain it or to disband it as Parliament had demanded. Hence, efforts to reconcile Crown and Parliament failed and earned Danby the enmity of France and the suspicion of the House of Commons.

In his efforts to allay the suspicions of Commons, Danby thought he could count on one ally, Sir William Temple. Temple was the architect of the Triple Alliance and as such he certainly was acceptable to the House. A most able diplomat and an ardent supporter of the Alliance, Danby hoped Temple could be brought into the government as Secretary of State. Danby was anxious to have Temple as his assistant; this would indicate to the country that the Government was truly sincere in its anti-French, anti-Papist policy. However, Temple was not willing to accept such a position and refused, even though Danby had pressed him, from mid 1677 to accept the office.

Now Danby not only had to cope with Temple's refusal, but had to answer the rival claims of Ralph

Montagu for the office. In October of 1677, Montagu hinted at the office of Secretary of State as a possible reward for his services to his government if Sir William Temple should not be appointed.[19] In the following months of November and December, Montagu offered himself to Danby as a candidate and for the next half year he pressed his suit employing the Lady Danby and his cousin, Charles Bertie, as his intercessors. Writing to Charles Bertie on March 29, 1678, "...but soe many things come Between the cup and the lip Especially at Court, that till things are done one must never despaire, noe more than I doe of being Secretary of State if my Lady Danby contrives her favor To me and Can work of Sr William Temple."[20] Again, on April 11th: "I am glad to heare that is such a Rubb in Sir William Temples way; Mr. Secretary Coventry [Henry Coventry] consented to me my self The Endeavoring for his place provided he had Ten Thousand pounds which I will lay donne when ever the king gives me his Consent to Come in."[21] Montagu felt that he could rely on Lady Danby's help, but he failed to reckon with Danby's inflexibility.

It is difficult to believe that Danby wholly trusted a man who was the constant flatterer. At times, Montagu's letters fairly exude flattery. In a letter dated June 4, 1678, Montagu related how he arranged to pay Secretary Coventry ten thousand pounds for the purchase of his office and now 'humbly' applied to Danby for confirmation in the office. He made sure to convey to Danby how much more service he could be to Danby in the office of Secretary of State than in an inferior post such as Ambassador to Paris (June 4, 1678).

... may perhaps put me in a Condition of being more usefull and serviceable to your Lordship in all your Concerns, than I Can be whilst I remaine soe insignificant as I am now; when I was in England I tooke the liberty; To propose to your Lordship my Coming into Mr. Secretary Coventrys place. But finding you lay under some obligation to your Lordships pleasure not Caring or Believing it was or is possible To Compasse it with out your good liking. ...and without flattering you as to your wisdome you have shoed your self Too goode a Lord Treasurer, to advise the king To give Ten Thousand pound for Sr William Temple so That now his chiefe meritt is your Lordships greate nicity of your word.... Mr. Secretary Coventry is willing to resigne To me if the king will consent as I will lay donne Ten thousand to satisfye him, without the kings being at any charge. I have noe friend nor will make no application in this matter To any person but your self, to whome I had rather owe it then To any body living, and I am sure you can recommend noe body whoe will alwaise be with more Trust and respect....22

Danby refused Montagu's overtures and Montagu was forced to accept his disappointment. However, he did not soon forget this affront; he did not forget that Danby had refused him, nor did he overlook Coventry's role. He thought that he had made a firm bargain with Coventry for the Office of Secretary of State and that the office belonged to him since Coventry had apparently agreed to its sale. It was, however, Danby who was the real villain and had caused him the loss of the coveted prize. Although he did not show any hostility immediately, this refusal made it clear he could not advance to a higher place while Danby was in office. With this in mind, Montagu continued to couch his further requests in his habitual fawning manner. In a letter to Danby on July 1, 1678:

> But I have had Too much Experience of your Lordships favour and kindnesse to me to Imagine you could be against a thing which I never desired but by your approbation and in which I hope I have Carried myself with all the regard and respect Imaginable to your Lordship, I am very unlucky that your Lordships Engagements to Sr W T. are like To deprive me, of your protection and assistance in my pretension it being a Thing which I am Confident his Majesty will be soe wholly directed by you in that it will be vaine for me to make the least step in it if you doe not find yourself free enough to recommend me all I begg of your Lordship is to believe that what will happen it shall not at all alter the professions I have made of being with all Trust and respect....23

Despite this effort, Danby chose Sir Leoline Jenkins, a career diplomat, who was instrumental in settling the dispute over the succession to Henrietta Maria's (Charles I's mother) property in favor of Charles, to be the next Secretary of State.[24]

Since 1675 Danby, in order to make his office of Lord Treasurer the chief office amongst the other offices of the government and to make his place secure, sought a rapprochement with Parliament by the use of gifts. By the offering of offices and pensions he hoped to form a nucleus of power for himself. However, Danby's efforts were wasted; he alienated some causing them to complain that they were not given their due. Further, Danby allowed them to organize themselves into an opposition party unfavorable to the Court. This opposition and Parliament's failure to meet in 1676 forced Charles to move more firmly into the French orbit. Knowing Charles' inclination toward France, Danby still continued his attempt to reinforce his position as Treasurer by his continuance of patronage. He hoped thereby to ensure his survival should Charles' attempted alliance with France become known and should Charles be blamed for the furtherance of a pro-French foreign policy.25

In an attempt to destroy both Danby himself and any negative influence that Danby might have had on Charles' pro-French policy, Montagu conceived the idea of replacing the current mistress of Charles, the Duchess of Portsmouth, with another mistress more favorable to France. Montagu reasoned that monarchs had their mistresses, and these ladies played a part in the political life of the nation; they enjoyed an important or not so important role in the governance of the people according to the will of the monarch or by reason of the attraction they had for the monarch. This fact was especially important to those who wished to be on favorable terms with the current favorite of the king. Charles and Louis each had their mistresses and these ladies held varying degrees of `control' over their monarchs.

Louis, like other monarchs, had his favorite; however, when it came to the fortune of his nation or his own gloire, it was not the favorite mistress who guaranteed the success of a petitioner, but merit. Louis had at this time successfully rendered the nobility ineffective. He allowed them their status and their ceremonial duties, but he gave offices of state, where the real power lay, to those not of royal or noble blood. In this manner Louis ensured not only loyalty, but dedication and service to himself and the country. Those who served well were greatly rewarded, those who did not suffered his displeasure.

The influence of the mistress on Charles was also a restricted affair. Charles had his mistresses, but it was well known that he did not allow them to color his judgment when it came to political affairs. The mistress might ask for and receive a favor for this or that noble, but Charles' favor usually was limited to the granting of a pension or a title. To Charles a mistress was a `thing of pleasure'-- not necessarily an advisor on domestic or foreign affairs.

Knowing this, Montagu welcomed Hortense Mancini, Duchess of Mazarin, to London, whom he, according to Charles de Marguetel de Saint Denis de Evremond, French critic, writer and soldier, knew rather well in Chambery. There is every reason to believe that this visit was not just a courtesy visit. It was Montagu's intention to replace the King's mistress, Louise de Keroualle, Duchess of Portsmouth, known to be a favorite

of Danby, with Hortense in the affections of the King.26
He, no doubt, hoped that she would destroy any influence
the Louise might have had on Charles. Montagu was
trying to destroy Danby and one sure means of doing this
was to break the alliance between Danby and the Duchess
of Portsmouth. Then a wedge could be driven between
Danby and the King. Hortense Mancini was to be that
wedge and her arrival signaled the beginnings of a new
political intrigue at Court.

> Her coming had caused a great stir, for it was
> whispered that there were political workings at the
> back of it. There seems little reason to doubt
> that this was so. St. Evremond, the exiled French
> philosopher, admits that he himself played some
> part in persuading her to accept the invitation,
> which seems to have been extended to her by the
> subtle and intriguing Ralph Montagu, who had known
> her in Chambery....27

> If her attractions contained nothing subtle, that
> was all to the good in the eyes of Montagu, who did
> not wish her to wield any political influence over
> the King, but only to destroy that of the Duchess
> of Portsmouth. Montagu did not even trouble to
> throw a veil of secrecy over his machinations. The
> reasons for the Duchesse Mazarin's coming were
> freely bandied about the Court and City.28

Conjectures as to the reasons for her coming over were
the subject of speculation even in the coffee-houses of
London. One unknown author pointed up the reasons for
her arrival in a burlesque conversation which had its
setting in Garraway's Coffee-house located near the
Exchange.

3 Coffist...But there are Reflexions about this Subject of a farr higher nature. A great wit, and profound Statesman, as well as lofty Poet, who is wont to Swear fearfully upon such great occasions, protests - By the living god - that the french king, finding Carwel [Keroualle] too weak, both as to Extraction and Interest, to wed throughly the concerns of France, Hath sent the king over a new Mistresse that Shall do it to the purpose.

2 Coffist... This is speculation Indeed too poetical.

3 Coffist... I Shall tell you another more reasonable one, and not so farr fetcht; It is Said for certain, That the Ingenious gentleman Mr. Ralph Montague (So lucky in remote contrivances) having made a great acquaintance with this Duchesse, while Shee resided at Chambry in Savoy, Hath, by concert with

Arlington, prevailed with
her to come over hither.
They are hoping that the
king taking to love her,
Shee may be a means of
ruining my Lord Treasurer
who is thought to bee much
strengthened by the Duchesse
of Portsmouth.29

Meanwhile, the Marquis de Ruvigny, French Ambassador to London, learned of the attempt to supplant the
Duchess of Portsmouth in Charles' affections. He
realized that Montagu was the chief instigator in this
scheme and had induced Arlington to join him in plotting Danby's destruction. Montagu counted on
Arlington's help. He knew how much Arlington disliked
Danby and Montagu planned to make use of this dislike
to serve his own purposes.30

As fate would have it, Montagu himself soon became
one of Portsmouth's victims and succumbed to her charms.
At the same time, as rumor had it, he was also carrying
on a affair with the socially prominent and lovely
Madame de Middelton, Jane Myddelton or Middelton (a
noted beauty of Charles II's reign, who at one time even
threatened the hold of the Duchess of Cleveland on
Charles), of whom it was said Montagu never complained
of `refusal.' Both affairs were, of course, natural
subjects for the wagging tongues.31 Montagu did not
seem too worried about the rumors or gossip; they did
little to stop him.

Montagu's sister, played the intermediary in the intrigue to replace the Duchess of Portsmouth; it was as her house that the King rendezvoused with the Duchess. In a letter to Arnaud de Pomponne, Minster of Foreign Affairs for Louis XIV, on July 20, 1676, Honore de Courtin, who replaced the Marquis de Ruvigny as French ambassador, wrote:

> I am told by Madam Harvey, sister of Monsieur de Montagu, the most intriguing and the cleverest woman in England, that Madame Mazarin is extremely satisfied with the conversation that she has had with the King of England, and that she is counting strongly on the protection and good offices of Monsieur de Montagu.[32]

Meanwhile, Montagu returned to Paris and put his time and talents to excellent use. And here we come once again to the long and devious tale of the French subsidy. In his letters to the Secretary he carefully let it be known that it was probable that Louis was taking advantage of Charles in the way of subsidies. Montagu claimed that he could obtain more money for Charles than was promised. He had previously written to Charles himself about this - June 21, 1677:

> ...and though after-games are hard to play, I thinke I understand this Court so well, and if you care to have it done I am confident I could gett you by agreement a million of‹ livres a yeare to bee paid whilst the war shall last, and foure millions six months after the peace shall be made.[33]

Aware that this letter, if it fell into the wrong hands, was of extreme danger to himself, Montagu, with his characteristic cleverness, suggested that if Charles should trust any of his ministers with this money matter it should be his Lord Treasurer; he was the best judge in such affairs. Montagu reasoned that should any difficulties arise from seeking the French subsidy, that is, if it should come to the knowledge of Commons, it would be the Lord Treasurer who would be the one to suffer the consequences. To further insure his own safety, Montagu asked the King that after showing his letter to the Treasurer, he should see to it that the letter be burnt by his sister.34

Charles, when informed of Montagu's claim to be able to obtain larger subsidies, instructed his Treasurer to grant Montagu every assistance to achieve this happy end. In letters dated August 12th and 30th, 1677 to Danby, Montagu is at his best.

...Mr, Courtin writes positively that he has agreed with your Lordship for two million of livres, where as I had heere insisted upon Two hundred thousand pound sterling you mention and could not faile having it granted Except the king himself has gon Back from the orders He gave me. I wish the king would have let this whole matter bin Transacted by so wise and faithfull a servant as your self. He would have found the Benefitt of it and either would have had noething or a larger Summe then a million of livers a yeare.

I congratulate very heartily with your Lordship that Mr. Chiffinch [William Chiffinch,
closest keeper and secretary to Charles II] is
to be the french Treasurer that office can
never doe you any goode and may doe you hurt.
You may be confident of my secrecy about this
whole affire, Both for the kings your Lordships and my owne sake for it would be noe
popular nor creditable thing if it were
knowne....[35]

Montagu set to work. He now thought better of his
original suggestion about a subsidy dependent upon the
peace (August 7, 1677). He had every hope of obtaining
the two hundred thousand pounds a year during the war
and at the same time avoiding any definite promise to
the French about the proroguing of Parliament.[36] He
began to negotiate for this sum when he was informed by
Arnaud de Pomponne, the French Minister of Foreign Affairs, that Charles was well satisfied with two million
livres (one hundred forty-five thousand pounds), a sum
that Danby had previously agreed to. It may have been
that Charles, who was in desperate need of ready money,
thought this lesser sum would be the more quickly given.
Montagu in his surprise wrote back to Danby (Aug. 30,
1677) that this sum was indeed far less than two hundred
thousand pounds sterling; "if you agree for two French
millions only," the King would stand to lose twelve
thousand pounds sterling a year at this rate of
exchange.[37] He could obtain more if given the
opportunity.

Pray, my Lord let me have your directions at
large and as soone as you can, for I doe tell

you very francly, and I hope the King will
pardon me since it is out of zeale for his
service, that if he had not Two hundred
thousand pound sterling it is his owne fault;
and if he has condescended to Two millions, I
can I am Confident Bring on my first proposition of foure millions after the peace.38

[Montagu] estimated this should bring [Charles] about
'five and fiftye thousand pound encrease' for the time
being and stop many a gap.39 However, he knew he could
obtain the four million. Indeed he was the industrious
servant making the talents multiply!

Meanwhile, [Honore de Courtin, French ambassador to
London], returned to France thinking that the subject of
the subsidy was settled: two million livres plus the one
hundred thousand crowns of the 1676 agreement. He was
somewhat perturbed to find that Montagu now, on Charles'
order, had reopened negotiations for a subsidy of two
hundred thousand pounds sterling (September 3/13,
1677).40 Montagu never doubted his ability to obtain
this new sum, but he refused to take any personal
responsibility for such a deal. He sought to have any
further negotiations carried out in London (September
25, 1677 and October 12, 1677).41 In a letter to King
Charles (September 25, 1677) Montagu said:

> ...I can only start the businesse, and have
> not credit enough to conclude it, ...except am
> I seconded by one of my Lord Treasurer's
> reputation and abilities.42

Considering the negotiations from the official position of Treasurer, Danby did not see things in so promising a light. He estimated that expenses incurred for the maintenance of armed forces as proposed by the Treaty of Dover (1670) would cost Charles over two million four hundred thousand pounds by Christmas of that year. So far Parliament had provided next to nothing, even with the granting of a Poll Bill (voting tax) which would bring in three hundred thousand pounds. Further, hidden in the Bill was a reduction of Customs due to a prohibition of the importation of French goods, thus lowering the possible return. By this reduction, the treasury lost at least two hundred ninety thousand pounds a year.43 Danby and the King were in dire need of money if the government was to continue to function.

Prospects indeed looked bleak, and it was just this bleak outlook that made the Anglo-French alliance all the more attractive. Danby was willing to join such an alliance if Louis was willing to pay him six hundred thousand pounds.44 Louis hesitated to commit himself outright to such a sum, but he did not close the door to further negotiations. Eventually, because of the skill of Paul Barrillon, the new French Ambassador to London, in handling these negotiations. Charles, in desperation, agreed to the smaller sum of six million livres, thus losing about one hundred and fifty thousand pounds sterling.45

Danby, taking his cue from Montagu that he could obtain a large subsidy, decided to do his best to either destroy the possibility of an alliance or force the last sous out of the French as the price of English friend-ship. He had been warned by Montagu (January 18, 1678) that Paul Barrillon was the French Minister of War's (Marquis Francis de Louvois) man and de Louvois desired war with England's help rather than her neutrality. With this in mind, Danby then insisted that a single payment of six million livres would not be sufficient to keep Charles from calling Parliament `out of necessity.' Only an annual subsidy for three years could prevent such a thing.[46]

To force a quick French decision in this matter Danby had to know what the French were planning to do regarding the peace feelers put out by the Allies (England, Holland, Spain) but he did not want to tip England's hand as which way the King would move. Montagu was instructed to offer peace terms to France, whose acceptance by Spain and Holland Charles himself was willing to guarantee.[47] Should peace be concluded according to the terms proposed by Charles, he would then expect to be given the payment of six million livres for the next three years for his good offices as mediator (March 25, 1678).[48] Louis rejected the terms and the rejection meant that the question of subsidy was, at least for the time being, closed. Charles, thus rebuffed, was forced to adopt a war policy for which he had no real desire. He then turned to forming a Quad-ruple Alliance of England, Holland, Austria and Spain against France (April 11, 1678).[49]

By May Charles had raised his army for war with France, but had all the while secretly negotiated for peace. Towards the end of May terms were agreed upon and a peace treaty was signed (May 17/27th 1678). With the treaty signed, there was now no longer any need for an army and the peace faction of the Commons began to clamor for its disbandment. The peace of Nijmegen had required that Charles be strictly neutral and withdraw his troops from Flanders, except for a small force to remain at Ostend. But unknown to Commons, France was secretly to pay Charles six million livres to disband his troops and to prorogue Parliament for not less than four months. Charles presented the signed treaty to the Parliament as something urged upon him by the Dutch.[50]

On the 27th of May, Danby wrote Montagu that Charles had gone before Parliament to ask for further supplies for the army and the House wanted to know if Charles wanted it for war or for peace. The proposition of supply was to be based on his answer. "But in theire debates they have shewed all the desire imaginable to a war, although both Spaine and Holland should have to go out of it...."[51]

Thinking peace was a certainty, Charles now awaited his subsidy from his illustrious counterpart. Louis, however, delayed the peace by refusing to return the agreed towns in Flanders to Spain until Sweden had also received some compensation. Charles sent Sir William Temple to Holland with instructions to conclude an alliance with the Dutch if Louis did not honor his agreement with England. The Dutch agreed and concluded a treaty which stipulated that unless Louis agreed to peace England and Holland would wage war upon him. Troops and monies were raised.[52]

After much recrimination and accusation, Charles awaited the first of his payments. Louis was not in a hurry to pay: he now blamed Charles for daring to thwart his plan in Flanders by forming a league with

Holland. To further show who was the master in this dangerous game of inflammatory politics, Louis sent instructions to his ambassador, Barrillon, to do his best to cause dissension between the King and his Parliament and supplied him with ample funds to accomplish this end.[53]

Montagu, was intimately involved in these matters. He knew of his master's secret military and financial dealing with Louis and knew the most sensitive and delicate details of agreements between the Courts. He was a veritable storehouse of knowledge which, if made public, could mean not only disgrace, but perhaps even bring imprisonment or death for those involved. Such information was dangerous in the wrong hands; an ambitious man possessing no scruples could use this information to his own advantage. Montagu was just that person. For some time he had been seeking appointment to the office of Secretary of State as a just reward for his faithful and zealous service. Yet, he had been overlooked and the prize given to another. He believed himself unjustly treated. Added to this curious mixture was his affair with a former mistress of the King, the Duchess of Cleveland, which became the talk of two countries and led to his dismissal from office and honors.

Meanwhile, Danby, to reassure the Commons of Charles' loyalty to the Protestant cause, once more reminded the House that he had persuaded Charles to agree to the marriage between Mary and the Prince of Orange, much to the annoyance of Louis XIV. When asked how Louis reacted upon hearing of the marriage, it was reported that he had taken the news "as he would have done the loss of an army."[54]

Parliament convened in January 1678 and immediately was asked to vote supply to Crown in its Protestant policy. Once again the specter of mutual mistrust plagued the session: Commons demanded that Charles declare war on France before they voted supply, Charles delayed for fear that Commons would force him into a war and leave him in it unless he agreed to their terms. Parliament then refused to vote subsidy fearing that the vote of a subsidy would put the House at a real disadvantage and render it ineffectual. Louis had won! Danby felt himself beaten; he could offer no effective substitute to the French alliance. At long last, he succumbed to the King's command which ordered him to set in motion definite negotiations for obtaining the French subsidy. Such was the situation at the end of autumn of 1678.[55]

Through all of this Charles had no desire to be separated from his brother monarch. He wanted Louis' friendship, and yet, at the same time, wanted to remain on good terms with his Parliament. But he had now gone too far to turn back. Therefore, to keep Commons pacified, Charles decided to accede to its demand and requested France to give up parts of Flanders, recently taken. Thus, with some justification, Louis could complain of Charles that he promised one thing and turnéd around and did another. To further complicate this situation, which just might have persuaded Charles to favor Commons, Charles had not received any payment from Louis other than a mere eighteen thousand pounds instead of the fifty thousand pounds promised that December, 1677.[56] Louis was equally as guilty; he was doing what he accused Charles of: saying one thing, and doing another.

What was Charles to do? He decided to bide for more time and adopted the pretence of a war-like attitude while he secretly maneuvered behind the scenes with Louis. Louis, in turn, decided to keep Charles off balance; he was well aware of Charles' quandary regarding Commons and intended to keep him dependent upon France. Using the old ploy of playing the King against Parliament, Louis kept them in constant opposition to each other while pretending to be friend to both. He hoped thus to reduce the country to impotence. Such was Louis's strategy even as late as 1680. The French ambassador, Barrillon, in a dispatch to Louis observed:

> My principal care and my first application has
> been to engage persons of credit in parliament
> to hinder the alliances being approved, and
> the granting of money to support them. This
> is the present interest of your Majesty; but
> with regard to the future, I see what your
> Majesty has most at heart is to prevent
> England from being reunited by accomodation
> between his Britannic Majesty and his
> parliament.[57]

It is inconceivable that Charles was ignorant of these doings.[58] The wisest thing, Charles felt, was to offer his services as a peace maker and bring about peace between France and Holland. As such, he could blunt Louis' efforts to drive a wedge between him and his Parliament and cause him real inconvenience. Besides, he thought, the role of mediator would make him appear to the Commons as a monarch free from French influence and one loyal to his Protestant nation. Thus, in order to appear his own man, Charles offered his good offices as mediator and peace maker between the warring factions.

Eventually Commons voted six hundred thousand pounds for war with France, but the sum did not satisfy Charles. Louis' offer of subsidy now appeared all the more attractive. He notified Danby that he was to ask for six million livres (approximately two hundred thousand pounds) a year from Louis for his endeavors as a mediator with Holland, Spain and France. Danby, not at all happy with his ruler's decision, saw it as extremely dangerous to his King, his nation, and of course, to himself. In order to forestall any danger to himself, he refused to write or send any letter until Charles himself added his approval in his own hand. Thus Charles addended two letters from Danby to Montagu with the words, "I approve of this letter," (January 17 and March 25, 1677/78).[58]

> In case the conditions of the peace shall bee accepted, the King expects to have six millions of livers a yeare for three yeares from the time that this agreement shall bee signed betwixt his Majestie and the King of France, because it will bee two or three yeares before the Parliament will bee in humor to give him any supplys after the maeking of any peace with France, and the embassador here has alwaies agreed to that sume, but for so long time. If you find the peace will not bee

accepted, you are not to mention the money att all, and all possible care must bee taken to have this whole negotiations as private as possible for feare of giveing offence att home....(March 25, 1678)59

From what is known of Danby, in his dealings with Montagu, it is hard to reconcile his actions with his suspicions--that he would enturst such delicate dealings to one whom he really did not trust and had every reason to suspect. What is truly amazing is that he put it in writing even with the counter-signature of Charles. He knew the mood of the Commons. Did he really think that such a stratagem would save him? Apparently he had not yet learned a lesson from the past: that the Commons, knowing it could not get directly at the King, was able to censor the King via impeachment of his ministers and counsellors. Danby, Charles and Montagu were tied together by their secrets--secrets that could undo one, both, or all. Only time could tell what would happen.

Despite the cares of his office, Montagu now entered into Parisian life with relish and gusto, for he was a man who had a definite predeliction for luxury and lavish entertainments. He even took Danby's son, Peregrine Osborne, Lord Dunblane, under his wing and showed him the 'sights and sounds' of the city.[60] Did he suspect it possible that Lord Dunblane was in reality his father's spy sent to keep watch on him? If so, perhaps it gave Montagu an ironic satisfaction to `educate' in the 'good life' the son of the man he had promised himself to destroy. Montagu may even have thought that he could keep a close watch on Danby through his son; the son could be a good source of information.

As an ambassador, Montagu was expected to lavishly entertain the best of the nobility and society. To do so in a proper and suitable manner, Montagu needed a hostess equal to the task. Ordinarily this position should have been undertaken by his wife, but during her stay in Paris Lady Montagu was oft times ill. She suffered from acute neuralgia and was treated for this condition by John Locke. Apparently she took up quite a bit of his time when he was in Paris, for he noted in his diary that he was frequently with the "Lady Ambassadrice whom I found crying out in one of her fits....".61 Due to her infirmity Montagu called upon his sister, who had remained in England although her husband, Sir Daniel Harvey, was ambassador to Constantinople, to act as hostess at the entertainments he gave as the representative of a great King. This position she filled with competence and delight. The role of hostess was a perfect cover for her to enter into every intrigue; nothing seemed to give her greater joy than the suspense of the secretive. The French knew of this penchant for Barrillon, in a dispatch to his sovereign on December 5, 1680, says of her: "Mrs Harvey, his sister, is as deep as he in all the intrigues: She is a woman of a bold and enterprising spirit, and had interest and connections with a great number of people in the court and parliament."62 Maurice Petherick, in his work Restoration Rogues, contrasts Montagu's wife with his sister:

...Elizabeth, the rich and lovely though fragile widow of Joceline Percy, Earl of Northumberland. She was virtuous and good-natured and very much a great lady, but often her health would not permit her to take part as an ambassador's wife. At these times, Montagu's sister, Lady Harvey, a bustling, dangerous woman, as lacking in scruple as her brother, would act as hostess and abet him in his steady and unremitting efforts, by any means available, to improve his own career.63

All seemed to be going well for the ambassador of Charles to the Court of Louis. However, there were unforseen difficulties ahead; things began to go awry for the clever manipulator of people. Through his own imprudence, Montagu ran afoul of the former mistress of King Charles, Barbara Villiers, the Duchess of Cleveland, then residing in Paris. She was to become the cause of his disgrace, dismissal from his post and the loss of other honors. In the spring of 1678, the Duchess arrived in Paris to take up residence, needless to say, at the expressed will of and to the definite relief of a King grown quite tired of her and her temper. Here she established a liaison with Ralph Montagu, who foolishly allowed himself to become romantically involved with her. Everything went well for them until she 'quit his bed' for that of Alexis Henri, Marquis de Chatillon. Naturally, this 'departure' led to bitter animosity between them.

The ill will created by the `leaving' of the Duchess was exacerbated by a quarrel that arose between Montagu's wife, the Lady Montagu, and the former mistress. The quarrel between the two ladies began one day as Lady Montagu went to visit the Duchess on order of the King to project a marriage. The projected marriage was to take place between her daughter,

Elizabeth, and one of the Duchess's illegitimate sons by the King, Henry Fitzroy, the Duke of Grafton, who was already contracted to marry Arlington's daughter, Isabella. Arriving at her house, Lady Montagu was denied admittance because the Duchess was 'engaged' with de Chatillon. Lady Montagu returned home in a high temper and related the incident to her husband. Montagu reproached Cleveland and accused her of bringing disgrace upon the King's children. It is certainly safe to say that, given her reputation for a violent temper, she flew into a rage at him. To defend himself, Montagu wrote the King of her intrigues with Chatillon using as evidence some letters she had imprudently written to Chatillon.64 Montagu knew well that Charles did not really care what she did or whom she slept with, but he did mind greatly if she brought disgrace on him or his nation.65 The Duchess returned to England was rather coolly received by the King--if she expected Charles to receive her warmly and to lend a sympathetic ear to her troubles, she was greatly disappointed. Naturally, she blamed Montagu for this cool reception and desired revenge. To some, her return to England was simply her attempt to try and break the marriage contract between her son, and Arlington's daughter. She wanted him to marry the Lady Elizabeth Percy and acquire the vast fortune of the Percys.66

Montagu was certainly aware of the damage he caused himself by his betrayal of the Duchess to the King and desired to minimize it. This is clear from a letter he wrote to his cousin, Henry Sidney (English ambassador to the United Netherlands), as quoted in Philip Sergeant's My Lady Castlemaine:

I am a little scandalised you have been but
once to see her--pray make your court oftener
for my sake, for no man can be more obliged to
another than I am to her on all occasions, and
tell her I say so, and, as my Lord Berkeley
[Sir Charles Berkeley, keeper of the Privy
Purse] says, give her a pat from me. If you
keep your word to come in June, I fancy you
will come together, and I shall not be ill
pleased to see the two people in the world of
both sexes I love and esteem the most.67

Even if Montagu did not fully realize the danger he
was in, he apparently was taking no chances. Cleveland's
wrath was too well known. Perhaps he hoped that Sidney
would show the letter to the Duchess to temper her
anger. In any case, he was just not sure of what she
would do or just how much influence she still had with
Charles. Charles might not be too happy with her and
her temper tantrums, but, after all, she was the mother
of his children. However, in this instance, Montagu
underestimated this lady's potential for destroying her
enemies; placed himself in an extremely vulnerable position. Incredible as it may seem, he compounded the
danger. He had the unbelievably bad taste and timing to
initiate, in the summer of 1678, in Paris, a `liaison'
with Cleveland's daughter, Anne, the Countess of
Sussex.68

Throughout these affairs, Montagu's wife,
Elizabeth, remained loyal to him. She did not add to
the already difficult situation by demanding an apology
either from the Duchess of Cleveland or her daughter,
the Countess of Sussex. To prove her belief in her

husband's innocence in the Sussex affair, Lady Montagu
entertained Cleveland's daughter as her house guest and
was only too happy for her to remain a time provided she
conducted herself properly. She even wrote Montagu, now
in London, declaring Sussex to be innocent of the affair, thereby implicitly stating her belief in Montagu's
guiltlessness, and asking him for instructions as to
what to do about the situation. Montagu's wife may well
not have believed the rumors of her husband's affair
with Lady Sussex. Both were in Paris at the same time
and if the Lady Sussex was guilty of an unsavory
relationship with Ralph, she certainly would have been
the first to have accused him of it. If she was
convinced of the truth of an affair she would hardly
have invited Sussex to her home.

In a letter to her husband, as quoted in Bernard
Falk, she believes Sussex to be innocent of any affair
with Montagu.

Since I sealed up my letter, Mr. Brisbane [a
government marine-agent in Paris] has been
here to speak with me. His business was about
Lady Sussex, to let me know that (by order) he
was last night to wait upon Lady Cleveland,
who(m) he found very positive about her [Lady
Sussex] going to Port Royal [nunnery] and she
had the king on her side, and that he thought,
according to his orders, it was fit for him to
persuade her to it, since if she should
disobey the king it would be mightly to her
prejudice, and it would be thought the advice
of others. So I told him that as for
disobeying the king, I thought it was very

unfit for her to do it, and could I pretend to
advise (which I did not) I should persuade her
to obey him in all things; but that was not
necessary, for I found her resolutions that
[so resolved]; but since Mr. Montagu was no
more here, and that the poor woman was really
ill and taking physic for her health, I
thought it would do very well if he that were
employed in it would represent that to the
king, and that she might make an end of that,
since a strange monastery, where she knew
nobody, was but a melancholy place to do it
in; but that I had nothing to say in it, but
that as she was in my house and I did believe
her innocent of all was said of you, so my
house was at her service for as long as she
thought fit, provided she lived as she ought
to in it.

Perhaps you may think me a little impertinent
in troubling you with all this strife, but it
is now so public a thing that I thought it not
amiss to let you know all that passes about
it, and to receive your orders what I shall do
or say further in it. Sure there never was a
more vexatious business, but I will say no
more. Pray God send we may meet quickly. ---
Yours for ever.69

The enmity of the Duchess of Cleveland was compounded by Montagu's tactical error of angering Charles
by blatantly recommending a French astrologer, Abbe
Pregnani, an Italian charlatan then living in France.
The Abbe reportedly made a number of marvelous predic-

tions, including one relating to Charles' restoration to
the Throne. The Duchess warned Charles that Montagu's
motives were far from pure and that he had definite
designs in recommending this astrologer. Cleveland
claimed that Montagu suborned the Abbe to fortell the
King what he wished to hear and not the truth: "...he
shall tell the King things that he forsees will infallibly ruin him...."[70]

When the Duchess returned to France, she made sure
that Charles knew of the disloyalty of his ambassador.
She heard rumors that her daughter had been 'debauched'
by Montagu much to the scandal of the court of France.
In her fury, she wrote Charles (May 28, 1678) telling
him of Montagu's frequent visits to her daughter's house
where he would stay till at least five o'clock in the
morning after having dismissed her servants.[71] There
seemed to be a great measure of spite in all this: she
was only too ready to destroy her daughter's good name
in order to avenge herself on the ambassador. Montagu,
on the other hand, defended himself by claiming that
Sussex was just trying to escape the clutches of her
rather over-possessive mother in order to obtain help
for her diseased condition, probably venereal disease,
from a physician.[72] In response, the Duchess replied
that the girl had joined the 'worst of men' and he
intended simply to ruin her. In the true fashion of a
woman scorned, she claimed that Montagu hated her
because she spurned his love.[73]

In a letter to the King she admitted to Charles
that she had a 'slight alliance' with Chatillon, but
claimed that it was really nothing. Continuing to vent
her anger, she went on to say that Montagu had expressed

some very disloyal statements concerning Charles and his brother, James. She repeated Montagu's plans of intrigue and asserted that Montagu intended to make his own the Secretaryship of State as a stepping stone to the office of Lord Treasurer.

> For he has neither conscience nor honour, and has several times told me, that in his hart he despised you and yr Brother; and that for his part he wished with all his hart the Parliament wd send you both to travell, for you were a dull governable fool, and the Duke a willful Fool. So that it was yet better to have you than him, and that you allwais chose a greater beast than yrself to govern you.... And in the mean time, because I will try to get Secretary Coventry's Place, when he had a mind to part with, but not to Sir Willm Temple, because he is the Treasurer's creature, and he hates the Treasurer; and I have already employ'd my sister to talk with Mr. Cook, and to send him to engage Mr. Coventry not to part with it as yet, and he has assured my Lady Harvey he will not. And my Ld Treasurer's lady and Mr. Bertie are both of them desirous I shd have it. And wn I have it, I will be damn'd if I do not quickly get to be Lord Treasurer; and then you and yr children shall find such a friend as never was. And for the King, I will find a way to furnish him so easily with money for his pocket and his wenches, that he will quickly out Bab May and lead the King by the nose.'[74]

The Duchess was fearful for her daughter's safety with such a person and she begged Charles to help her get Anne out of Montagu's clutches. Of course, in this whole affair, she claimed her conduct to be irreproachable and she hoped that Charles would not heed the ambassador's malice towards her. It was simply a matter of his spite. One of her observations in these letters seems to sum up the attitude of the day to such goings on. Such `gallantries' were so common that they are hardly to be wondered at.

> And that he could not imagine that you ought
> to be so angry, or indeed be at all concerned;
> for that all the World knew, that now all
> things of Gallantry were at an end with you
> and I; that being so, and so publick, he did
> not see why you shd be offended at my Loveing
> any body.75

She closed with this remark:

> I promise you, that for my conduct
> it shall be such, as that you nor nobody shall
> have occasion to blame me; and I hope you will
> be just to what you said to me, which was at
> my House, when you told me you had letters of
> mine; you said 'Madam, all that I ask of you,
> for your own sake is, live so for the future
> as to make the least noise you can, and I care
> not who you love.'76

If ever Charles believed that Montagu was a loyal and trustworthy servant, there was now cause for doubt. Even if he ignored half of what the Duchess said, taking it as an act of spite by a woman scorned, he must have thought that there was a grain of truth in her complaint. Quite annoyed with all this, Charles made known his displeasure to her for allowing the royal name to be sullied by such an affair.

Meanwhile, Montagu became suspicious of the motives for the Duchess' return to England and he certainly learned the displeasure of his master over this affair from official channels at the French Court. Fearful for himself and his freedom, he was at his wits' end as to what to do. Montagu petitioned for permission to return home and received a negative answer (July 1, 1678).[77] He then daringly left his post in Paris and hurried to London to force an audience with the King in order to plead his cause. Desperation guided his action, for this was a dangerous gamble which might well have put him in the Tower.

Montagu's arrival in London did not go unnoticed. Montagu's cousin, Charles Hatton, in a letter to his sister, Mary Hatton (July 1, 1678), stated that Montagu was the subject of local gossip. His return to England is noted as well as the reason for it.

> My cosen Montague is come over to vindicate
> himself agst several accusations lay'd to his
> charge by ye Duchesse of Portsmouth and ye
> Duchesse of Cleaveld, who accuses him of to
> great kindnesse with her daughter Sussex and
> taking her out of ye monastery in wch she had
> placed her and putting her into another....[78]

Mary Hatton replied in a letter to Charles (July 18, 1678):

> What I have to aquiaint you withall of
> Paris news is our cosin Montagues being gon
> last Monday post towards Ingland, opon my Lord
> Sunderland's being sent hither ambassador,
> which bussness they say my Lady Cleveland has
> intrigued, out of revenge to the ambass. for
> being soe jealous of her for one Chevalier
> Chatillon as to wright it wheire he thought it
> might doe her most prejudice, which she being
> advertised of, and attributing to it and cold
> reception she found when she was laitly in
> Ingland, has, as they say, acussed him of not
> being faithfull to his master in the imploy-
> ment he gave him here; too which there is
> another particular that dus much agravate her,
> and that is that, whillest she was in Ingland,
> the ambas. was every day with her daughter
> Sussex, which has ocationed such jealousy of
> all sides that, for the saffty of my Lady
> Sussex, it is reported the ambass. advissed
> her to a nunnery, and made choice of Belle
> Chase for her, where she is at present and
> will not see her mother.79

Directly upon his arrival in England, Montagu went
to see the Lord Treasurer and asked him to arrange a
meeting for him with Charles. Charles refused to see
Montagu. Montagu then prevailed upon Danby to arrange a
'chance' meeting with Charles at his home, Hampden
House, in Whitehall.80 Here Montagu tried to plead his
cause but Charles cut him short by saying that he did

not want to hear more on the subject. He then put Montagu on the spot by asking him why he left his post without royal permission. Having no answer to this question, Charles ordered Montagu to leave the Court. Charles then commanded that Montagu be removed from his post as ambassador, that his name be stricken from the roll of the Privy Council and that he be stripped of his office of Master of the Great Wardrobe. His post in Paris was given to Robert Spencer, Earl of Sunderland (July 12, 1678).[81]

Incredibly, Montagu still thought that all was not lost and that he could work his way back into Charles' good graces. Charles may have come by this time to dislike or mistrust Montagu. He may have thought to get rid of him in the easiest manner by dismissing him from Court and from his office of Master of the Horse to the Queen Consort. In this way, he hoped to force him out of politics and forestall any possibility of Montagu doing him harm with the knowledge he possessed through his embassy in France.

Charles directed Queen Catherine to dismiss Montagu from her service.

> Yesterday His Majesty spoke to the Queen to
> discharge Mr. Montagu of her service; she made
> answer that Mr. Montagu having not given her
> any offence it would be hard for her to punish
> him, but if he were criminal to His Majesty he
> had full power to do what he thought fit.
> This was all which then passed, but everybody
> concluded that Mr. Ralph Montagu will lose
> that station at least. Mr. Saville is

restored to grace having kissed the King's
hand and is departing in quality of mediator
to compose matters between the Duchess of
Cleveland and the Countess of Sussex.[82]

Sensing that his future was in jeopardy, Montagu
decided upon a definite course of action to restore
himself to power, and from this time until Charles'
death, past or present association with Montagu definitely involved personal peril.

Montagu's quarrel with the Duchess of Cleveland and
the revelation of his political plans through his
"pillow talk" cost him dearly. He lost the good graces
of Charles: he was stripped of his position in the Privy
Council and his office as Master of the Wardrobe. Danby
and the Duchess were, in Montagu's opinion, allies and
thus equally his enemies. Considering Montagu's
vindictive and vengeful nature, his opponents or victims
displayed a surprising lack of foresight. Those who
knew him were aware that this self-serving, unabashed
flatterer and sycophant was not to be trusted and should
have realized that Montagu was dangerous.

His plans now formed, Montagu now intended to
destroy Danby, but to do this he needed the aid of
France. First, however, he must protect himself from any
possible prosecution for his proposed destruction of the
Lord Treasurer and the only way to secure his immunity
in this affair was to have himself elected to the House
of Commons and thus shield himself with the Parliamentary privilege. This he would do and thereby sieze the
initiative. Danby was to be caught off guard. He spent
the summer in comparative quiet forgetting his political

worries and concerned himself with the marriage of his daughter, Bridget, to Charles' illegitimate son, the Earl of Portsmouth (September 19,1678).83

In desperation, then, Montagu decided that if Court and King would not reward him he would join the opposition in Parliament. What was to transpire there forms one of the most important chapters in English political history and for once Montagu was on center stage.

CHAPTER IV

Footnotes

[1] Andrew Browning, Thomas Osborne, Earl of Danby and Duke of Leeds. (Glasgow: Jackson and Sons, and Co., 1951), I, 224.

[2] Thompson, p. 65.

[3] Lionel H. Cust, "Verrio, Antonio (1639?-1707," Dictionary of National Biography, XX, 284.

[4] Henry B. Wheatley, ed., Diary of John Evelyn (London: Bickers and Son, 1906), II, 318.

[5] Manchester, p. 272.

[6] Rawlinson, MSS. A. 255. ff. 565-71; Dalrymple, I, 153; Mignet II, 529, 572; firth, p. 710.

[7] B.M. Add. MSS. 25119 - Instructions and Official Letters to the Ambassadors at Nimoegen.

[8] Lockyer, pp. 344-48.

[9] B.M. Add. MSS. 39757, f. 69; B.M. Add. Mss. 28054, f. 91; H.M.C. IX, 2 452;_____,Copies and Extracts of Some Letters Written to and from the Earl of Danby (now Duke of Leeds) In The Years 1676, 1677, and 1678. With Particular Remarks Upon some of them (London: Published by his Grace's Direction 1710), p. 26; Browning, II, 286-89.

[10]B.M. Add. MSS. 39757, f. 66; B.M. Add. Mss. 28054, f. 93; Letters, p. 30-33, Browning II, 290-93.

[11]B.M. Add. MSS. 39757, f. 84; B.M. Add. MSS. 28054, f. 99, 101; Letters, p. 326; Lockyer, pp. 349-50.

[12]B.M. Add. MSS. 28040, f. 41.

[13]B.M. Add. MSS. 39757, f. 86; Browning, II, 303-04.

[14]Longleat, Coventry Papers--a few of Montagu's Letters containing such information: April 21, 1677; May 12, 1677; May 19, 1677; June 23, 1677; July 17, 1677; July 31, 1677; Jan. 12, 1678; Jan 29, 1678; Feb. 2, 1678; Feb. 12, 1678; Feb. 26, 1678; March 12, 1678; June 22, 1678.

[15]B.M. Add. MSS. 39757, f. 88; 28054, f. 115; Letters, p. 38-43. See also letters of Jan. 5, (f. 92), Jan 10, (f. 95), Jan. 17, 1678; B.M. Add. MSS. 38849, f. 130; B.M. Add. MSS. 28054, f. 134; 38840, f. 146; Letters, p. 56; Browning, II, 299-303.

[16]B.M. Add. MSS. 39757, f. 88; B.M. Add. MSS. 28054, f. 115; Letters, 38-43; Browning, II, 299-303.

[17]B.M. Add. MSS. 39757, f. 88; B.M. Add. MSS. 28054, f. 115; Letters, p. 38-43; Browning, II, 299-303.

[18]Longleat Coventry Papers, Vol. XXXIII, ff. 418, 420, 424, 434, 449, 461. A review of the State Papers, Domestic/104/185/ff. 82, 86, 88, 89, 117, 118, 171, 132, 136, 145, 146, 151, 158, 166, 200, 201, find Montagu engaged in the attempt to redress the grievances of the London merchants concerning their ships and contents,

e.g.: the Mayflower, the King's Arms of Dover, Unity of Deale, the Friendship of Dover, the Speedwell of London, the Golden Lyon of London, the Royale Oake, the Resolution of Poole, the William.

[19]B.M. Add. MSS. 39757, f. 79; Letters, p. 36, p. 83, p. 88; Browning, II, 293-295.

[20]B.M. Add MSS. 39757, f. 102; Letters, p. 78; Browning II, 344-45.

[21]B.M. Add. MSS. 39757, f. 105; Letters, p. 83.

[22]Osborn Collection - Yale University - June 4, 1678; see also Letters, pp.88-90.

[23]Osborn Collection - Yale University - July 1, 1678; see also Letters, p. 90.

[24]Firth, p. 710.

[25]Mignet, IV, 377-80; Lockyer, pp. 346-47; Sidney Lee, "Osborne, Sir Thomas, Earl of Danby and Duke of Leeds (1631-1712," Dictionary of National Biography., XIV, 1190.

[26]C.A. 117, f. 114 - Ruvigny to Pomponne, Jan. 2, 1677; Cyril Hughes Hartmann, The Vagabond Duchess: The Life of Hortense Mancini, Duchesse Mazarin (London: George Routledge and Sons, Ltd., 1927), p. 152.

[27]Hartmannm The Vagabond Duchess, p. 151.

[28]Ibid., p. 152.

[29]P.R.O. State Paper, Domestic Series 29/376/f. 198; Cal. S.P. Dom. 1675-776, pp. 474-75; (Mignet, IV, 404-06; Hartmann, The Vagabond Duchess, p. 156.

30C.A. 117, f. 14 - Ruvigny to Pomponne, Jan. 2. 1676; Hartmann, The Vagabond Duchess, p. 158.

31C.A. 119, f. 15 - Courtin to Pomponne, July 2, 1676; Hartmann, The Vagabond Duchess, p. 182.

32Hartmann, The Vagabon Duchess, p. 187. See also C.A. 120 A, f. 168.

[33]B.M. Add. MSS. 28054, f. 66; Letters, pp. 1-7; Browning, II, 265-68.

[34]B.M. Add. MSS. 28054, f. 66; Letters, pp. 1-7; Browning II, 265-68.

[35]B.M. Add. MSS. 39757, f. 56; Letters, pp. 17-18; Browning, II, 279-80.

[36]B.M. Add. MSS. 39757, f. 50; Browning, II, 274-76.

37B.M. Add. MSS. 39757, f. 60; - Letters, p. 21; Browning, II, 282-83; Aug. 12, 1677 - B.M. Add. MSS. 39757, f. 53; Letters, p. 13; August 12, 1677 - B.M. Add. MSS. 39757, f. 56; Letters, p. 17.

38B.M. Add. MSS. 39757, f. 60; see also - Letters, p. 21-24; Browning II, 282-83.

[39]B.M. Add. MSS. 39757, f. 66; B.M. Add. MSS. 28504, f. 92; Letters, p. 30; Browning, II, 290-92.

[40]B.M. Add. MSS. 28054, f. 89; Letters, p. 24; Browning, II, 284-85.

[41]B.M. Add. MSS. 39757, f. 69; B.M. Add. MSS. 39757, f. 66; B.M. Add. MSS. 39757, f. 77; B.M. Add. MSS. 28054, f. 91; B.M. Add. MSS. 28054, f. 93; Letters, p. 26, p. 30, p. 34.

[42]B.M. Add. MSS. 39757, f. 69; B.M. Add. MSS. 28054, f. 91; Letters, p. 26.

[43]Browning, I, 270-71.

44Browning, I, 271. Mignet, IV, 536.

[45]Browning, I, 271. Mignet, IV. 571.

46B.M. Add. MSS. 39757, f. 99; Letters, p. 61; Browning, II, 321-24; B.M. Add. MSS. 28054, f. 136; B.M. Add. MSS. 28054, ff. 138-47; Letters, p. 59.

[47]B.M. Add. MSS. 28054, ff. 50-2; Cal. S. P. Dom., 1678, p. 61, p. 67.

[48]B.M. Add. MSS. 38849, f. 140; B.M. Add. MSS. 38849, f. 146; B.M. Add. MSS. 28054, f. 168; Carte MSS 72, f. 369; H.M.C. Hodgkins MSS., 194; C.J. IX, 560; Russell, p. XIV; Browning, II, 346-49.

[49]B.M. Add. MSS. 38849, f. 150; H.M.C. Hodgkins MSS.,

196; <u>Letters</u>, p. 81; Browning, I, 273, II, 350-53.

50Petherick, p. 125.

51B.M. Add. MSS. 28054, f. 176.

52Petherick, p. 127.

53<u>Ibid.</u>, p. 128.

54Burnet, I, 132; Manchester, p. 278; Mignet, IV, 318-19.

55Lockyer, pp. 347-48.

56B.M. Add. MSS. 38849, f. 118.

57Dalrymple, I, App. 359. (Barrillon to Louis XIV-Dec. 5, 1680.)

58B.M. add. MSS. 38849, f. 121; <u>Letters</u>, p. 53; Browning, II

59B.M. Add. MSS. 38849, f. 140; B.M. Add. MSS. 28054, f. 168; 38849, f. 146; <u>Letters</u>, pp. 72-76; Browning II, 346-49.

60B.M. Add. MSS. 38849, f. 130; Falk, p. 102, p. 116.

61Lough, p. xvii, p. 183.

62Dalyrmple, I, App. 357.

[63]Petherick, p. 369.

[64]H.M.C. Ormonde Collection. IV, 443-44; Petherick, p. 370.

[65]Brian Masters, The Mistresses of Charles II (London: Blond and Briggs, 1979), pp. 88-89.

[66]Petherick, p. 370; Falk, pp. 110-111.

67Philip S. W. Sergeant, My Lady Castlemaine: Being a Life of Barbara Villiers Countess of Castlemaine, afterwards Duchess of Cleveland (London: Hutchinson and Co., 1912)) p. 219; Petherick, pp. 128-130.

68Sergeant, p. 218; Firth, p. 710.

[69]Falk, pp. 110-111.

[70]Sergeant, p. 223, Burnet, II, 143; Firth, p. 711.

71Harleian MSS. 70006, f. 171; B.M. Add. 21505, ff. 32-38.

[72]Harleian MSS. 7006, f. 173; Petherick, p. 372; Firth, p. 711.

[73]Harleian MSS. 7006, f. 173; Firth, p. 711.

74Harleian MSS. 7006, ff. 171-173; Sergeant, pp. 222-26;

Firth, p. 711.

[75]Harleian MSS. 7006, f. 174; Sergeant, p. 225.

[76]Harleain MSS. 7006, ff. 175-76; Sergeant, p. 227.

[77]Osborn Collection - Yale University - Letter to Danby from Montagu - July 1, 1678.

[78]Edward M. Thompson, ed., Correspondence of the Family of Hatton: Being Chiefly Letters Addressed to Christopher, First Vicount Hatton, A.D. 1601-1704 (London: Camden Society, 1878), II, 167.

[79]Ibid., p. 168.

[80]Letters, pp. 92-93; Petherick, pp. 129-130; Firth, p. 711.

[81]H.M.C. Ormonde Collection, IV, 445; Petherick, p. 130; Firth, p. 711.

[82]H.M.C. Ormonde Collection, IV, 445.

[83]Browning, I, 289.

CHAPTER V
Honourably Acquited of Suspition

Upon reading these Letters, it was immediately resolved in Parliament, that there was sufficient Matter of Impeachment against Thomas Earl of Danby Treasurer of England, and his Grace was honourably acquited of suspition.[1]

The Fall of 1678 found Montagu once again out of favor. As in 1673 when he had been sent to the Tower, he had angered his sovereign. To survive politically, he decided to enter Parliament and join forces with the adversaries of the King. Parliament provided protection and freedom of speech to each member. and it even offered Montagu the opportunity to attack the one man whom he considered most responsible for his dismissal as ambassador: The Lord Treasurer, Danby.

Before one can discuss this exciting episode in Montagu's life, it is necessary to review the power situation in Europe, domestic affairs in England, the career of Danby and the role of Parliament.

European politics were dominated by the unbridled ambitions of the King of France, Louis XIV, who ruled a France which had replaced Spain as the greatest power in Europe. Louis possessed the finest army in Europe, had unlimited funds, and enjoyed absolute power of rule. He early decided to employ these assets to make France the arbiter of Europe. He desired to extend the borders of his realm at the expense of the German and Spanish

Hapsburgs and Spain. In short, Louis intended to make France the dominant power in Europe and became a "universal monarch."

Charles was even eager to align himself with Louis whom he envied and admired for his power and glory. As a sign of his friendship, Charles gave in marriage his sister, Henriette Anne, to Philippe, Duke of Orleans, Louis XIV's brother, in 1661. As another sign of this friendship, Charles then married Catherine of Braganza, daughter of the King of Portugal and an enemy of Spain, in 1662, and sold back to France the city of Dunkirk for four hundred thousand pounds in the same year. This policy of friendship was prompted not only by admiration for Louis, but by Charles' intense dislike for the Dutch, whom both he and the English merchants viewed with deep mistrust and hatred as England's most serious trade rival. Because of this rivalry, Charles and the Parliament thought a war with the Dutch both necessary and desirable and did not hesitate to enter into a second Dutch war in 1665. The war was ended in 1667 by the Treaty of Breda with the English emerging as victors.

Although successful in this war, Charles still feared the Dutch for their economic strength and hoped to gain French support in another war against them. However, Parliament cooled its anger toward the Dutch and regarded Louis' increase in power as dangerous and began to view the United Provinces as its natural ally against the French. Besides, the Dutch were Protestants and France was Catholic. This alone was enough for Parliament to consider France its mortal and permanent enemy.

In 1667, Charles joined the Triple alliance with Sweden and the Dutch against France. Although an apparent contradiction, this was actually a stroke of his political genius. Through this show of strength he hoped to demonstrate to Louis that England was a strong nation and its alliance was worth having. Louis accepted this assessment, ended his invasion of the Spanish Netherlands, and concluded a peace with Spain; then Louis turned his attention to the Dutch, whom he despised as a notion of Protestants, merchants, and republicans.

Despite the Treaty of Breda, Charles remained hostile to the Dutch and the years 1667 to 1674 were years devoted to a policy which had as its objective the destruction of the United Provinces. The cornerstone of this policy was the Treaty of Dover (1670) between France and England in which the two kings agreed to conquer and partition the Dutch Republic. England was to provide a fleet and soldiers, Charles was to declare himself a Catholic and Louis was to give him one hundred and fifty thousand pounds and provide six thousand French soldiers with which to suppress any opposition when he declared for Catholicism.

Louis invaded the United Provinces in March of 1672 and Charles sent his fleet to Louis' aid. Meeting stiff resistance from the Dutch under the leadership of William of Orange, who organized a coalition of the States against Louis, the French king realized he was involved in a general war with most of Europe. Charles' alliance with Louis drew him into this conflict to the extreme displeasure of Parliament. Parliament viewed this whole affair as an attempt on Charles' part to restore the Catholic faith to England and to govern without it. Under great pressure, Charles withdrew from the war and concluded the Treaty of Westminster in 1674. Withdrawl from the third Dutch War had ended Charles' military alliance with France, but did not change his basic policy of friendship with Louis, nor did it end his reception of subsidies from Louis in return for England's neutrality in the continuance of the war.

From 1674, Charles's chief concern became his struggle with Parliament for a financially independent government. He continued his arrangement with Louis for English neutrality and the deliberate proroguing of Parliament whenever it pressed too hard for a war against France in return for a large subsidy. Charles no longer played any official role in Louis' war with the Dutch, and the Treaty of Nijmegen, which ended the war in 1678, caused England to view with great anxiety his continued successes.

Domestically, Charles was having his problems, especially with Arlington. Early in his tenure as Secretary of State (1660s), Arlington was not effectively to execute his office because of his lack of resolution and absence of unity amongst his followers. He often launched a policy in one direction only to be forced to retreat that position and to set off in another. He even had to suffer being accused by his detractors of guiding foreign poliicy in the direction of France in order to obtain this much needed commodity in return for a promise of the prorogation o dissolution of Parliament. Under such circumstances, it was difficult to resolve the main problem facing his Government: the lack of money. However, even if a large sum could be found, by which to run an independent government, who was competent enough to administer it wisely to maintain fiscal independence? Ralph Montagu petitioned for the office, but was refused. Instead, Thomas Osborne was chosen as Lord Treasurer.2 Osborne (later Earl of Dangy), serious, diligent and attentive to duty, did not attempt to hide his anti-French and anti-Catholic sentiments.

Osborne, as the Lord Treasurer to Charles II, occupied one of the most important offices, if not the most important office in Government, exercising control over almost every other governmental department, including that of the Secretary of State. The Lord Treasurer, in time, came to be regarded as the King's First Minister. Members of the `diplomatic corps' looked to the Lord Treasurer not only in financial matters, but also as the Chief Diplomat for direction in carrying out their embassy. The diplomat had not yet reached a level of great importance; he was still solely regarded as one who carried out the will of his monarch. It was now the responsibility of the Lord Treasurer to coordinate their efforts in the accomplishment of that task.

Danby was well aware of Charles' need for money. He also knew where Charles intended to obtain it and he made known his opposition. With the disorderly adjournment of the Parliament in 1677, Charles became more and more inclined to move into a closer union with the French for the financial help so desperately required. When Danby pondered the situation of the finances, however, he concluded that if Parliament was postponed until the Spring of 1678, as the French insisted, Charles would need no less than two hundred thousand pounds a year to continue an independent Government. Secretly, Danby hoped that this sum would be too much for the French and force them to back away from their offer. His hope was fulfilled; negotiations came to an impasse.[3]

On June 21, 1677, Montagu told Charles that he need not be satisfied with the original sum agreed upon; a much greater sum could be obtained. He could obtain a larger subsidy--an extra million livres (some three hundred thousand pounds or more) a year while the war (French against the Netherlands and Spain from which England had withdrawn by the Treaty of Westminster, 1674) lasted and four million livres (some one million pounds or more) six months after the settlement of a peace as the price of English neutrality. Montagu asked if he should proceed. Would the King authorize his efforts in writing? He hesitated to implement this dangerous idea on his own. He wanted protection. As a further means of self-preservation, Montagu also asked that Danby be brought into the dealings; Montagu wanted Danby to oversee the operations.[4] Was he forcing Danby's cooperation, at the King's command, in order to be sure of his own survival in the event of discovery of the transactions?

Danby now committed his most serious political blunder. He entered the negotiations. What he had so assiduously avoided hitherto he was now forced to embrace. Had he kept to his official policy of total independence of the French orbit of influence, he might have emerged triumphant in the coming conflict. Had he been truly dedicated to his principles of an anti-French and anti-Catholic policy and left it to the King and Montagu to manage the affair themselves, he might have survived the debacle that followed. Danby at first thought he had a chance to win Charles to his way of thinking, but the obstacle to this policy came in the person of Buckingham with his pro-French inclination. Buckingham's return to the good graces of Charles set to naught any hope of success for Danby and foretold disaster for his own political career.[5]

But haste was to decide the outcome of the affair. What if France ceased her warring activities in Flanders and considered England's neutrality no longer necessary to her expansionist plans? A decision had to be made! Charles feared that should Louis no longer need England, Charles would lose all hope of the subsidies from France which would keep him independent of his Parliament. Finally, deciding for acceptance of Louis' offer, Charles ordered Danby to draft a letter to his ambassador in Paris, Montagu, and gave his permission to undertake such negotiations as would lead to the granting of the monies. Taking Montagu at his word, Danby ordered him to seek the additional sum of a million livres during the war and four million at the signing of the peace. He added that the million by itself would not be enough, and, unless four million at the peace could be confirmed, a subsidy of two hundred thousand pounds a year during the war was of absolute need (July 15, 1677).[6]

Danby wrote his letter the day before Parliament adjourned, July 16th. It was not to sit again until December 3rd; it was an adjournment that brought back memories of the May 28th adjournment with the loud and boisterous behavior of its members.7 Having dispatched the letter at the King's order, Danby had every reason to feel secure in the knowledge that the King would surely protect him for doing his duty. Yet, he did not have a sense of well being and in his uneasiness he wrote another letter to Montagu. He expressed his personal, not `official feelings' about the subsidy: he was extremely unhappy that he should be the `receiver of any subsidies obtained.' Furthermore, Danby expressed his total hostility to France and asked Montagu to relay instances of France's misuse of England's trust to him that he might offer them to the King as examples of the dangers of an alliance with Louis and his Court.8

Danby was not the only one thinking of self-preservation. Montagu, too, sought the protection of the royal mantle. He obtained in writing the direct command of Charles to follow the orders given him by `my Lord Treasurer.'

> July 18, Whitehall.--"I have directed my Ld Treasurer to tell you my minde in answer to your letter, and would haue serve you follow those directions, so as I have nothing more to add, but to thanke you for the industry wth which you serue me in the station where you are, and to assure you that I will allwayes be your assured frind.
> "Charles R."9

Accordingly, Danby was aware that Montagu possessed letters in which he seriously compromised himself. But he may have thought that Montagu would not dare to use the letters that passed between them during the last

years because they also seriously compromised him.
Montagu was as deeply involved in the affair as Danby.
Had he been more politically astute, Danby might have
recognized the signs of impending disaster when Montagu
put himself up for election in Parliament for Northamptonshire.   Montagu opposed Danby's son-in-law, Lord
O'Brien, who eventually withdrew from the election.

Montagu should have been a candidate for
Northampton, his family seat, where his father had great
influence politically,10 but he found himself opposed by
Sir William Temple, once a candidate for the office
Montagu so desperately wanted, the Secretary of State.

Montagu and his father, Edward, took no chances as
to whom the preferred candidate was to be. They saw to
it that those who voted did not thirst as they cast
their vote; they spent nearly a thousand pounds on ale.
Apparently Montagu's election did not come cheaply;
Montagu knew the way to a man's vote was through his own
pocket:

> "1678, October 17. I found all things in a
> merry posture. Mr. Montague was that day
> there, and it was a holiday. They were very
> busy about the election of a burgess, there
> are four that stand, my Lord O'Byron, Sir
> George Norris, Mr. Montague and of late Sir
> William Temple. Mr. Montague is the only man
> who treateth, and they say it had cost him
> 1,000 pounds in ale, let who will believe it,
> but certain it is, as the townsmen themselves
> say, both he and his father spend 100 pounds
> per week, but they say to no purpose, for

whomsoever the King will recommend they are resolved to choose, and there coming a letter in favor of Sir William Temple, he, it is thought, will be the man."[11]

Temple lost the election, but was certified the winner by the Sheriff, while Montagu was certified to be the winner of the election by the Mayor. Montagu then petitioned against the return. His petition was presented to the House of Commons on November 6, 1678, and it was decided on November 11, 1678, in Montagu's favor. Without a dissenting vote, Montagu was declared duly elected.[12] The sheriff was placed in custody "for his misdemeanor in making an improper return."[13]

As a member of this Parliament, Montagu was now entitled to immunity. At last he felt himself secure! Not long from his return from Paris, in the Summer of 1678, Montagu began his conspiracy with the opposition party. His plan for revenge and profit now began!

Now a protected member of the House, Montagu initiated his plan for Danby's fall. On Oct. 24, 1678, Barrillon wrote Louis that Montagu had approached him with the boast that he had it within his power to ruin Danby by attacking him in Parliament. He would do this, however, only on the condition that he be assured of some sort of protection from Louis and at the same time be indemnified for his troubles. He was attacking Danby, he said, in order to protect himself. The Lord Treasurer hated him because he refused to demand of France excessive subsidies as an alternative to war with England. Montagu said he could prove to Parliament how the money (the six million livres for the next three years) was to be used, and further, he could show how really reluctant the French King was to enter into such a scheme to satisfy Charles' desire to reduce English liberties to a mere plaything of his will.

Barrillon wrote Louis a rather long letter telling of Montagu's intent.

Mr. Montagu and I have had many occasion of talking upon the present state of affairs. ... This engaged him to speak openly to me, and tell me it was in his power to ruin the high Treasurer, and that he would attack him in parliament, and accuse him of treason, if he was assured of the protection and good will of your Majesty in case of the consequences which this accusation might have. He pretends to prove so from this minister's letters, that he ordered him on the part of his Brittanic Majesty to ask a sum of 18 millions from your Majesty, and to declare that it was the only means to prevent his joining your enemies, and without it that he should be obliged to enter into the league against France and to declare war against you. He alleges that his refusal to obey an order so extraordinary and so unreasonable an order, and which was unknown to the Secretaries of State, drew upon him the enmity of this minister, and that it would be easy for him to shew the parliament for what design 18 millions were wanted; and at the same time the parliament will see that your Majesty was not willing to enter into the schemes which were forming for the oppression

of England, and the change of government. Mr.
Montagu believes this accusation will
infallibly ruin the high Treasurer. ... The
King of England can receive no greater embar-
rassment than to see a man attacked who has
all his confidence. ... No one can ever be
sure of anything in this country: But this
accusation cannot be entirely fruitless,
because it is not destitute of foundation.
... However, he does not believe he shall be
able to bear the weight of such an undertaking
if your Majesty will not also contribute to it
on your part. He asks that whatever your
Majesty would do to traverse the designs of
the court of England, and hinder the keeping
up of the army, may be employed at the same
time to favour what he undertakes. His
demand is, that your Majesty will make a fund
here of one hundred thousand livres, which
should be employed to gain votes, and to make
sure of seven or eight of the principal
persons in the lower House, who may support
the accusation as soon as it shall be begun.14

In return for his services, Montagu demanded:

Mr. Montagu hopes that your Majesty will
recompense him for the service he shall do,
and indemnify him for the loss he will
infallibly suffer in his fortune and posts.
The King of England will probably use all his
efforts to revenge himself of a man who in the
person of his Prime Minister has attacked
himself. Mr. Montague asked in this case that

your Majesty should cause the sum of one
hundred thousand crowns to be paid him, or
that your Majesty would secure him an annuity
of forty thousand livres, on the Hotel de
Ville, payable out of the funds that have been
last settled. ...he shall not sell or
alienate it without your permission. If
neither of these propositions be agreeable to
your Majesty, he will content himself with
your promise of a pension of fifty thousand
livres during his life: Thus it is in your
Majesty's choice to give either the sum of one
hundred thousand crowns in hand, or an annuity
of forty thousand livres upon the Hotel de
Ville, or a pension of fifty thousand livres
during his life; and in this case only that
the accusation succeeds, and the Treasurer is
removed from Court in six months, for if this
happens, Mr. Montagu does not think he should
be exposed to the King of England's hatred, as
he will be, if what he attempts succeeds. Six
months time is taken, because it is presumed
that his Brittanic Majesty will use his
efforts to preserve his minister, and that at
first he will support him.15

Montagu made his decision and threw his lot in with the
French in his effort to destroy Danby.

Thereupon, Barrillon, faithful to Louis XIV's
desires, began to distribute his master's funds where
they would do the most good: to certain members of the
English Parliament, including Montagu, whom he believed
favorable to the French position.16

Montagu demanded a large sum of money, but he thought that he was worth it. His self-estimation would not allow him to sell himself for a lower sum. Besides, he had sold out to a foreign power; in simple terms, Montagu was now guilty of treason. However, not satisfied with putting his own head on the block, he drew his sister into the intrigue. A born intriguer and devoted to her brother in all things, she did not hesitate for an instant. At Montagu's request, she centered her attentions on the Duchess of Portsmouth, an ally of Danby.[17] With the removal of the King's favorite it would be the easier to get at Danby; the King would unwittingly aid in the removal of his first minister. However!

> ... the ambassador thought money a more
> efficient influence than a woman whose
> politics might not always follow the lines
> indicated by Louis XIV. A somewhat coarse man
> Barrillon, of his own accord, attempted to buy
> people and distributed large sums of money to
> many Englishmen, among whom Ralph Montagu was
> the greediest.[18]

Had he seen the danger of Montagu's movements, Danby would have been hard pressed to meet the challenge. His attention was focused on another plot which affected the very life of the King: the Popish Plot, so called because of a supposed Papist plan, revealed by one Titus Oates, to murder both the King and Duke of York. Danby's attention was diverted and this augured well for Montagu and his intrigue.[19]

Charles was convinced that the plot was sheer nonsense, a complete fabrication, and ordered Danby to ignore it so as not to cause alarm and to allow for time to get at the truth. Instead, Danby brought Oates's deposition concerning the affair before Parliament. He hoped, thereby, to strengthen his position with the Protestant cause and convince the House of his anti-Papist and anti-French policy. But Danby's plan had the reverse effect; it actually hastened his down-fall. Had he followed orders instead of trying so desperately to prove the plot true, he might have made political capital out of the situation and thus strengthened his place as Lord Treasurer and first minister of the King. As a result, Danby lost political credibility.

Danby's deliberate revelation, in opposition to Charles' expressed prohibition, to the Council of some letters to a Fr. Bedingfield, Confessor to the Duke of York, from some Jesuits, supposedly containing 'treasonable' designs, could hardly have preserved the secrecy that Charles wanted concerning this whole affair.[20] In bringing this plot to light Danby also incurred the enmity of the Duke of York. It was his Confessor who was accused, and in doing so, Danby had indirectly accused the Duke of a part in the Plot. The affair only served to point up the gulf that had been constantly growing between the Duke and the Lord Treasurer.[21] Danby had made another enemy! Further, the murder of Sir Edmondberry Geoffrey, the justice of peace who had taken the depositions of Oates, did not help matters. Many soon believed that this was the first of many victims of the Catholic conspiracy and if nothing were done there would be thousands more. Panic seized the city of London and Charles could not refuse a Parliamentary investigation.

Meanwhile, Mr. Baker, Montagu's agent, informed Montagu's sister that there was talk all over London of French money being spread about with a view to procuring a favorable public opinion towards France. She was of a mind that her brother had a right to some of that money because of his attempt to destroy Danby and so aid the French policy. She intended that he should have his share.

> Upon her returne [August of 1677] she was immediatly visited by the French ambassador, Mounsieur Barrillon, who constantly afterwards made her very frequent visits allmost every morning. The Parliament then sitting, a great noise was about towne of a bargaine made by somebody for a peace instead of warr with France. In August following, Mr. Montague came suddenly and privathy over, and was imediatly mett at his sisters by Mounsieur Barrillon, where they generally were four or five time a weeke privately togeather.
> ...
> Amongst other things when the talke of French money encreased in the towne, I telling her what I heard of it, she freely told me she was clearly for her brother's driving the bargaine, and that she told him soe when she was with him there, for if they wou'd have money, said she, why should not he have some of it as well as anybody else, and a great more to that effect, &c.22

At the outset of this drama of betrayal and intrigue, Barrillon was not entirely convinced that Montagu's plan would produce the desired effect: the impeachment of Danby. But later when victory seemed in sight, Temple feared he might became a victim of Montagu's vindictiveness, especially since he was once a viable candidate for the office of Secretary of State and Montagu was not. Temple observed:

And this went so far, that Mr. Montague went a great way from Man to Man in the House to know whether if such an Accusation were brought in, they would be against me. Several went into it upon Hatred of the Late Treasurer, whose Friend they took me to be, and upon Envy at my being design'd for Secretary of State; but yet in no such Numbers that Mr. Mountague could hope to make any thing of it: And when some of my Friends acquainted me with it, I only desir'd them to obtain Leave of the House, that I might hear my Accusation at the Bar of the House, and assur'd them that I should be glad to have that Occasion of telling there both Mr. Mountague's story and my own.[23]

The more Montagu pressed his case, the more Barrillon saw the benefit that could come to the French cause from such a coup. The accusation of treason against Danby might work since Montagu claimed he had the evidence in writing. Judging the situation from these perspectives, he assessed the chances of success and then agreed to Montagu's scheme.[24] However,

Barrillon would not hand out his sovereign's money without some kind of `escape clause.' To protect himself
from his master, he warned Montagu that if Montagu's
scheme did not work and Danby survived the attack,
Montagu would then have to trust to the generosity of
Louis. But if the plan worked within six months,
Montagu could then hope for a fitting reward for his
`loyalty' to Louis. Both came to an agreement and the
plan for the destruction of the Lord Treasurer was set
in motion. Barrillon also considered the possibility of
Charles' proroguing Parliament as soon as Danby was
attacked, but such action would leave no money to maintain or disband his army, the constant thorn in the side
of Commons.25 Further, Louis would not be inconvenienc-
ed in regard to Montagu. If Montagu's part should become
known, it would be his head on the block. Montagu knew
full well what he was doing; he knew that his actions
were truly treasonable.

Meanwhile, on the other side of the Channel, Louis
relished the possibility of the dismissal of his enemy,
Danby, and the continued dependence of Charles upon him
for funds. With the election of Montagu to Parliament
the plan could now go ahead in earnest. Further, with
Montagu enjoying the privilege of immunity, there was
little that could be done to him by Charles. Louis may
have wanted to give Charles a lesson in diplomacy by
using one of his own servants against him. There also
remained, happily, the distinct possibility that Montagu
might be of further service to Louis for the right
price. Added to all this, Louis delighted in the specta-
cle of an England in the throes of the Popish Plot. The
confusion caused by this crisis might be the added
ingredient to the plan that could insure its success.

Barrillon's dispatches of October 20, 24, 27, November 24, and December 14, 22, 1678 reveal that, following Montagu's offer to destroy Danby, he was continually involved in extending the opposition to Danby and that he believed Danby deliberately accepted the validity of the Popish Plot in order to make France the more hated in England.26 The dispatches further indicated that a fair number of members of Parliament knew of Danby's impending impeachment. George Savile, Lord Halifax, knew of it, as did his cousin, Algernon Sidney, brother of Henry Sidney, the English ambassador to the United Netherlands. Yet the leaders of the party were unsure about the exact timing of their attack on Danby. They insisted upon disbandment of the army as a necessary condition for the attack.27

It was November (1678). Chaos reigned. The conspirators were not seemingly too anxious to launch their attack for fear that Danby would reach a reconciliation with the Duke of York, and that together with Charles, they might present a united front which the Commons might find difficult to topple. If only the three protagonists could be separated the success of the plan would be assured! Accordingly, not knowing Charles' intent, whether he would or would not prorogue Parliament, Barrillon was slow to parcel out the promised reward to Montagu. He claimed the reason for his parsimony was the lack of results so far. If Montagu wanted his money, he had better deliver the promised outcome.28

In December 1678 the Treaty of Nijmegen was signed and Charles began arrangements to call his troops home, troops which had been levied in the spring of that year to fight France. This army was the constant source of irration between the two monarchs and also between the English King and his Parliament. But if Louis kept faith with the terms of the peace, there was little need or excuse for Charles to retain these troops under arms. Parliament realized this, but it also realized how loath Charles was to disband his army. Commons, in its frenzy to remove Danby, believed his pro-French sentiments explained the slowness to dissolve the men at arms.

During the negotiations for the Treaty of Nijmegen, Sir Leonine Jenkins, one of Charles' envoys to the peace conference, wrote to Danby that the Swedish representative to the talks, Olivenkrantz, reported that Charles was "ill served" by his former ambassador to Paris. Olivenkrantz claimed that some time previously Montagu had several late night private meetings in Paris with the Pope's Nuncio. He said he received the information from the Swedish envoy in Paris, who, in turn, had it from the master of the house in which the conferences were held. Perhaps there were reasons for these visits. He did not know, but he thought it wise to pass along this information (November 5, 1678).

> ...and that he did not know how well the King had been serv'd by Mr. Montague while ambass- ador lately in France. The reason why he doubted was, he sayd, for that Mr. Montague had had, about a year and a halfe agoe, several conferences in a private house in Paris, and at late houres in the night, with the Popes nuncio there, and that he (Monsieur Olivecrantz) had this notice from the envoye

of Sweden in France, and that that envoye had
had his information from the master of the
house himself where Mr. Montague and the
nuncio mett.[29]

Danby replied to Leonine Jenkins (November 22,
1678) that neither he nor the king had any knowledge of
these meetings and that Montagu had no authority or
orders to visit the Nuncio.

As to what concerns Mr. Montagu, I perceive
his Majestie knows nothing of this conference
with the Popes Nuncio; and for what Monsieur
Olivencrantz supposes might have been the
occasion of these conferences, viz., a treaty
of marriage betwixt the King of Spaine and the
Duke of Orleans daughter, his Majestie saies
hee never entered into any such treaty, nor
ever gave Mr. Montagu any instructions about
itt. You may also say in your letter that in
twelve or fifteen dais Monsieur Olivencrantz
would probably bee able both to tell the time
more precizely of those conferences, and
perhaps something more of the designe against
our religion in England, which gives us great
impatience till we heare againe from you of
that matter, being under so great apprehen-
sions of the papists att this time what wee
can apply our thoughts to no other businesse,
of what importance soever itt bee, either att
home or abroad.[30]

Inquiring further into this matter, Danby learned
that there were three such meetings over a two week

period and they were held at the house of the Abbe Siri
(December 3, 1678).

> As to the precise time of the Conference
> between Mr. Montague and the nuncio, he had
> this to adde,...; 2. that they were had in the
> house of the Abbe Siri, the same Siri that
> hath written a Generall History in Italian in
> severall volumes in quarto 3. that there were
> three conferences between them, had within the
> space of fifteen dayes or thereabouts.[31]

Aided by this information, Danby now thought he
could defend himself, in case of attack, through the
revelation of this link of Montagu with the Catholic
cause.   In the intense anti-Catholicism prevailing this
was certainly formidable and dangerous evidence of
collusion.   Danby wrote to Temple (November 19, 1678):

> ...and the ill practices of Mr. Montagu to
> debauche them. Since his coming to the House
> I have heard more of his ill practices of
> other kinds, and some of them particularly
> against yourselfe, which I am hunting as
> eagerly as I can to find out; and I heare that
> Monsieur Olivekrans can tell us some things if
> hee pleases, of Mr. Montagu, which would both
> spolie his plotts and his seate in Parliament,
> and which would do well to informe yourself
> of, if you meete with a fitt occasion.[32]

It is rather curious that the government did not
act before it did. Why did it wait till December before

making any sort of move? Perhaps Charles and Danby were looking for some other piece of evidence which they felt was absolutely damning to Montagu. Had Danby been more politically atuned he could have `scotched the snake before it bit him.' He persisted, however, in his belief that Montagu had nothing to gain by incriminating himself in such an affair. Unfortunately, Danby waited until after Montagu became a member of Commons before he acted. Danby was warned by Sir John Reresby, of impending danger but chose to ignore the warning.

> I acquented his lordship that Monsieur de Croc (the said resident) had assured me the day before that the Commons would certainly fall upon him, and that it was in his power to take of the edge of one most violent against him. I tould him more that I heard from others, that my cozen Ralph Mountaigue, since Lord Mountaigue (lately recalled from being embassadour in France and now member of our Hous), would accuse him ther. My Lord rejected both, saying the latter durst not impeach him , for he had letters to show from him, whilst embassador, that made out, how endeavouring he was to persuade him to accept the French Kings mony, but he absolutely refused it.33

Apprised of Montagu's intention to reveal Danby's letters to the House, the King acted to defend his minister. At Charles' command, the Council dispatched its couriers to Montagu's house (December 19,) with orders to seize his papers. The seizure of Montagu's papers brought instant reaction. The House went into conference about the violation of the privilege of the

House; to seize the papers of members was equal to the seizure of the member.

> Dec. 19, 1678. The K. acquaints the H. by Mr. Stage (?) that having received Information that Mr. Mountagu, his late Embassad'r in France a member of this H., had private conferences with the Pope's Nuncio there without any Instructions from his M., That his M. might know ye truth of the matter, he had given order for the seizing of Mr. M's Papers. The H. declares they cannot make any Judgment either in violation to their Member, or the Privilege of the house, which may be invaded, till they knew whether the Information agt Mr. Montagu was on oath, and of what nature the offense is, that is there complain'd of. And they ordered some of their Members attend his M. with this vote.[34]

The King then notified the Chancellor of the Exchequer that he was to inform the House that such action had been taken because of Montagu's direct violation of his instructions: Montagu had had unauthorized conferences with the Papal Nuncio in Paris.[35]

The commandeering of the letters may have been prompted by a hope on the part of the King and Danby to recover any incriminating letters they had written. The Government's only hope now was to discover something that would incriminate Montagu.[36] But Montagu had been clever enough to remove anything detrimental to himself and left only that which would help his case. The debates that followed upon the seizure, of Montagu's

papers served to divert the attention of the House from
the Popish Plot and centered it upon the problem of the
Lord Treasurer.37

But if the King and Danby entertained any hope
that Montagu would incriminate himself, it had little
possibility of fulfillment. Besides, the letters in all
probability had been read by others by this time.
Montagu must have used them as evidence to induce others
to vote his way.

In the House Montagu stated his belief about the
seizure of his papers.

Mr. Montagu. I believe, that the seizing of
my cabinets and Papers was to get into their
hands some Letters of great consequence, that
I have to produce of the designs of a Great
Minister of State.

Mr. Harbord. This has been intended for three
or four days, but, I believe, they have missed
some of their aims; and I would not for 40,000
l. they had those Papers. And, freely, this
was my great inducement to stir so much to
make Mr. Montagu a Member of this House. In
due time you will see what those Papers are.
They will open yours eyes, and though too late
to cure the evil, yet they will tell you who
to proceed against, as the authors of our
misfortunes. I desire that some persons of
honour and worth may be present at the opening
these Cabinets, lest some of the Letters
should be there. For they are of the great
consequence that ever you saw.[38]

The more temperate of the House proposed that the papers of Montagu be examined the next day (Dec. 20); however, the more radical would not have it so and professed their anxiety as to what the morrow would bring and demanded that proceedings begin at once. Grey recorded in his Debates:

> Sir John Lowther. For ought I know, Montagu may be served as Sir Edmundbury Godfrey was; therefore I would not have him go out of the house for the papers. He knows by what practices these negotiations with France have been done. I am of the opinion that we shall not sit here to-morrow. I move therefore to have the Papers sent for now.
>
> Sir Henry Capel. I second that Motion. ... I know not what may become of us tomorrow; therefore, I would have Montagu's Papers brought to-night.[39]

Present at these debates, Montagu informed the House that he had in his possession certain damaging evidence against Danby. But just previous to this calculated announcement to the House, Montagu had selected the 'pertinent' letters and carefully set aside any letters which might be deemed injurious to himself.[40] Lord Russell, Mr. Harbord, and Sir Henry Capell were then sent by the House to fetch the chest wherein Montagu claimed to have placed them.[41] They went to Montagu's house and returned with the startling news that his papers had already been 'carried off' in four cabinets, which were sealed and were not to be opened unless in Montagu's presence. The 'Box of Writings' was opened in a tension-filled House and Montagu selected two letters to be read to a now rather angry House: the two notorious letters of January 17 and March 25, 1678, wherein it was claimed that Danby sold England to France.42

The incident of the "opening of the box" is recorded in the Journal of the House of Commons:

Mr. Montagu acquainting the House, That he had in his custody several papers, which he conceived might tend very much to the Safety of His Majesty's Person, and the preservation of the Kingdom;

Ordered, That the Lord Russell, Mr. Harbord, Sir Scroop How, and Sir Hen. Capell do take Mr. Montagu's Directions; and repair immediately to the Place where the said Writings are lodged; and bring the same to the House.

Ordered, That the Box be opened; And that Mr. Montagu be present: And that he do select such Writings as he thinkes may be for the Service of the House; and dipose of all other Writings which properly concerns himself, as he shall think fit.43

These must have been tense and uneasy moments for Montagu, perhaps even moments of fear and panic. He knew full well the very real possibility existed that at any moment he himself might be found out and that he could be arrested and imprisoned for treason. The charges he leveled against Danby could be, in fact, also leveled against him, and with greater justification. He knew that the letters he wrote to Danby over the last two years concerning the subsidy were in Danby's possession and if provoked enough Danby would use them. Such thoughts must certainly have crossed Montagu's mind during his disclosures to the House of Danby's wrongdoing. However, what Montagu counted on was that Charles would not allow treasonous documents relating to the secret negotiations of subsidies to be produced in public. With this in mind, he had carefully separated the letters and allowed only those dealing with Danby's part in the negotiations to be made public.

While pretending great reluctance in obeying the command of the House, Montagu opened the cabinet and selected two letters which he calculated would produce the desired effect: the impeachment of Danby.

Grey (Debates) recounted the reading of the letters:

> Lord Cavendish. I believe, it will appear by those Papers, that the War with France was pretended for the sake of an Army, and that a great man carried on the interest of an Army and Popery; and Montagu gives you the convenience of this discovery. I move, therefore, "That he brings the Papers in as soon as can be."

> Colonel Titus. I suppose Montagu had those Papers in his custody; else neither he nor his friends would have informed you of them. I

would therefore have some Members go with him
and fetch them.

Lord Russel. Montagu has imparted some of the
contents of those papers to me; and I was
required by him not to impart them to anybody;
but now it is no secret. Montagu cannot come
at the originals, for the present, he has but
a copy of them.

Mr. Harbord and some others were ordered (Mr.
Montagu having acquainted the House that he
had [in his custody] some Papers which concern
the Peace of the Government) to receive directions from Mr. Montagu where to find those
papers.

The House sat till the Gentlemen returned with
Mr. Montagu's Papers.   Then

Mr. Harbord reported, That they had repaired
to the place where Mr. Montagu directed them,
and had brought the Box of Papers which Mr.
Montagu mentioned; but that the key is carried
to Whitehall, locked up in the Cabinets; and
that they have sent for a smith to break it
open.

Mr. Montagu went up to sort the papers.

Mr. Montagu. I am sorry that so great a
Minister has brought this guilt upon himself.
It was my intention (making reflections upon
your apprehension of a standing Army) to have

acquainted Mr. Secretary Coventry with the Papers. I will now only tell you, that the King has been as much deluded as the Dutch or Spain: and you have been deluded too by this great Minister. This I should not have done, out of duty and respect to the King, but by command of the House.

[The box being ordered to be opened] Mr. Montagu [selected and] presented to the House two Letters, which were read [by the Speaker,] the one dated [January 16, 1677-8; the other] March 25, 1678. The principal matter therein is contained these words: "In case the conditions of Peace shall be accepted, the King expected to have six millions of livres [300,000 l.] yearly, for three years, from the time that this agreement shall be signed between his Majesty and the King of France; because it will be two or three years before he can hope to find his Parliament in humour to give him supplies, after your having made any Peace with France, &c."

Subscribed "Danby"

"To the Secretary you must not mention one syllable of the money."
[At the bottom of this Letter were written these words: "THIS LETTER IS WRIT BY MY ORDER. C.R."]

Mr. Bennet. I wonder the House sits so silent when they see themselves sold for six millions of livres to the <u>French</u>. Some things come home to Treason in construction. I would have the Lawyers tell you, whether this you have heard be not worthy impeaching the Treasurer of Treason. Now we see who has played all this game; who has repeated all the sharp Answers to our Addresses, and raised an Army for no War. You Know now who passes by the Secretaries of State. I would impeach the Treasurer for High Treason.

Mr. <u>Williams</u>. Will any member aver this to be the Treasurer's letter?

Mr. <u>Montagu</u>. I conceive it to be the Treasurer's hand. I have several letters from him of the same hand.

Mr. <u>Williams</u>. If this be his Letters, there cannot be a more constructive Treason than is contained in it. You have heard of Religion and Property apprehended in danger, in several speeches. But when your Laws are contemned by a Great Minister, and they miscarry are laid dead--(<u>A great cry from the House</u>, "Name him, name him, name him.")

The Letters name the person sufficiently. Nothing ought to be imputed to the King -- But this man, unless he clears himself upon some body else, must take this crime upon him. The project of Peace is what you have prophesied all along. This agrees with <u>Coleman's</u> Letters, this great engine Money. Now when this great person is on this point to make Parliaments useless, it is Treason. And the Parliament may declare a Treason, without making any. For any Minister to destroy a confederacy, and to make the King a Pensioner to France, I would impeach him of Treason.

Mr. Harbord. I hope now Gentlemens eyes are open, by the design on foot to destroy the Government and our Liberties. I believe, if the House will command Mr. Montagu, he will tell you more now. But I would not press it upon him, because poisoning and stabbing are in use. Therefore I would not examine him farther now, but let him reserve himself till the matter comes to Tryal before the Lords. As to the danger of the King's person, there is something much more extraordinary. But I will not name him yet--The thing has taken wind -- A Witness has been taken off with 300 l. and denies his hand. I protest, I am afraid that the King will be murdered every night. A Peer, and an intimate of this Earl's said, "There would be a change in the Government in a year." He has poisons both liquid and in powders -- But I would ask Montagu no more questions now, but have an Impeachment drawn up, and I doubt not but this great man will have condign punishment, when the matter comes before the Lords.44

Montagu's plan worked; the selected letters produced the desired effect: the House decided to censure and impeach Danby.

The House of Commons for the most part supported Montagu, yet, he must have feared for his safety. He did not know how Danby would respond; he might produce a stunning defense and turn the House around.

The letters produced were only two in a long chain of letters dealing with subsidies. These letters were really taken out of context, and, in fact, were rather innocuous in themselves. These facts, however, escaped the notice of the House, or if they were noticed, the House simply did not care.[45] The House wanted Danby impeached. Even had the Commoms known the depth of Montagu's involvment, it is probable that they would not have censured him. Commons saw what it wanted to see and any revelation concerning Montagu would have made little difference.

Charles sent the House several letters he had received to give them satisfaction in the matter of Danby. The letters were read but had no effect on the mood or tenor of the House. Commons continued in its determination to impeach the Lord Treasurer.[46] Montagu was aware of the fact that much French money had been used to suborn many of the opposition and that the very ones who vented their fury and indignation were the ones who had been the first to take the French "gifts." They could hardly accuse him.

On December 20, 1678, the Duke of York wrote William, Prince of Orange about Montagu's perfidious action:

I believe you will be surprised to hear what Mr. Montagu has done; for being yesterday accused in the Council of having had secret conferences with the Pope's Nuncio at Paris, he to revenge himself of that, produced letters written to him by the Lord Treasurer by his Majesty's command, when he was Ambassador in France and shews them to the Commons, who upon it ordered an impeachment to be drawn up against the Lord Treasurer upon the matter contained in those letters, and other things they had against him. I am confident there was never so abominable an action as this of Mr. Montagu's, and so offensive to the King, in revealing what he was trusted with when he was employed by his Majesty; all honest men abhor him for it.47

What really confirmed the guilt of Danby in the eyes of Commons was that the letter of March 25 was written five days after the House had voted Charles supplies to raise an army to fight France. After a heated debate Danby was loudly condemned: (1) for entering into affairs outside the province of his competence, that is, his encroaching of royal powers in foreign affairs in defiance of King and Parliament by issuing orders to the King's ambassador; (2) for the selling of England to France for money by the putting off of Parliament; (3) for arbitrary government by raising an army on pretense of a war and continuing it in existence in spite of an Act of Parliament calling for its disbandment. Found guilty of high treason, Danby was held over for impeachment and imprisonment. On December 21st, 1678, Articles of Impeachment were formally drawn up and issued against the person of the Lord Treasurer.[48]

Danby's defense was weak. He might have used the letters written him by Montagu in his own defense and shown the House that Montagu was far more deeply involved in the question of subsidy from the French. To do so, however, might have complicated matters all the more, and, perhaps, even made it appear that he was only bringing forth more proof of his guilt. He did, however, try to show that many of his accusers were in league with the French and were on the payroll of the French ambassador in England, the recipients of French money. On December 20 Danby sent the Speaker two of Montagu's letters (January 11 and January 18, 1678) to prove his point, but these letters were not specific enough in detail and identified only Lord Russell, who was one of the most respected members of the House. If Danby hoped that these letters would change the mood of the House, he was sadly disappointed. So little effect was achieved. The letters were not even read into the House Journal.[49]

Charles saved his first minister from impeachment by proroguing Parliament on the 30th of December. Realizing that he was not doing himself or the King any good by protesting his innocence and remaining in office, Danby resigned his office on March 16, 1679.

Montagu had won! He had his revenge. That this personal quarrel had cost his country the loss of its Lord Treasurer and caused the proroguing of Parliament disturbed him not at all; to Montagu, the important thing was the satisfaction of his desire for revenge.

In the face of such a monumental ego, everything else meant little. Perhaps Lord Macaulay was right when in his History of England (p. 218) he called Montagu "a faithless and shameless man."

Barrillon was also successful. His enemy was disgraced and was soon to be impeached. However, given the mood of the House and the anger of the King, Barrillon thought it best that he should have as little public contact with Montagu as possible. In like manner, Montagu kept out of harm's way and avoided Barrillon.

Montagu also wisely decided to make himself "hard to find," should Charles want him arrested. When Parliament is not sitting, parliamentary privilege is in abeyance, and those who had treason on their minds had to look to their own safety. Montagu was no where to be seen.[50]

Montagu's sister related that when her brother's papers were seized he was very much afraid; much afraid of a prorogation and of his arrest.[51] However, Montagu had planned for such an eventuality. His agent, Baker, assumed the responsibility of watching and informing Montagu of events. If news of an impending arrest arrived he was to convey this news to Montagu immediately. Wearing a cloak, Baker was to attend the House every day, and, if Montagu were at any time threatened, he was to "...clasp a cloak about him (which I was enjoyn'd not to be without), and carry him away by water into London, or where else I thought fitt...."[52] Lady Harvey told Baker that she would rather trust her brother's life to him than to anyone else and Montagu echoed this sentiment when he intimated that his life was in danger and that he might be at any time sent to the Tower "...and swore he had noe mind to eate meat of other's dressing where he must either eate poyson or starve."[53]

After the letter esisode Montagu did not go to the House, but felt it best to `return' to a house in Fleet Street and then to a lodging in Lime Street belonging to a friend of his intimate Baker. Here he remained in hiding for over about two where his friends, including Barrillon, often visited him there. "The nights being then long and darke, wee went often out to some taverne, or private house of my acquaintance, where the French ambassador and others of his freinds severall times mett him."[54]

Barrillon also remained in constant touch with Lady Harvey, who visited her brother on a daily basis. After the first days of hiding, Montagu became frightened and proceeded to make arrangements to cross the Channel. He persuaded Baker to charter a boat, the Dort, and prevailed upon him to accompany him into exile. He hoped to escape prosecution, but had every intention of returning when the emergency ended and Parliament had reassembled. Baker hired a vessel and made all arrangements for the journey. The boat was to clear Gravesend, about twenty miles east of London, and to wait for them on the 'hether side of the Hope.'[55] Montagu may have had some second thoughts about the trip; he was fearful of such a journey, but at last made up his mind to make it. Early one morning they took a coach and on the way to Deptford met Sir Thomas Armstrong, also a member of the opposition party, who awaited Montagu with servants, horses and arms.[56]

They embarked for France late one evening. Rounding Margate Roads, some sixty miles or so east of London, a violent storm arose. Upon being informed that they would have to ride the storm out at anchor for some time, Montagu would have none of it. He was extremely seasick and "...he had rather I would throw him in the sea then keep him there in that condition, for he was very sick."[57] Baker suggested that they make for Holland, but Montagu refused and they returned to Queenborough Water, "where it was very quiett." Montagu wished to spend the night ashore and in the morning go by coach to Dover. Baker left him at Canterbury and riding through the night arrived at Dover, where he hired a small boat for Calais. He then returned to Canterbury to fetch Montagu. Just as they were embarking, they were seized by officers who had been warned of the planned flight by a member of the boat's crew.[58]

> News came this morning that Ralph Montague is taken in a disguise at Dover, where he was endeavoring to get into France. He hired a small vessel in ye river and went aboard it as a servant to his own man, and the wind being agst them hee put into Quinborow and so went over land to Dover.[59]

Montagu and Baker were arrested at Dover (January 19th)[60] and placed in custody. William Stokes, the Mayor of Dover, wrote to Sir William J. Williamson:

> I will observe your orders as to the stay of Mr. Montague; he has been treated with respect and seems satisfied, except with the guard, civil men of the town, placed in the house

where he is. I dare not release him on
parole, though he earnestly presses it. I
enclose affidavits relating to his seizure. I
have promised a reward to the two seamen that
made the discovery.61

Here they remained for the better part of a week
awaiting the disposition of Whitehall.

... "Mr. Montague was stopt at Dover in his
passage for France -- but not taken in woman's
clothes as was reported: -- a messenger is
sent to summon him to appeare at Court, not to
take him into custody, soe that great care
seems to be taken not to break privilege.62

Montagu was obliged to give a security of one
thousand pounds that he would not try to leave the
country. Upon doing so, he was returned to London.
When entering the city he received a warning from his
sister to be on guard for his safety as it was rumored
that he was soon to be made a `close prisoner.'
However, nothing came of this and Montagu went to his
home in Bloomsbury.63 Perhaps the Court thought it best
to ignore him for the time being, at least until it
could determine what to do next. A few days later
Montagu was elected for Huntingdonshire (February-July
1679) and with this new sitting of Parliament Montagu
felt safe once again. The House, triumphant and feeling
all the more independent of Royal influence or control,
once more assured Montagu of its protection.

With Montagu's flight and subsequent house-arrest,
Danby did his best to defend himself, but his efforts

were futile. His speeches before Parliament in his defense were useless. They fell on deaf ears. Parliament wanted his banishment. To save himself, Danby waged a propaganda campaign by a series of pamphlets to make his position clear and justify his actions to the populace. Of course, the opposition was not slow to counter with its rebuttal.64

During all this, it was business as usual for the Court. In the first weeks of February, news reached the Court of the breach between the Dutch and the French. Charles was delighted. This meant an end to the mistrust between him and his French counterpart. However, in contrast to Charles' delight, it looked as if the elections were likely to go against the Court.

Montagu had some difficulty in being elected. He could not win Northamptonshire's endorsement and so tried Huntingdonshire.

1678-9, February 4.   ...Mr. Montague for Northamptonshire....65

1678-9, February 15. - Mr. Montague is chosen for Huntingdonshire. He had intended to stand also for Northamptonshire but was chosen here. Yesterday he was before the King and Council upon summons. The King told him that he understood that he was chosen a member of Parliament. That they were shortly to sit, and therefore he would say nothing to him now; hoping that they would do him right, and so discharged him of attendance.66

1678-9, February 20. - Mr. Montagu (I mean
Ralph) being said to be gone into Northamptonshire to manage his election as was thought,
was pursued with a message to appear at the
Council Board. Which was accordingly sent to
his father's house. But being invited into
Huntingdonshire by the gentlemen there to
avoid the opposition that was raised against
him in Northamptonshire, and to gain time,
embraced the invitation, and was chosen without trouble with one night's stay, and had the
advantage thereby, to be absent when the
summons came. Howbeit he had it afterwards,
but being now under privilege the stile in
which it was directed was very modest, viz.,
to appear when he conveniently could. Which
he did forthwith, and was asked why he left
Paris before his orders came for his return.
To which he said he had advice that his return
was ordered, and being indebted upon the
King's account 8000., and fearing an arrest,
he went to meet his orders at Callis, which he
did accordingly. Then he was questioned about
his correspondence with the Pope's Nuncio
which he denied. And last of all he demanded
the keyes of his cabinet (which it seems they
had not opened, though seized you know when);
but he said he remembered not then where he
had hid them, and so he was dismissed with
this only that he should send them when he
could find them.67

In the meantime in order to forestall any
unpleasant reaction from the House due to the Popish

Plot and James' Catholicism, Charles thought it best that James be sent abroad to Brussels. James refused to leave except by direct order and this the King gave in order to keep him out of reach of his enemies. James loyally obeyed Charles' order. A wise move on his part given the virulent anti-Catholicism of Parliament.

Meanwhile, Montagu was not sitting idly by. The first rumblings of the Monmouth rebellion were beginning to be heard and Montagu was involved. He supported Monmouth financially and even importuned Barrillon for a sum of money to be used in gaining support for Monmouth's bid for the Throne. Nor was Montagu slow to remind Barrillon that Louis had promised him one hundred thousand francs and had as yet to pay even half the promised sum.68

On March 22nd Charles delivered a speech to both Houses in which he declared that he had given Danby full pardon for any misconduct, and would, if the need arose, pardon him ten times over. He declared that the letters produced by Montagu were written at his direct order. He then informed them of his dismissal of Danby from his Court and Councils and then recommended that the Parliament settle down to business. The House chose to ignore the pardon and began to question both the validity of the pardon and the power of the King to pardon in such a case. It continued in its demand that Danby be impeached. The Lords, however, accepted the pardon as valid and drew up a Bill of Disqualification of Danby but not of impeachment. This touched off a series of hot debates between the Houses and ended with the Commons drawing up a Bill of Impeachment against Danby and a demand for his committal to the Tower.69

Fearful of the current mood of Commons, Montagu consistently urged secrecy on Barrillon as to their joint venture, and found, to his consternation, he was received with indifference and even contempt by the ambassador. Montagu sought from Barrillon his full money, but to no avail. Barrillon did succeed in obtaining half of the promised one hundred thousand crowns, but, if he had his own way, Montagu would have received less. However, Barrillon realized the necessity of paying something since he had not given up hope of a further engagement of Montagu's services in the cause of France.[70]

On March 26th Danby resigned his Treasurership and Henry Guy was appointed Secretary of the Treasury.[71] Danby's resignation provoked a literary response on the action:

A Pun

(1679)

Take a turn

Upon my word

And into five parts cut it,

And put it

Into a pie,

To convince

Our good Prince

What it can be

To mince

Thomas Earl of Danby

Into five commissioners and a Guy.72

Unashamed, in April, Montagu declared to Barrillon that his campaign against Danby was a success and he petitioned for his money in full. Barrillon replied that he was awaiting Danby's impeachment for treason, but Montagu replied that he had only promised to have Danby removed from office and not condemned to death. He wanted his money; he considered the money as earned and therefore his by 'right.' On December 14, 1679, Barrillon wrote to Louis of the difficulty he had in defending himself from Montagu's solicitations during the last six months:

I ought to give your Majesty an account of what regards Mr. Montagu separate from the others, being engaged as he is in your Majesty's interests by particular considerations. I have had trouble enough to defend myself these six months against his solicitations for the payment of the sum which was promised him for the ruin of the high Treasurer, He alleges that the condition is fulfilled on his part. I have always endeavoured to make him understand that it was an affair not entirely finished, and that being full assured of what had been promised to him, he ought not to make himself uneasy whether the payment be made a little sooner or later. He does not give way to my reasons. The two journeys which the Sieur Falaiseau had made to no purpose, would have made him resolve to go himself to solicit the payment of the sum he pretends to a right to, if he could have left England at a time when affairs are in so great commotion, and in which he has acted so great a part. Your Majesty will remember, if you please, that Mr. Montagu spoke to me in the month of January last, to try if you would favour the Duke of Monmouth's pretensions: It was the principal motive of his journey to France when seized at Dover.73

Barrillon continued:

> He has often spoken to me of getting Lord Shaftesbury into your Majesty's interests, and alleges that it would not be impossible if a considerable sum were employed. ...it would be a proper means to stir up new embarrass- ments to the King of England, and Lord Shaftesbury would be still more bold, if he found himself secretly supported by your Majesty:....74

Barrillon then suggested that a date be set for payment to Montagu. He hoped the suggestion would both quiet him and cause Montagu to be once more eager to serve Louis; he would be helpful in dispersing money to the other Members of Parliament. He could think of no other

persons better equipped for this than Montagu and his
sister; they would be of great help in contravening the
designs of the English Court.75

The following years were to see Montagu annoyingly
badger the ambassador for his wages. However, present,
Barrillon thought he might be of some further use to the
French and so on December 5, 1680, he wrote to Louis:

> Although Mr. Montagu has been in your
> Majesty's interest a long time, and the sum of
> which he expects the payment is alone suffic-
> ient to prevent his taking any contrary
> step.... All I said did not persuade Mr.
> Montagu, but the money I paid him by your
> Majesty's order makes his mind very easy. I
> believe it will be necessary to make him a
> second payment of fifty thousand livres, for
> the excuse of the bills of exchange not coming
> fast enough is not sufficient, and in the
> present conjuncture he may be of great use to
> me in your Majesty's affairs.76

Apparently Montagu received his money, but not all of
it.

Barrillon also wrote that he had made connections
with a number of the opposition party who were also
members of Parliament through Montagu and his sister.
This group included Mr. Harbors, Mr. Hampden, and
Montagu's cousin, Algernon Sidney. They and others,
although they openly professed to be anti-French and
Protestant in Religion, had little difficulty in accepting French money to overlook any qualms they may have

had in their directions. These men, in essence, said
one thing, as was evidenced in their accusations in the
debates in the House concerning Danby and his pro-French
and pro-Papist policy, and did another, as proved in
their willingness to accept the gifts of money from the
French ambassador to destroy the Lord Treasurer. They
easily accepted duplicity as a normal way of acting.
Apparently, they saw nothing immoral in suborning themselves. In fact, they were almost eager for the French
money, and, thus basically were representative of the
dualistic morality of their age. These and others,
Barrillon boasted, he had easily suborned for the French
advantage. He regarded Lady Harvey as a most important
ally in his venture to rid France of an enemy. She was
deep in the affair and seemed to thrive on conspiracy.77

However, he warned Louis about what he perceived to
be Montagu's true sentiment: he would be gladly of the
Court party and would be quite happy with another
appointment by the King, especially an ambassadorship to
France.

> Mr. Montagu would willingly be well with the
> court, and have a great place if it were
> possible; he would be very glad first to go
> ambassador extraordinary to France for some
> time. He declared himself openly against the
> Duke of York, and is entered into an intimate
> confidence with the Duke of Monmouth; he is
> also united with Lord Russell and Lord
> Shaftesbury.78

Confidence in one's ability to survive is
admirable, but in Montagu's case it was certainly

extraordinary. He was somewhat sure that the King did not know about his treacherous dealings with Barrillon for Danby's betrayal. But to believe that after producing secret correspondence which led to the impeachment of Danby he could still hope for a position of trust, such as an ambassadorship, was indeed an extraordinary naivete or unbounded audacity.

From his actions in this affair, Montagu appears as a schemer, not a real planner; an intriguer, not a statesman. Had he put such effort and energy into the true services of his King and Country, and had he served Danby faithfully as the representative of the King, Montagu might have left a different mark in history. Rather, he chose to serve himself. His attempts to advance himself show a mind that was strong and decisive. He had an iron will, by which, in spite of obstacles, he determined to obtain a higher place. To this end he was not above deceit, which eventually turned into treason. Montagu's immorality was not unique, however; duplicity and greed were the acceptable standards of conduct in the seventeenth century. Montagu was representative of his times.

CHAPTER V

Footnotes

[1] The Court in Mourning, p. 7; Boyer, Annals, VIII, 370-71.

[2] Lee, p. 1190.

[3] Mignet, IV, 476-98; Browning, I, 237.

4B.M. Add. MSS. 28054, f. 66; Browning, I, 237-39; Letters, pp. 7-8; William Harris, An Historical and Critical Account of the Lives of Oliver Cromwell and Charles II (London: Printed for F.C. and J. Rivington et al., 1814), 231, 235.

[5] B.M. Add. MSS. 28054, f. 87.

6B.M. Add. MSS. 28054, f. 70; Letters, p. 7; Browning, I, 237-38.

[7] Cal. S.P. Dom. 1677-78, p. 149; Anchitell Grey, Debates of the House of Commons: From the Year 1667 to the Year 1694 (London: T. Becket and P.A. de Hont, 1769), VI, 391; Browning, I, 239.

[8] B.M. Add. MSS. 28054, f. 72; Letters, p. 9.

9Buccleuch MSS. I, 418.

[10] H.M.C. 13th Report. App. Part VI, 13-14.
pp. 9-10.
Montagu first tried for East Grinstead, but met with no
success. (B.M. Add. MSS. 28044 f. 33; Letters, p. 114.)
His victory at Northampton was due in great part to
Danby's propensity to favor family first: his son-in-
law, Lord O'Brien, whose father's death caused the
opening. O'Brien was, however, considered too young and
also suffered from parental interference; his mother
refused to allow him to stand. (Caret MSS. 103, f.
236.)

[11] H.M.C. Egmont MSS. II, 76-77.

[12] C.J. IX, 522, 537; Grey VI, 186; H.M.C. Ormonde MSS.
N.S. IV, 471; H. of Lords R.O. - H. of C. Carol 2
Journal Oct. 21-Dec. 30, 1678, ff. 170-171, 214-15.

[13] T.H.B. Oldenfield, The Representative History of Great
Britain and Ireland: Being a History of the House of
Commons, and of the Counties, Cities, and Boroughs of
the United Kingdom from the Earliest Period (London:
Baldwin, Cradock and Joy, 1816), p. 279.

[14] Dalrymple I, App. 249-50.

[15] Dalrymple I, App., 251-52; J.J. Jusserand, Recueil Des
Instructions Donnees Aux Ambassadeurs Et Ministres De
France (Paris: F. De Boccard, ed. Anciennes Maisons
Thorin & Fontemoing, 1886) XXV Angleterre. Tome Deuxieme
1666-1690, 265; Firth, p. 711.

[16] Jusserand, p. 265.
...Montagu a offert de se tourner contre son roi:...
"comme le Grand Tresorier [Danby] faisait les derniers
efforts pour gagner les membres de cette assemblee.
...qu'il repandait beaucoup d'argent pour arriver a sa

fin. ...pour cela de gagner quelques membres du Parlement. ...que pour cela il etait necessaire que j'eusse en Angleterre une somme considerable."

17Delpech, p. 132.

18Delpech, p. 145; Dalrymple, I, App. 249; Firth, p. 711.

19Petherick, p. 131.

20Ibid., p. 132.

21Dalrymple, I, App. 257-8; Lee, p. 1192; Browning, I, 290-301; Petherick, pp. 131-32.

22B.M. Add. MSS. 28044, f. 33; Letters, p. 114-15; Browning, II, 375-76.

23_____, Letters Written by Sir William Temple, Bar. and Other Ministers of State, Both at Home and Abroad (London: J. Round, 1731), Part II, 338.

24B.M. Add. MSS. 28044, f. 33; Letters, p. 116.

25Dalrymple, I, App. 252; H. of Lords R.O. Journal ff. 392-93.

26Dalrymple, I, App. 253.

27H.C. Foxcroft, The Life and Letters of Sir George Savile, Bart. First Marquis of Halifax &c. (New York: Longmans, Green, and Co., 1898), I, 136; Dalrymple, I, App. 253.

[28]Petherick, p. 140.

[29]B.M. Add. MSS. 34274, f. 99; Browning, II, 610; Cal. S.P. Dom. 1678, p. 579.

[30]B.M. Add. MSS. 34274, f. 102; Letters, p. 266; Browning, II, 612-614.

[31]B.M. Add. MSS. 34274 f. 104; Browning, II, 614-15.

[32]B.M. Add. MSS. 28054, f. 196; Letters, pp. 264-65; Browning, II, 501-02.

[33]Andrew Browning, ed., Memoirs of Sir John Reresby (Glasgow: Jackson, Son, and Co., 1936), pp. 158-59.

[34]House of Lords Record Office: Speaker Bromley's Precedent Book, p. 242, p. 261.

[35]P.C. Reg/66/f. 483; C.J. IX, 559; Grey, IV, 33-45; Boyer Annals, VIII, 369; W. Cobbert, Parliamentary History of England (London: B. Bagshaw, 1809), IV, 1054.

[36]Cobbert, p. 1054, footnote.

[37]Elias F. Mengel, Jr., Poems on Affairs of State: Augustan Satirical Verse, 1660-1714 (New Haven: Yale University Press, 1965), II, 107-09; cobbert, pp. 1064-67; Burnet, p. 183; Grey, VI, 337-87.

[38]Grey, VI, 345-46; Cobbert, pp. 1058-59.

[39]Grey, VI, 346-47; Cobbert, p. 1060.

40Cobbert, p. 1054.

[41]C.J., IX, 559.

[42]Osmund Airy, ed. Burnet's History of My Own Time: Part I, The Reign of Charles the Second (Oxford: Clarendon Press, 1897), I, 183; Grey, VI, 337-45; Colbert, p. 1958; Browning, I, 304.

[43]C.J., IX, 559.

44Grey, VI, 347-50.

[45]Grey, VI, 338, footnote.

46Grey, VI, 387-89.

[47]Dalrymple, I, App. 260.

[48]C.J., IX, 561-62:_____,Memoirs Relating to the Impeachment of Thomas, Earl of Danby (Now Duke of Leeds) in the Year 1678 (London: John Morphew, 1710), pp. 40-48:_____,The History of England During the Reigns of K. William, Q. Anne, and K. George I (London: Daniel Browne, 1744), pp. 403-04; John Lingard, The History of England from the First Invasion of the Romans to the Accession of William and Mary in 1688 (London: Charles Dolmen, 1855), IX, 195.

49B.M. Add. MSS. 38849, f. 121 (Jan. 11, 1678); B.M.

Add. MSS. 28054, ff. 121-23; H.M.C. Hodgkin MSS;, p.
187; Letters, p. 53; Browning, II;, 318-19; B.M. Add.
MSS. 28054, f. 136 (Jan. 18, 1678); B.M. Add. MSS.
28054, ff. 138-47; Danby, Earl of, Memoirs Relating to
the Impeachment of Thomas, Earl of Danby (Now Duke of
Leeds) In the Year 1678. Wherein Some Affairs of Those
Times are Represented in Juster Light than has hitherto
appear'd (London: Printed for John Morphew, 1710), pp.
230-34; Grey, VI, 359-64; Browning, II, 325-26. Sir
John Reresby, the Diarist, claims they were read
(Memoirs, pp. 164-65); and it is so confirmed in the
Journal of the House (C.J. IX, 561).

[50]S.P. Dom. 44/334/f. 536.

[51]B.M. Add. MSS. 28044, ff. 33-37; Letters, pp. 114-22;
Browning, II, 375-80.

[52]B.M. Add. MSS. 20844, ff. 33-37; Letters, pp. 114-22;
Browning, II, 375-80.

[53]B.M. Add. MSS. 20844, ff. 33-37; Letters, pp. 114-22;
Browning, II, 375-80.

[54]B.M. Add. MSS. 20844, ff. 33-37; Letters, pp. 114-22;
Browning, II, 375-80.

[55]B.M. Add. MSS. 20844, ff. 33-37; Letters, pp. 114-22;
Browning, II, 375-80.

[56]B.M. Add. MSS. 20844, ff. 33-37; Letters, pp. 114-22;
Browning, II, 375-80.

[57]B.M. Add. MSS. 20844, ff. 33-37; Letters, pp. 114-22;

Browning, II, 375-80.

[58]B.M. Add. MSS. 20844, ff. 33-37; Letters, pp. 114-22;
Browning, II, 378-79.

[59]Hatton Correspondence, II, 170; Firth, p. 711.

[60]B.M. Add. MSS. 32095, f. 133 - Warrant for Montagu's
arrest; S.P. Dom. 29/411/ff/87, 89; 44/43/ff. 63-64. -
Dover; Cal. S.P. Dom. 1679-80, pp. 42-43, 46; Reresby,
p. 167 - "In a disguise."

[61]Cal. S.P. Dom. Charles II 1679-80, p. 46.

[62]H.M.C. 12th Report, Appendix; Part IX, 182.

[63]B.M. Add. MSS. 28054, f. 33; Letters, p. 121;
Petherick, p. 158; Cockayne, IX, 106; Cal. S.P. Dom.,
1679, p. 53.

[64]An Impartial State of the Case of the Earl of Danby,
in a Letter to a Member of the House of Commons.
London. Printed in the Year, 1679. (S.P. Dom./30/Case
G.)

An explanation of the Lord Treasurer's Letter to Mr.
Montagu, the King's Late Embassador to France, March
25th 1678. Together with the said Letter: and The Two
Letters of Mr. Montagu, Which were read in the House of
Commons. Printed in the Year, 1679. (S.P. Dom./30/Case
G.)

Two Letters from Mr. Montagu to the Lord Treasurer: one
of the 11th, the Other of the 18th of Jan. 1678/9, Which
Were Read in the House of Commons Together with the Lord
Treasurer's Speech in the House of Peers, upon an

Impeachment of High Treason, &c. Brought up Against His
Lordship by the House of Commons, Dec. 23, 1678.
London. Printed and are to be sold by Johnathan Edwin at
the Three Rose in Ludgate Street, 1679. (b.M. Add. MSS.
38849, ff. 241-48.)

Some Reflections Upon the Earl of Danby, In Relation to
the Murther of Sir Edmundbury Godfrey. In a Letter to a
Friend. 1679 (B.M. Add. MSS. 38849, ff. 249-50.)

A Letter to a Friend in the Country. Being a
Vindication of the Parliaments Whole Proceedings this
Last Session with the State of the Plot, and the Manner
of Its Discovery. (B.M. Add. MSS. 38849, ff. 281-84.)

An Examination of the Impartial State of the Case of the
Earl of Danby In A Letter to a Member of the House of
Commons. London. Printed and are to be sold by Walter
Davis, Bookbinder in Amen Corner neer Pater-noster-Row.
1680. (B.M. Add. MSS. 38849, ff. 262-80.)

An Account at Large of the Right Honourable, the Earl of
Danby's Arguments at the Courts of the King's Bench at
Westminster Upon his Lordship's Motion for Bail, the
27th Day of May, Term Pasch. 1682, Together with the
Judges Answers and the Earl's Replyes As They Were Truly
Taken. London. Printed for Chirles Mearue, 1682 (B.M.
Ass. MSS. 38849, ff. 383-97.)

65H.M.C. 13th Report, Appendix, Part VI, 12.

66H.M.C. 13th Report, Appendix, Part VI, 13.

67H.M.C. 13th Report, Appendix, Part VI, 14.

68Dalyrmple, I, App. 384; Petherick, pp. 161-62.

69Cal. S.P. Dom. 1679-80, p. 106; H.M.C. Ormonde MSS.

N.S., IV, 368-70; <u>Lindsey</u> <u>MSS</u>. p. 404; Grey, VII, 19;
Reresby, pp. 172-73.

[70]Dalrymple, I, App. 384.

[71]David Ogg, <u>England</u> <u>in</u> <u>the</u> <u>Reign</u> <u>of</u> <u>Charles</u> <u>II</u> (London:
Oxford University Press, 1963), p. 285; <u>The</u> <u>London</u>
<u>Gazette</u>, March 24-29, 1679, Num. 1393; April 24-28,
1679, Num. 1452.

[72]Mengel, II, 113.

73Dalrymple, I, App. 340-41.

[74]<u>Ibid</u>., p. 341.

75<u>Ibid</u>., pp. 341-42.

[76]<u>Ibid</u>., pp. 355-57.

77<u>Ibid</u>., p. 357.

Mrs. Harvey is described as an intriguer: Mrs. Harvey,
his sister, is as deep as he is in all the intrigues.
She is a woman of a bold and enterprising spirit, and
has the interest and connections with a great number of
people in the Court and Parlaiment.   It was through her
I engaged Mr. Hampden and Mr. Harbord, who are two of
the most considerable members of Parliament.

78<u>Ibid</u>., p. 355.

CHAPTER VI
Montagu: A Man Who Had a Price in
Search of One Willing to Pay It

I cannot find that his Grace [Ralph Montagu]
was much at the Head of Affairs during that
Reign, tho' he continued his Place under that
King,1

After Danby's resignation in March 1679, Charles
thought that an election might give him a more favorable
House of Commons. But the Popish Plot and its ensuing
panic resulted in the election of numerous supporters of
the Country Party. Charles tried to make peace with the
Country Party by bringing Shaftesbury, its accepted
leader, into the Government. This move, however, failed
and the Country Party introduced a Bill designed to
exclude James from succeeding to the Throne. However,
Commons was divided on the issue. Some desired Mary,
James' daughter, as successor, while others, including
Shaftesbury, wanted the Duke of Monmouth, Charles'
illegitimate son, to succeed to the throne. Charles,
sensing that the Bill might pass the House of Commons,
dismissed Shaftesbury from the Government and dissolved
Parliament in July 1679.2

With the dissolution of Parliament in 1679, the
Country Party recognized Charles as its enemy and the
champion of a pro-French, pro-Papist policy and of
legitimacy. The Country Party opposed him and intended
to deprive James of his legitimate right of succession.

But this deprivation was to be done in a legal manner: a Bill of Exclusion would be introduced into Parliament and accompanied by a bill favoring a monarch who both was anti-French and anti-Papist.[3]

The Country Party's obvious candidates for succession were James' daughters, Mary and Anne. Mary, the wife of William of Orange, Protestant and an enemy of France, was the more popular and logical choice. However, Shaftesbury championed the Duke of Monmouth, Protestant and illegitimate son of Charles by Lucy Waters, as the successor. Monmouth was Protestant, but he may be obnoxious to many because of his vanity, stupidity, greed and illegitimacy! Shaftesbury tried to strengthen Monmouth's claim to the Throne by asserting that Monmouth was the legitimate son of Charles and that the certificate of marriage could be found in a 'black box' in the Palace. But such a story gained little creditability with the people; they believed that Charles should be succeeded by one of James' daughters. Charles flatly rejected this scheme in favor of Monmouth; and he sent Monmouth into exile.[4]

Montagu took part in these debates. His speeches were emotional and self-serving rather than the pleadings of cold logic. He desired the Bill's passage not from any overpowering devotion to his nation or King or from any intense attachment to the Protestant religion. His declaration that until the Bill passed the King would not be safe; that Charles would continue to be exposed to the malice of the papists and the cunning evils of the friends of the Duke of York, was viewed as hypocritical. Such sentiments, from one who was willing to, and, in fact, did betray King and Country for monetary gain, cannot have been taken as totally altruistic by his fellow members, who were themselves involved with the French. They knew that the only reason he was not in the Tower at the present time was due to the protection of the immunity of the House of Commons.

On November 4, 1680, Montagu, in a debate in the House of Commons on the Exclusion Bill, addressed the Speaker of the House and urged its passage:

> Sir, the Honourable Member that spoke last, may understand very much of the Laws of other Countries, and Foreign Affairs, but I am apt to think not much of the Laws of this Nation, or else he would not argue that this is a Popish Bill, when it is the only thing, that can save this King and Kingdom, and the Protestant Religion, which I hope will never come to that extremity as to need any thing that is Popish to save it. For my part, I am so far from thinking that this Bill is so unanswerable as hath been argued, that I think this House of Commons will get as much Credit by passing of this Bill, as that in 1660 did by passing that which brought home the King. For as the one restored him, so the other may preserve him and nothing less. And therefore I think, Sir, you ought not delay in giving it a second reading, but appoint a speedy day for it.5

The second Bill of Exclusion reached the House of Lords on November 15, 1680. The deciding debate in the

Lords, whose sessions Charles customarily attended, was a strident affair. Charles declared himself willing to accept limitations on the monarchy but not exclusion in the event of a popish King. Nor would he accept the banishment of James to a spot five hundred miles away from England for five years or for the duration of Charles' life. Further, Charles refused Shaftesbury's urgings that he divorce Catherine, who was barren, and marry someone capable of bearing a Protestant heir.

Charles' principal advisor, George Saville, Earl of Halifax, under intense attack by the opposition, led the fight to defeat the exclusion measure,[6] which caused Montagu an intense fit of pique. He actually accused Halifax of favoring Charles' limited exclusion.[7] He accused Halifax of being one of the leading figures in the urging of the dissolution of Parliament by Charles in July of 1679.[7]

Montagu openly called Halifax an enemy of the King and Kingdom:

It was not for want of zeal (he began) that I did not trouble you the last Debate. I am sensible of the miseries we lie under through the loss of our Bill in the Lords House -- It has been always the Privilege of the House of Commons to use Common Fame as an Information of things ... Common Fame says 'That Lord Halifax advised,' and since he has owned the Dissolution of the last Parliament. I think therefore, that in justice you can do no less than vote him an Enemy to the King and Kingdom, and address his Majesty, that he

would be pleased to remove George Earl of
Halifax from his Councils.

. . .

Mr. Montagu: ...I think that is time long
enough for this Lord to have a share of the
Prorogations.9

On December 20, Commons again demanded the
exclusion of the Duke of York and an Association to
guarantee it as well as the expulsion from office of all
who favored the succession of James. If this were
done, Commons would then grant subsidy to defend Tangier
(a prized port in Northern Africa, part of the dowry of
Catherine of Braganza, which was under constant attack
by the Moors since 1678) and give consent to alliances
with other foreign powers. To assure these provisions,
Commons further asked that judges be appointed who would
ensure compliance with these measures.

Not willing to be left out of these important
proceedings, Ralph Montagu, leading a group of Whigs,
approached the King with a petition for his approval of
the Exclusion Bill and the grantings of important offices in the government. Montagu himself still hoped
for the Secretaryship of State. If Charles acceded to
their wishes, they in turn would agree to a large
subsidy on his behalf. Such dealing could not long
remain secret. When the other members of the House heard
of these plottings on the part of some of their members,
they immediately voted a prohibition for any member to
accept any Crown office or place without approval of the
House.10

At this time, as the issues crystallized and the members of Parliament grouped themselves around one or the other of the opponents (King Charles and Shaftesbury), political parties came into being. Shaftesbury became the leader of what was first known as the Country Party, a party which represented the country (gentry) against the Crown. It soon came to be known as the Green Ribbon Club (since the members wore green ribbons in their hats) in London, where it devoted its energies to organizing mob violence and disseminated anti-royal, pro-exclusionist propaganda in the form of pamphlets. Since it petitioned that the King summon Parliament, its members also became known as `petitioners'. Charles in turn rallied his supporters and those who supported James' right to the Throne. These were eventually joined by the moderates who were disenchanted by the violence of the Country Party. The King's supporters were first known as the 'abhorrers' since they detested the petitions of their opponents. These parties, in time, became known by the popular names of Whigs and Tories. Originally these were terms of derision, a Whig was a 'humorless convenanter' and a Tory was an `Irish Roman Catholic robber'. The Whigs espoused exclusion, Parliament and Protestantism, while the Tories represented legitimacy, the royal prerogative and the Church of England.[11]

On January 7th, 1681, Montagu once again addressed the Speaker of the House urging the passage of the Exclusion Bill.

> Sir, the truth is, we committed a great Error
> in the beginning of this Session; when we went
> about to look into the Popish Plot, we went

into the Tower, whereas we should have gone to the Court; for it is plain, that the Duke's Friends which are there, do still carry on the Plot against the Protestant Religion, as much as ever the Lord Bellasis, Powis, or any of those Lords in the Tower did. And we may reasonably conclude by the little success we have had against Popery this Session, that until we can remove that Interest from the King, we shall take pains to no purpose.[12]

Lest James rule arbitrarily when he came to the Throne, Commons must take caution:

Sir, being the house is inclinable to hear of Expedients, I will crave leave to offer you one. In case the Duke should outlive the King, I think it by an Act of Parliament the Prince of Orange were appointed to administer the Government jointly with him, with such powers and limitations as might be thought convenient upon a serious Debate, it might give great satisfaction, and probably secure the Protestant Religion.[13]

This provision was one which Montagu, in all probability, inserted for his own protection. He assuredly did not want James to continue Charles' policy of distrust towards him. He probably believed that he could hope for kinder treatment from the Protestant William.

Later that January, Charles dissolved Parliament and called a new one to assemble in Oxford in March of that year. Charles feared that unless he came to some kind of agreement with the Whig faction he could face the possibility of another Civil War. He no doubt remembered the fate of his father and he deemed it best to move Parliament out of its stronghold in London and have it sit in a territory more favorable to himself and his cause. The trial of Lord Stafford for treason before the House of Lords in December, the attacks on the Earl of Halifax and other Councillors as 'evil advisors of the King' who were guilty of pernicious advice, and the propaganda campaign critical of governmental officials caused Charles to fear not only for the succession of James but for the very safety of the Throne itself.

Montagu was present representing Northampton. Again, it was Exclusion which occupied the attention of the debaters and Montagu's attitude towards King, Duke, Parliament and Religion was evident to his fellow Members of Parliament.

> Montagu, although rightly suspected by many of being mercenary and dishonest, acquired great influence during the session of 1680 as the most extreme and outspoken opponent of the Court.14

On March 26, 1681, Montagu addressed the House:

> The security of the <u>Protestant</u> Religion, and the preservation of the King's Person, is great weight, that we should not have staid to this day to Exclude the Duke; but I am sorry to hear that Language, that because the King

has said in his Speech, he will stick to his
former Resolution in not altering the Succession, &c. and proposes a kind of Expedient,
&c. but in this we are not used as an <u>English</u>
Parliament, but a <u>French</u>, to be told what we
are to do, and what not; `tis the greatest
Arbitrary Power in <u>England</u> to cow a Parliament, which may be was in design to bring us
hither; but be we called to <u>York</u>, or any part
of <u>England</u>, I believe we shall be the same men
we are here and were at <u>Westminster</u>. My Lord
<u>Danby</u> Dissolved the long Parliament, and said,
he had spoiled the old Rooks, and had took
away their false Dice; and then started in the
new Ministers, and they shuffle and cut again,
and Dissolve Parliaments till they can get one
for their turn. I have heard much weight
laid upon Disinheriting the Duke; sure no
Father would scruple to Disinherit a Son, or a
Brother, nor turn away Servants that would
ruine him. If Bishops and Counsellors would
speak plain, they cannot answer deferring our
security so long. But neither the Ministers
of the Gospel have endeavoured the preservation of our Religion, nor the Ministers of
State the Government, both acting against
Religion and Safety of the King's Person: and
I have no expectation of our safety, but the
Bill to exclude the Duke; and therefore I move
for it, &c.[15]

Montagu's professed devotion to the Established
Religion was admirable. Whether or not it was prompted
by genuine religious belief is open to question. Had

this been a speech delivered by his father, Edward, the second Baron of Montagu, its genuineness would not come into question. It is probable that Montagu's zeal for the Established religion served as a cloak under which he hid his dealings with the French ambassador and his acceptance of French money and thus remove any suspicion of treason. His espousal of the exclusion of James from the Throne on religious grounds also served as a smoke screen for his own protection from persecution by James, should he come to the Throne, for his part in the betrayal of Charles.

Again Charles told Parliament that he was willing to accept the limitations upon James that Parliament would propose, but he would not accept exclusion. In turn, Shaftesbury and the opposition clung to their original intent of exclusion. Thinking that if sufficient pressure was applied to Charles he would give way, the Commons went ahead with the Bill. They were mistaken! On March 28th, Charles went to the House of Lords with his royal regalia following in a sedan chair. Both Houses were completely surprised to hear the King, in royal dress, convene and summarily dissolve Parliament. Had the opposition been forewarned, it might have been better organized and had Parliament sat in London, it possibly might have taken the initiative into its own hands. But Charles had brought his Life-Guards to Oxford and indicated that, if necessary, he would fight. Charles returned to London and the opposition dispersed quietly. Charles he called the opposition's bluff and averted civil war.16

The opposition came to Oxford expecting victory. Charles would have to concede to the House or go bankrupt. But what the opposition, including its leader, Shaftesbury, did not count on was that the royal revenue had risen, due to the revival of trade, to beyond one million two hundred thousand pounds per annum. Further, Charles had been promised a supply by Louis. Alarmed that the opposition might succeed and thwart Louis, desire to keep England impotent in international affairs, lent his support to Charles.[17]

With the Oxford Parliament dissolved, Charles enjoyed popular support. Shaftesbury was in disgrace, and James, Duke of York, was again restored to favor. Charles now decided to destroy the Whigs and the nonconformists. Shaftesbury was put on trial for treason, was acquitted, and fled to Holland, where he died in 1683. Charles then revoked the charters of London and other major centers. He then remodeled these charters in such a manner as to increase his control over them, especially in the municipal elections. With these measures, Charles was able to weaken in a very marked manner the strength of the Whigs, particularly in the towns, and thus insure that they sent representatives to Commons that were royal supporters.[18]

With deprivation of the constitutional means of opposing the King, the extreme members of the opposition party turned to violence. In June 1683, a number of them, including Lord Grey, Sir Thomas Armstrong, Major John Wildman, Arthur Capel, the Earl of Essex, and James Scott, Duke of Mommouth, plotted to kill Charles as he returned to London from the races at Newmarket. However, the conspirators were unable to carry out their

plan. There had been a severe fire at Newmarket that
March and Charles decided to return home earlier than he
originally intended. The Rye House Plot (the name of
the spot where Charles was to be murdered) was discovered. Monmouth successfully escaped, but most of the
ring-leaders were captured. Essex committed suicide and
Lord Russell and Algernon Sidney, Montagu's cousin, were
executed even though they were not involved in the plot.
Charles, now in control, took strong measures to remove
the Whig leaders and thus ensured his personal rule.[19]

During the Parliament in which he was so occupied
in the defense of his King and his Religion, Montagu was
not in the least hesitant in petitioning Barrillon for
the unpaid balance of the sum owed him for the downfall
of Danby. The years 1680 and 81 saw Montagu almost on
the point of degrading himself with his incessant
importunities of the Ambassador. Barrillon reported
Montagu's request for payment to Louis and urged the
King to pay Montagu with a view to insuring future
service from the Englishman.

With the realization that Charles' wrath might soon
comme down on his head and desiring to be prepared 'to
travel,' Montagu met with Barrillon and again asked for
his money. Barrillon wrote to Louis (September 22,
1681):

... he told me that he was at present in a
capacity to do you as considerable a service
as he had done in accusing the High Treasurer;
that he would do it with a great deal of zeal,
but could not engage in any new affair till
the first was finished, and till he saw

himself certain of entire and complete payment. ... and what he had to say to me was to put you in a condition not to be hurt by England for a long time: That he would not capitulate with your Majesty, but refer himself to you for such a recompense as you might think he deserved for what he had to propose: But he stuck fast to having positive assurances of being paid what was due to him, and that without it he could not again hazard his fortune and his head. I pressed him much to open himself further, but it was impossible for me to get any thing more from him, except that when he was sure of his entire payment, your Majesty would find he was not an imposture, and that he would not for any thing in the world lose your Majesty's esteem and good grace.[20]

Montagu had to be careful. He did not yet have his money, and, if he were too insistent, he might not get it. He had to keep Barrillon and Louis interested; he had to offer something worth bargaining for. Hence, he carefully avoided any impression of excessive independence or of hostility and created the illusion of dependence and a willingness to continue in their service. "... and the sum (one hundred thousand crowns) of which he expects the payment is alone sufficient to prevent his taking any contrary step...."[21] Montagu made his offer of betrayal more specific on Nov. 24, 1681, as recorded by Barrillon to Louis XIV:

He told me it appeared, from all the steps taken for some time past, your Majesty had formed a design of having Luxembourg; that if it was so ... he would do his utmost with his friends to hinder the parliament from doing any thing against your Majesty, or giving one farthing to help the Spaniards; that to this end measures ought to be taken in good time, and things not delayed till the ministers and the Prince of Orange had formed all their cabals to cause their design to succeed.22

The danger of such collusion must have occurred to Montagu. It was, to say the least, perilous, for it could mean a trial for treason and even the block. Judging from his letters to Barrillon, Montagu knew exactly what he was about; he was engaged in treason. No other interpretation is possible. Phrases such as: "he would do his utmost with his friends to hinder Parliament," and "put Your Majesty in a position that England could not harm you for a long time," admit of no other interpretation. However, Montagu's services came at a high price: 50,000 Crowns.23

But fear now forced Montagu to seek a rapprochement with Charles.24 He knew he must return to the good graces of his sovereign if he were to live peacefully and fulfill his dreams. Montagu must have considered Charles a real fool to think that he would forgive and forget and then reward someone who had publically humiliated him by causing Danby's resignation. Even so, there still remained the question: when and how to reach this desired rapprochement? As things stood, Montagu felt that he would have to await a more favorable time than the present.

Montagu now tried to play the King-mother by encouraging false hopes in both Portsmouth and Monmouth, but purely from selfish motives. Along with Shaftesbury, Montagu shared a dislike for the Duke of York. He thought him to be a strong supporter of the former Lord Treasurer. This dislike caused Montagu to try to plant a like antipathy in mind of the Duchess of Portsmouth by encouraging her in the hope of the possibility of her son, the Duke of Richmond, being proclaimed the legitimate successor to Charles should James be declared ineligible. He hoped to win her over to the side of the exclusionists and perhaps influence Charles to accept the Bill. If his efforts succeeded, and James was excluded, Montagu would then have an invaluable ally at Court from whom he could hope to expect a generous reward.[25]

Montagu also tried to encourage in Monmouth a belief that Parliament considered him the suitable heir to the Throne. He offered, for a price, to get Monmouth to support the French interests and even suggested to Barrillon that his pretentions should receive Louis' attention. Montagu claimed that these pretentions could cause a civil war, which would well be in the interest of France.[26] This hope was engendered more from personal reasons and preference than from solid logic. Montagu felt that he had much more to gain if Monmouth were chosen then if James came to rule. In view of his open espousal of the Exclusion Bill, Montagu could hardly have believed that James had much liking for him. Montagu must have come to realize that he would truly have to fear for his life once James ascended the Throne.

Montagu also tried to enlist the aid of Louis in his designs.[27] He hinted to Barrillon that King Charles wanted to declare Monmouth the Prince of Wales, but lacked French support for this. If this help was forthcoming, Louis could then expect a disputed succession which could only be of benefit to France, for it would keep England out of Continental affairs. Also, if Monmouth were chosen there would then be no hope of the Prince of Orange coming to the English throne. Montagu then slyly suggested that the strict enforcement of the penalties against Catholics would cease or lessen once Monmouth were King.[28] Montagu then asserted that Monmouth would gladly support the Exclusion Bill. "The Duke of Monmouth having said, in a speech in the House of Lords upon the exclusion, that he must vote for it, because he thought the King's safety was involved in it,...."[29]

Montagu's involvement as a member of Parliament in the Exclusion Bill naturally brought him into constant contact with the Whig faction, and its leader Shaftesbury. As a leader of the Whig faction, Shaftesbury did much to popularize Monmouth's cause knowing of Charles' displeasure, Montagu confidently informed much to Charles' Barrillon that he could influence Shaftesbury for the French interests.[30] A rather empty boast, since Shaftesbury detested Montagu and considered him a rogue and a potential opponent.[31]

Montagu overestimated his ability to persuade. The dowager Countess of Sunderland writing to her brother,

Mr. Sidney, on March 22, 1680 said of the supposed relationship between Montagu and Shaftesbury: "My Lord Shaftesbury says, he never had anything to do with Mr. Montague, nor never will."32 It was pure politics not friendship that brought them together. They shared a common dislike and distrust of Charles and James, even though at one point, Montagu, along with Sunderland and Sydney, with Charles' blessings, tried to bring about an accomodation between James and Shaftesbury to put aside the Exclusion Bill and allow James to return to Court from Scotland.33

His involvement in the Danby affair, his advocacy of the Exclusion Bill and his relationship to Shaftesbury and other Whig members of the House, and his championing of Monmouth did not contribute to making Montagu a welcome person at Court. He knew that he was a persona non grata. As early as March 22, 1680, he began to feel the coolness of royal disfavor. In a letter of March 22, 1680 to Mr. Sidney, the Dowager Countess of Sunderland wrote: "Mr. Mountague goes no more to Madame Mazarine, the town says he is forbid; whether his love or his politics were too pressing, I know not. I hear he has lately endeavoured to make his peace at court; but it will not be, and he is reduced to spend much of his time at my Lady Oxford's."34 Previous to this Montagu found indications that he was beginning to be received coldly in the circles he hoped to penetrate. He wrote his cousin Sidney: "...that a letter from a man that is out of them, and that is in town when the Court is at Windsor, cannot be of much use to you. ...and I am going into the country to be chosen if I can of the new parliament...."35

Lack of loyalty on the part of Montagu to anyone
but himself led to his advocacy of the cause of Monmouth. He did not act from any conviction of the
justice of the cause. Montagu sensed that the only way
to survive under the present circumstances was to seek a
protector, and his espousal of Monmouth's cause gave him
that protector, a protector in the highest circles.
But Montagu now underwent a phase of ambivalance. He
began to show sign of restlessness and independence.
Might it not now be time for Montagu to be his own man?
He would never be really free as long as he stayed in
the service of the French. Perhaps he had best declare
his intention. Could it be that he was, after all,
having second thoughts about where his loyalties lay?
Were these the stirrings of a conscience long considered
dead? Or was it resentment at being snubbed by the
French in his demand for payment for services rendered?
Be that as it may, Barrillon was not too anxious to
lose such a valuable asset. He wrote Louis on September
22, 1681:

> ... incidents may happen to make him service-
> able, to overturn the projects that have been
> formed against your interests. ...and think
> that in the mean time I ought to manage Mr.
> Montagu with care, because he may in the end
> be useful to your Majesty's service. For this
> purpose it is necessary to pay him soon what
> is due to him; and I see no other way to make
> him serviceable for the future than to satisfy
> him for the past.[36]

Barrillon may have sensed a certain stirring of
'conscience' in Montagu, and thus convinced Louis to re-

tain his services. If Montagu was dropped from the
French payroll Louis might be the loser. Louis would no
longer have such an easy means with which to bribe
members of Parliament. But Louis had first to pay
Montagu what was owed him if Louis wished to retain him
in his service.

> It may be thought if he should be entirely
> paid, he would be less zealous to act, and
> would not care to expose himself for your
> Majesty's interest; but on the other hand, I
> do not see a possibility to make him act
> without satisfying him, and I believe he will
> not find his advantage in abandoning your
> Majesty's interest, from whom he will always
> expect a powerful protection, and new advant-
> age when he does new services.[37]

Further Montagu was now cautious in rendering any future
service.

> I endeavoured to penetrate, through Mrs.
> Hervey, into what Mr. Montagu had to propose,
> but by what she said, I find he will not trust
> her with the matter.[38]

Although Montagu was unwilling to tell Barrillon anything more until he was paid, Barrillon suspected the
possibly of an amnesty from Charles for the opposition;
was a new design afoot to reconcile the King with his
people.

Barrillon now thought that Montagu really had something

worthwhile to offer that might just neutralize the
effect of the intrigues of the Prince of Orange. He
hoped to get more news but first he would await Louis'
orders on what to do about Mr. Montagu.

> ...I shall endeavour to manage his spirit, and
> draw from him something more than what he has
> as yet told me; He is a man who may be of very
> great help, and by whom I can do more than by
> many others. To speak the truth, he is not
> contented, and thinks he has been neglected;
> but all this may be removed, if your Majesty
> gives orders for the payment of what is due
> him.39

But Montagu continued to prove his loyalty to the
French even as late as November. He suggested to
Barrillon the possibility of helping Louis obtain Luxembourg. Once Louis had this he could have an easy entry
into the Low Lands. Montagu offered to see to it that
certain members of Parliament would not impede this
design. Barrillon replied that Louis might not be
interested in this project especially if it cost French
blood.

Barrillon must have wondered how Montagu and just a few
others could bring Parliament to heel, especially with
strong pro-Spanish and anti-French factions which were
so difficult to handle. Montagu, ever thinking of the
practical, answered that such a thing was possible if
handled properly. He suggested that Parliament would
refuse to vote supply, press for Danby's condemnation,
bring charges against the Duke of York and other
ministers, put the King in a condition where he would

obtain no supplies and force him to dissolve Parliament. Barrillon was not impressed. He preferred cordial relations between England and France. If England proved untrue then there would be time enough for men like Montagu.40

During the years 1679-1681 Montagu was plagued by fear of royal retaliation for his role in bringing down Danby. Moreover, he had not been paid the full sum by France for his treason and was kept dangling in hopes of securing all the money. He now occupied himself with importuning Barrillon with pleas for the full amount, while promising ever greater treasons. He dallied with the fanciful hope of restoration to royal favor, he declaimed earnest parliamentary speeches for the exclusion of James and tried to attach himself to the coattails of Monmouth. It was a frenetic, fearful period in which he found himself as much buffeted and manipulated by the times as well as by those in authority. In all his actions Montagu simply revealed himself to his contemporaries as a man who had a price in search of one who was willing to pay it.

CHAPTER VI
Footnotes

1The Court in Mourning, p. 7.

2M.A.R. Graves, England Under the Tudors and Stuarts, 1485-1689 (London: Bell and Hayman, 1965), p. 316.

3Graves, pp. 316-317.

4Ibid., p. 317.

5_____, An Exact Collection of the Debates of the House of Commons, Held at Westminster, Oct. 21, 1680 (London: R. Baldwin, 1689), II, 53.

6Airy, Biomet's History of My Own Time: Part I, p. 258; Grey, VIII, 21; Maurice Ashley, Charles II (Frogmore: Panther Books Ltd., 1973), pp. 275-76.

7Haley, p. 606; Sidney, Diary, II, 13; Firth, p. 711.

Haley says: It should not, however be lightly assumed that Shaftesbury was behind these attacks. Indeed he and Russell [William Lord Russell] specifically disowned any responsibility for the address against Halifax.... The truth was that the House was slipping out of control. Some of those who were new to the House were prone to dislike the advice of the older leaders of the 'Country Party' and to prefer the more extreme courses advocated by others like Ralph Montagu.

[8]K.H.D. Haley, The First Earl of Shaftesbury (Oxford: Clarendon Press, 1968), p. 606.

[9]Foxcroft, George Savile, I, 252-53; Grey, VIII, 21; Airy, Burnet's History of His Own Time, Part I, 258-60; Reresby, Memoirs, p. 193; Sidney, Diary, Nov. 16, 1680.

[10]Ormonde MSS. V, 541; J.R. Jones, The First Whigs: The Politics of the Exclusion Crisis, 1678-1683 (London: Oxford University Press, 1961), p. 153; Ashley, p. 277; Haley, p. 615.

[11]Graves, p. 317.

[12]Debates of the House of Commons, II, 241-42.

[13]   Ibid., p. 246.

[14]Jones, p. 149.

[15]Debates of the House of Commons, II, 318-19.

[16]H.M.C. Ormonde MSS. IV, 561-62; Grey VI, 354-55, 435-37; Airy, Burnet's History of His Own Time; Part I, pp. 275-78; History of England During the Reigns of K. William, Q. Anne and K. George I, 155, Lockyer, pp. 352-53.

[17]Lockyer, p. 352.

[18]Graves, pp. 318-319.

[19]Ashley, pp. 308-309; Graves, p. 319.

20 Dalyrmple, I, App., Pt. I, Bk. I, 87. Baschet Transcripts - P.R.O./31/3/150, Vol. 143, f. 298.

Transcripts of Barrillon's correspondence with Louis are contained in the copied manuscripts of the Baschet Collection (P.R.O./31/3/--). His correspondence dealing with Montagu is found mainly in volumes 138-155, covering the years 1678 to 1683. Comments concerning Montagu mainly relate to the value of Montagu's continued service to the French King, and his constant pleading for payment of the money he claimed was owed him for his service to France.

[21]Dalrymple, I. App., Pt. I, Bk. I, 356; Dalrymple, I, App. 334, 384; Firth, p. 711.

[22]Dalyrmple, I, pp. Pt. I, Bk. I, 90-91. Baschet Transcripts - P.R.O./31/3/150, Vol. 143, f. 220.

[23]Dalrymple, I, App. 384.

In Barrillon's letters there are several relations concerning money sought by Buckingham and Montagu, and sometimes given, but oftener refused to them. Montagu did not receive more than 50,000 of the 100,000 crowns promised him for ruining Lord Danby.

24Dalrymple, I, App. 335; Sidney, *Diary*, II, 12; Firth, p. 711.

[25]Airy, II, 266-67.

[26]Jones, p. 82, p. 149, p. 152; Firth, p. 711.

27Jones, p. 82, p. 149.

28Dalyrmple, I, App. 312; Baschet Transcripts - P.R.O./31/3/152, Vol. 133, f. 132.

29Dalyrmple, I, App. 280.

30Jones, p. 149.

31Ibid., p. 149.

J.R. Jones says: Montagu undertook to manage Monmouth in the interests of France. There was some plausibility in this claim, but none whatsoever in his further assertion that he could also influence Shaftesbury. The latter was never at any time manageable by anyone, and detested Montagu, not only as a rogue but as a potential rival.

32Sidney, Diary, II, 13; Firth, p. 711.

33J.P. Kenyon, Robert Spencer, Earl of sunderland (London: Longsman, Green and Co., 1958), p. 33.

34Sidney, Diary, II, 12.

35Sidney, Diary, I, 67-69.

36Dalyrmple, I, App. Pt. I, Bk. I, 92-93. See also - Baschet Transcripts - P.R.O./31/3/150, Vol. 144, f. 220.

4

[37]Dalyrmple, I, App. Pt. I, Bk. I, 88. See also -
Baschet Transcripts - P.R.O./31/3/150, Vol. 143, f. 298.

[38]Dalrymple, I, App. Pt. I, Bk. I, 88. See also -
Baschet Transcripts - P.R.O./31/3/150, Vol. 143, f. 298.

[39]Dalrymple, I, App. Pt. I, Bk. I, 90. See also -
Baschet Transcripts - P.R.O./31/3/150, Vol. 143, f. 298.

[40]Dalrymple, I, App. Pt. I, Bk. I, 90-93. See also -
Baschet Transcripts - P.R.O./31/3/150, Vol. 144, f. 220.

CHAPTER VII

He Began to Increase Vastly in His Estates

"... and by the Death of his Father Edward
Lord Mountague of Boughton, succeeded him in
his Honour and Estate, and began to encrease
vastly in his Estate."[1]

Though he was out of royal favor and now forced to
look to his future haunted by a sense of fear, Montagu
did not give up hope entirely of returning to the life
he had come to know and love both at Court and as
ambassador. However, he knew that for the present such
was impossible--he had no one at Court to favor his
cause and his Whig proclivities and his French connec-
tion had made him a persona non grata to the King.
Affected by these adverse circumstances, Montagu thought
it best to retire from active involvement in politics
for the time being and devote himself to things of a
less dangerous nature. He now gave himself over to
domestic activities.

Even with the great wealth that came to him by his
marriage to the Countess of Northumberland,plus his own
annuity from the office of the Great Wardrobe and the
amount settled on him by his father at his marriage,
Montagu's income, which came to about twelve thousand
pounds, was not sufficient to meet his expenditures.
The main reason for this insufficiency of funds was the
construction of Montagu House, his London residence.
Begun in 1678 and finished in 1683, the house was
reputed to be one of the finest in the city.

Oct. 10th. Visited the Duchesse of Grafton, not yet brought to bed, and dining with my Lord Chamberlaine (her father), went with them to see Montagu House, a palace lately built by Lord Montagu who had married ye most beautiful Countesse of Northumberland. It is a stately and ample palace. Signr Verrio's fresca paints, especially the funeral pile of Dido, on the stayrecase, the labours of Hercules, fight with the Centaurs, effeminancy with Dejanira, and Apotheosis or reception among the gods, on ye walls and roofe of the greate roome above, I think exceedes anything he has yet don, both for designe, colouring, and exuberance of invention, comparable to ye greatest of the old masters, or what they so celebrate at Rome. In the rest of the chamber are some excellent paintings of Holbein and other masters, The garden is large, and in good aire, but the fronts of the house not answerable to the inside. The court at entrie, and wings for offices, seeme too neere the streete, and that so very narrow and meanely built that the corridore is not in proportion to ye rest, to hide the court from being overlook'd by neighbours, all which might have ben prevented had they plac'd the house further into ye ground, of which there was enough to spare. But on the whole it is a fine palace, built after the French pavillion way....2

Judging from the description the house was truly tastefully and expensively appointed. The cost of the house, together with furnishings, although not known, must have been staggering even for a person of Montagu's income. Unfortunately, the house burned in 1686. The damage was put at forty-six thousand pounds.[3] It is no wonder that Montagu, despite his precarious position at the Court, sought to obtain his back salary and even hoped to make his peace with Charles.

For some reason, Montagu failed properly to interpret Charles' displeasure during the early years of the eighties. In March 1680, he was forbidden to visit the Duchess of Mazarin, now one of Charles' mistresses.[4] Montagu had hoped, with the help of his sister, to influence her to change Charles' mind in his favor. His scheme failed and he was left with a royal prohibition against visiting her. Perhaps Charles feared that Montagu would try and bring her into some sort of political intrigue with Charles himself as the victim of the endeavor.[5] Another sign of Charles' displeasure with Montagu was his refusal to renew the appointment of his father, Edward, as Recorder of Northampton (1681) which he had willingly granted previously. Charles refused to confirm Lord Montagu as the Recorder once he was informed that Ralph had promised the town five hundred pounds if his father were chosen for the office. Further, Montagu apparently stirred up the opposition, almost to the point of violence, to refuse the King's nominee and to choose his father. Of course, Charles refused to confirm the election.[6] Montagu's action only served to deepen an already marked distrust of Montagu on the part of the King.

Political disfavor did not hinder Montagu's social life. Nor did being a married man stop Montagu from having his affairs and when these pecadilloes became known they caused him little shame.

> Mr. de Montagu who had a mind to conduct an
> intrigue for the king with her [Hortense
> Mazarin] has himself fallen into her toils,
> and malicious tongues here say that he is
> being unfaithful to the beautiful Madame de
> Middleton, with whom he is said to have been
> in love for a long time.7

Jane Middleton, an `intimate' of Montagu, one of Hortense Mazarin's friends, could have caused Montagu serious problems had he offended her and directed his attentions towards Hortense. Hartmann in The Vagabond Princess says that friendship between the ladies seemed to prevent a rivalry from arising between them. He maintains that Montagu's interests were largely political and that he did not want Mazarin so much for himself as to obtain her for Charles. At any rate, Montagu used his sister as the medium for this intrigue and her house became the rendezvous for Mazarin's and Charles' frequent meetings.8

> Lady Harvey wife of Sir Daniel Harvey ....
> belonged to the country or opposition party,
> which was opposed to the court. She has been
> described as "a woman of bold and enterprising
> spirit". An ardent intriguer, she sought to
> gain power over `Charlemayne' [Charles II] by
> supplying him with a new mistress.9

Marriage and the birth of his first son Ralph on August 7, 1679 did not prevent him from his affairs, nor did this seem contrary to his sense of the conventions of the day. Perhaps Montagu sought these affairs as a welcome diversion from the all too proper and decorous society that his wife must certainly have introduced into their London home. She was possessed of a virtuous character and was a loyal wife as she well proved by her patient and forgiving conduct during the affair between her husband and the Duchess of Cleveland.

Nor was Montagu's life style at this time safe from the wit's pen. His conduct outside the political arena soon became the object of biting criticism. In his poem Colin (1679) Charles Sakville, Earl of Dorset, attacked him, his sister, Mrs. Middleton and their 'strange' relationships.[10]

That Montagu and his sister were the subject of satirical prose is hardly surprising. With the Restoration there was a definite reaction in almost every sphere of life to the former Cromwellian rule with its opressive Puritan morality. Nowhere was this reaction more evident than in the literature of the period; literary tastes became more mellow and almost reached the point of frivolity. Satire became the common vehicle for frivolity and almost no subject was left untouched. The doings of the Royal family, particularly of the King and his mistresses, members of the Court and their relatives became the object of the wit's pen. The main focus of these satires was the `love-life of the Restoration', and as a consequence, was often crude in treatment and unpolished in style. In reality, the satire of the period simply became an obscene attack on

person or deed. No wonder then that Montagu and his
sister felt a deep bitterness toward the author of a
poem which satirized their sexual process.

Montagu was not the sort of person quick to
forget an injury or insult. The former Lord Treasurer
could attest to that. What Montagu failed to realize
was that his daily life was under close scrutiny. His
part in the prosecution of Danby and Exclusion made his
name well known, and if this were not enough notoriety
for him, the marriage of his step-daughter, the Lady
Elizabeth Percy, brought him into prominence once again.

In attempting to arrange the marriage of his step-
daughter, Montagu followed the custom of his age.
Arranged marriages were common to the propertied class
to prevent doubts about the legitimacy of offspring and
to protect property rights. He was also a practical
man; love was not a concern when it came to a fortunate
marriage. His own `courtship' of Lady Montagu was proof
that the overriding concern was that he marry wealthily.
However, arranged marriages did not necessarily mean
that they were loveless. Often the contrary was true,
and the arranged marriage worked out as well as that
born of romantic love, probably because the expectations
of happiness were not too high. Many believed that if
love was directed along socially acceptable lines to a
man or woman of like background the marriage would be
successful. Of course, it was necessary that there be
some degree of physical attractiveness, not too great a
gap in age and that the marriage was not arranged out of
purely mercenary motives.[11]

Montagu's marriage was such. Although there is no evidence that he was in love with his wife, the marriage apparently worked out to the satisfaction of both. From appearances they may have even grown genuinely fond of each other over the years. At any rate, whatever the years brought, she remained loyal to him till her death in 1690. Montagu had his affairs, and of this there was ample proof, but she forgave him these. For her to do so is not totally surprising considering the morality of the age. The enjoyment of a mistress while married was condoned and even expected of the man, but the wife was to regard these affairs as `venial sins' best over-looked. Adultery and fornication were often regarded as the male prerogatives of the seventeenth century.[12] But the roles could be reversed.

Montagu alone was not in this dualistic moral approach of his age. He had the example of his monarch when it came to the keeping of mistresses. Charles had few equals in this respect and his love escapades were well known to the nation.

> ... Charles II was extremely sexually attract-
> ive, or, as he put it more modestly to Sir
> John Reresby, "because that his Complexion was
> of an amorous sort" women offered themselves
> to his embraces ... --women were the aggres-
> sors, for mercenary reasons--it can be
> answered that there is plenty of evidence of
> this attraction. Barbara Castlemaine--who
> certainly knew what she was talking about--
> confided to a friend that the King was except-
> ionally well endowed physically to make
> love.[13]

Few, at least amongst the male population, found any difficulty in accepting this double standard of morality of marriage and mistress. The intellectuals of the population reveled in the cynicism of the age about emotion, religion and conventional morality. They enjoyed the sex-intrigue and decried love as the oldest aspiration of man and considered marriage as a mere concession to "family necessity." The escapades of sex were either dressed in wit, cleverness, and fine language, or in a rough, bawdy farce, replete with obscene jests and put upon the stage as comedy which came to be known as Restoration comedy.[14]

Montagu had occasion to reflect on this apparent casual acceptance by society of the arranged marriage and on its shortcomings. In the fall of 1679, when only twelve, Elizabeth Percy was courted by Henry Cavendish, the sixteen year old Earl of Ogle, third and only surviving son of the Duke of Newcastle. Their marriage took place on March 27, 1680. The marriage was, to all intents and purposes, one of convenience uniting two great families of the land and admitted of little pretense of love. There was no honeymoon for the newlyweds; the groom was of a sickly disposition and his health caused its postponement. Henry's weak condition forced him to travel to the Continent in search of his health. The journey was futile; he died six months later on November 1, 1680.[15]

Scarcely had young Cavendish's body been in the grave than the new Lady Ogle was besieged by a crowd of suitors. Some of the most aristocratic names were to be found amongst those seeking her hand: the Duke of Somerset, Lord Northumberland, the Earl of Kingston,

Lord Cranborne (son of the Duchess of Cleveland) and Thomas Thynne, the wealthy squire of Longleat, "Tom of Ten Thousand."16

Thynne had little to recommend him. He was not himself a peer nor the son of a peer. He was much older than the girl of thirteen and of a dour temperament. Yet, all the suitors were passed over but Thynne. His attempt to ingratiate himself into Lady Elizabeth's good graces led him to seek the aid of the Dowager Duchess herself through ample use of his family money. Eventually he gained the young widow's hand and she consented to the marriage. After the customary year of mourning, which she strictly held to, the marriage took place on October 30th at a rather quiet ceremony at Sion House, the Isleworth (Middlesex) home of the Northumberlands, performed by a clergyman brought from Longleat. True to her rather odd nature, the bride did not wish to live at Longleat but desired to live with her grandmother. It was on this basis that she could later claim that she was married de jure but not de facto.17

Montagu could hardly have been unknowing of all that was happening. He made no attempt to interfere much as he would like to have the final say in the matter. He certainly could not call upon Charles for help. In all probability, he remained silent because of the former Lord Northumberland's will restricting custody of the step-daughter to the Dowager Duchess including her marriage and the disposal of her fortune.

Society's and perhaps Montagu's, expectations were soon fulfilled. The family was touched by scandal. It seems that the marriage was short-lived. The lady left her husband "on the conclusion of the ceremony to meet no more."[18] She departed for the continent and not long after her name became linked in a romantic manner with that of a Swedish nobleman, the Count Johann von Koningsmarck. In order to win the Lady, Koningsmarck decided to rid himself of Thynne. Meanwhile, Elizabeth sought an annulment of her marriage on the grounds of Thynne's supposed previous marriage. Matters seemed to lie quiet for a time until the night of February 12, 1682 when Thynne was murdered while driving down Pall Mall Street in London.[19] The Diarist, Sir John Reresby, described the event as follows.

> 12 February, 1682 -- There happened the most barbarous Murder that has taken place in England for some time. Mr. Thynne, a gentle-man of 9,000 a year - lately married to my Lady Ogle, who, repenting of the match, had fled from him into Holland before they were beded - was set upon by three ruffians and shot to death as he was coming along the street in his coach. He being one deeply engaged in the Duke of Monmouth's interests, it was much feared what construction might be made of it by that party - the authors escaping and not known.[20]

Koningsmarck planned the murder to be attributed to political motives since Thynne was a member of Mon-mouth's Party and an Exclusionist. Therefore, the idea was current that he fell to the Duke's enemies.[21] Koningsmarck was eventually acquitted, however, the others involved were convicted at the Old Bailey. Sir William Montagu, Chief Baron of the Exchequer, Ralph

Montagu's uncle, was one of the presiding judges of the case.[22]

Koningsmarck could have saved himself the trouble. Elizabeth did marry again, but not him. Not allowing herself to mourn Thynne for an over-long time, Elizabeth married Charles Seymour, sixth Duke of Somerset. As a result of this marriage, she eventually became the First Lady of the Bedchamber to Queen Anne.[23]

For some time now, Montagu was troubled with some `complaint' of health which caused him to `take the waters of Tunbridge Wells' rather often.[24] He apparently gave the impression of one overly concerned with his well being and this concern caused Dorothy Spencer, Dowager Countess of Sunderland, to comment that he was so taken up with his own health, to the point of downright selfishness, that he hardly gave any consideration to his wife's illnesses.[25] However, her health must have given Montagu some anxious moments. She was delicate and suffered some form of neuralgia dating beyond her days in Paris. This condition worsened and consequently his anxiety increased. Montagu wanted to father a line of earls or even dukes and the continuance of the family line depended on her good health. Although she preferred to live in southern France for reasons of health, her wifely duties caused her to remain in England to be with her husband who, at this time, was still involved in his political plotting.[26]

Montagu was present at Shaftesbury's trial for treason for conspiring to wage war against the King at Oxford. In July of 1682, Montagu, the Earls of Salisbury, Clare, Essex and Macclesfield, Lords Grey and

Russell and Sir Scrope Howe were in court and offered themselves as 'sureties' for Shaftesbury's good conduct. "The more fashionable members of the audience included Monmouth, Essex, Russell, Montagu and Armstrong, all lending their patronage to Shaftesbury's cause."27 In October of that year Montagu, Charleston, Russell and Tom Thynne were chosen by Sheriffs Pilkinton and Shute as members of the grand jury (Westminster panel) to adjudge the case.28 With a Whig jury the outcome of the trial was a forgone conclusion. In November Shaftesbury was acquitted and "conceded bail, on his own surety of 13,000 and those of Russell, Montagu, Sir William Cooper, Sir John Sydenham and Francis Charlton for L 1,500."29 Shaftesbury's acquittal sent a signal of definite personal danger to Montagu; it was best to put distance between himself and a King most displeased with the trial, its results and those concerned with it. So far he had been fortunate. He had avoided arrest.

About this time, the Montagus moved into their fine new mansion, so admired by Evelyn, at Bloomsbury. At Bloomsbury they were able to enjoy the closeness of friends and relatives: the Russells of Southhampton House, the Shaftesburys and the Daniel Harveys.30 There was the giving of dinner parties, visiting and the exchanging of the niceties common amongst those of comfortable means and high station. Almost certainly, politics was the subject most discussed by the men: the King, the Duke of York and his exclusion, the Duke of Monmouth and Parliament. The women most likely confined themselves to the usual topics of the feminine world: home, children, husbands, social happenings and the enjoyment of family games.31

Montagu, living in such close proximity to two of the leading members of the Whig party, walked the proverbial tightrope. Caution was his watchword. Politically, he stood for the Exclusion Bill and offered Monmouth encouragement, but at the same time he was very careful not to go beyond the limits of Charles' endurance. The specter of Charles' vengeance was never very far from his mind. In such circumstances, it is reasonable to assume that Montagu was very circumspect in his dealing with the Whigs, Shaftesbury and Russell. Very probably he restricted his actions in the political sphere fearful they be construed as offensive to the King.[32]

Montagu, as a Whig, supported that faction of the party that sought the removal of certain ministers of the King whom it considered dangerous and hoped to exchange these offensive ministers with men friendly to their political philosophy. While professing loyalty to Crown and Country, in reality, money and power were their primary goals. This group contained many men like Ralph Montagu and William Harbord; men who had, at one time, held office under the Crown and were familiar with the ways of the Court. By denunciation of the King's ministers (e.g., The Lord Treasurer Danby) and the use of extreme measures (e.g. in writing of the Second Exclusion Bill Montagu and his associates deliberately left out the clause in favor of legitimate succession), the extremists tried to offset any impediment to the leadership of the party. However, they were never quite able to eradicate the legitimate suspicion by the rank and file of the party that they would, if given the opportunity, cross over to the Court. Barrillon's suspicion that Montagu was willing to come to some sort of reconciliation with Charles had, therefore, some grounds for justification.33

With the threat of Charles' displeasure ever present, Montagu continued his political activities, but kept a low profile. Having failed in his boast to bring Shaftesbury to the French cause,34 Montagu now hoped for acceptance of his services to Charles by tempering his zeal and advocating a limited exclusion. He still wanted the office of Lord Treasurer. However, the baseness of his desire and the means he employed to realize it, (e.g., to supplant the ministers), was quite evident to his contemporaries and he became hated and despised both by the King and by members of his own party.35 The basic reason for this intense dislike of Montagu's scheming nature was probably best stated by the Dowager Countess of Sunderland who was probably most accurate and correct in her assessment of Montagu and his sister when she wrote Henry Sidney on March 12, 1679/80: "I am not apt to think they do any thing out of good-nature or generosity."36

Ever the political opportunist and survivalist, Montagu had in 1682 attempted to bring Shaftesbury over to the King's side - solely with a view to self-preservation. In an attempt to have Shaftesbury agree to their plan of compromise with Charles, that is, the passing of a limited Exclusion Bill and the granting of a large subsidy in exchange for offices of government, the Whigs promised Shaftesbury the office of Secretary of State. Shaftesbury refused to have any part in such a scheme.37 He suspected that this was really a plan by Charles to split the Whig opposition in two: Shaftesbury and Monmouth on the one hand, and the Southampton Whigs (from Southampton Place) led by Russell and Montagu on the other.[38] Such an arrangement would have split the leadership of the party from the rank and file of the Commons. Commons replied by forbidding any such compromise.[39]

Charles also had refused this compromise. He reaffirmed his opposition to the Exclusion Bill, and his promise to preserve the Protestant Religion. This, however, did not satisfy the more radical of the leadership of the Commons; Charles' stand was regarded as inflexible. Commons believed itself to be the representative of the people and Charles, in his inflexible stand due to his `evil advisors' compromised its existence. Charles, in turn, responded by declaring that the passage of the hated Exclusion Bill would force him to share his power, a thing he was very unwilling to do. He complained that should such a bill pass into law, not only his power would be effectively diminished but that of his successor as well. Things were now at a stalemate.[40]

Charles then took the initiative out of the hands of the Commons by restructuring the Privy Council. He appointed some leaders of the Whig Party to the Privy Council and thus effectively sowed the seeds of dissension amongst the leadership itself and between it and the membership. He nurtured in them the belief that many of those so loud for the cause of the people were, in reality, simply careerists who, when offered the right inducement, would abandon their `high' principles. As was to be expected, Commons received this reform of the Council with suspicion and resentment. But for many the resentment stemmed from being passed over for royal favors.[41]

Montagu expected to be appointed to the Council and was angered when not included. R. J. Jones in The First Whigs says that this was rather naive of Montagu.[42] Perhaps such an assessment is an over simplification. Montagu was too experienced a politician to be naive; he knew "you rendered no service without its reward." He had been in the diplomatic service and had dealt with some of the best of the ministers of Louis XIV (Colbert, Pomponne, Louvois and Barrillon). Most certainly anyone who was naive in the ways of politics would not have lasted very long in such a climate of intrigue and secrecy. Nor did Montagu believe that anyone in his age would put his own interests aside in favor of an associate, especially if wealth and position were involved. Montagu was a man of the world and certainly knew how self-interest governed men's actions; he himself was a prime example of this practical morality. Any naivete in political matters on Montagu's part was apparently feigned and had a definite purpose to it. Montagu intended to keep his enemies off balance and thus pursue his goals.

Charles' rejection of any compromise regarding the Exclusion Bill and the revaiding of its proponents must have indicated to Montagu that Charles was in an ill mood and that it was best not to anger him. Montagu, thought it the more prudent course of action to leave England; he therefore left for France in 1683 to take up `his old quarters in Paris.'[43] Presumably, he had permission from Charles to leave the country and the permission must have been willingly granted. Things were not going well for: Charles refused to reconfirm his father as Recorder of Northampton,[44] Montagu's brother-in-law was executed as a result of the Rye House

Plot in the summer of 1683 and Shaftesbury was in exile in Holland, where he died in January of 1683.

Montagu fled to France, but his flight did not go unnoticed. His movements and activities came `under the scrutiny' of the English ambassador at Paris, Lord Preston, who, in turn, reported back to George Savile, Earl of Halifax, known to be anti-French. Montagu was suspected of pro-French inclinations and so bore watching. Also, Charles may have ordered that he be observed so that he might know what Montagu was up to. Not long after his arrival Montagu attempted, at least on two occasions, to secure an audience with Louis XIV to petition for the money he claimed Louis still owed him.45 Louis refused to grant his request on the grounds that he wanted to continue the good relationship that he now had with Charles. Unabashed, Montagu shifted tactics, asked for the money as a gift and again was refused with the maxim that `gratification presup-posed service.'46

While in peaceful retreat in France, Montagu, far from the cares and worries of English politics, met and became friendly with Bishop Gilbert Burnet. Bishop Burnet, a Scot divine, went into exile in France after his defense of his friend, Lord William Russell, who was executed for his part in the Rye House Plot of 1683. Realizing that to remain in England posed a definite threat to his own safety, Burnet left for Paris. A Whig in political philosophy, he was anti-Catholic, exclusionist and an enemy of James. (Burnet remained in exile until befriended by William of Orange. He accom-panied William to England in 1688 and was created Bishop of Salisbury, William's first episcopal appointment).

Burnet was both a writer and a critic and it was while in exile that he put his literary talents to work and composed his famous History of My Own Times which he published in 1723-24.

Burnet and Montagu were often in each other's company. "I spent much time with my Lord Montagu and by his means I knew many of the secrets of the court of England...." 47 Burnet met Montagu and `conversed much' with him in the summer of 1685 and during these conversations Montagu was supposed to have revealed many a `state secret.' Montagu supposedly revealed: the `secret' of the Duchess of Portsmouth being so much for the exclusion of James and Burnet expressed his belief that Montagu had a definite part in this.48  He also revealed to Burnet the `secret' of the Danby incident, and the true secret of the Prince of Orange's marriage in all its circumstances.49 However, it is rather evident that Burnet did not believe all that Montagu revealed as being true for he says that Montagu was: "the most accomplished liar of a not very scrupulous day."50

While in France, Montagu received word of the death of his father on January 10th, 1683/84.51 The specific nature of the relationship of Montagu to his father is not clearly known. His father was not at all pleased that he went into service at the Court, however, he eventually reconciled himself to the fact of his son's service there, but he did not offer Ralph his support. Ralph may have felt this lack of patronage, recognition and support from his father and may have resented it somewhat, but he never openly stated this. At any rate, Ralph continued to keep in contact with his father by letter and by visiting him at the family estate at Boughton.52

His father's reaction to Ralph's marriage to the Countess of Northumberland was one of delight and he settled an annuity on him. What his reaction to Ralph's part in the Danby incident was is unknown, but if he knew of Ralph's true part, his reaction would have been one of deep indignation with his son for being untrue to his religious principles. It does not seem that there was any rift between them at the time of the father's death.

Montagu's father was never raised to the rank of an Earl, a fact that made a deep impression on Montagu, and caused him to harbor a deep resentment towards Charles. His father's criticism of the King for his lewd and lascivious conduct, and of the Restoration Court for its total lack of morals, made him unwelcome at Court and brought him no honors. In addition, Montagu believed that Charles blamed his father for the actions of his brother, Edward, in the `disgraceful conduct' with the Queen consort. In an ironical reversal of the biblical interpretation: the sins of the son were visited on the father.

With the death of his father Montagu succeeded to the title of Baron and thus became the Third Baron of Boughton and the inheritor of his father's vast estates. Now a peer of the Realm, the Lord Montagu, Montagu "began to encrease vastly in his Estates."53

In retrospect, Montagu's need for money originally arose out of his expenditures to prove his worth as ambassador to Louis XIV. This need increased further due to the great sums required to build and furnish his palatial home at Bloomsbury and his failure to profit from a financially favorable marriage for his step-daughter. To recoup some of his losses, he turned to the French and offered his services to disrupt the English government. Relying on the promise of French money, Montagu, the intriguer, set about his task. He achieved partial success, but thereby incurred the anger of both Charles and James. However, dreams of wealth and position seemed nearly to vanish with his voluntary exile in France with Charles' `blessing'. Montagu, once in France, could not free himself from the need of French assistance much as he desired to do so.

But with this elevation to the rank of a Peer, the Lord Montagu saw his release from the necessity for French funds and the possibility of his returning to England. `In England, he could continue the pursuit of his designs for wealth and position. Entrance to the ranks of the Peerage now offered him this long sought opportunity! In spite of the apparent insurmountable opposition of the displeasure of Charles and James, Montagu determined to use this opportunity of his Peerage to restore himself to royal favor.

CHAPTER VII
Footnotes

[1]The Court in Mourning, p. 7; Boyer, Annals, VIII, 371.

[2]Evelyn, Diary, II. 420-21.

[3]Falk, p. 113.

[4]Sidney, Diary, II, 12.

[5]S.P. Dom. 29/376/f. 138; C.A. 122, f. 204 (Courtin to Pomponne, March 4, 1667; C.A. 120A, f. 168. Courtin to Pomponne, July 20, 1676); C.A. 119, f. 15 (Courtin to Pomponne, July 2, 1676); Hartmann, Vagabond duchess, p. 218, p. 187, p. 182, p. 231.

[6]Cal. S.P. Dom. 1680-81, pp. 633-34, p. 641, p. 646; Cockayne, IX, 105.

[7]Hartmann, The Vagabond Duchess, pp. 182.

[8]C.A. 119, f. 15. Courtin to Pomponne, July 1, 1676; Hartmann, The Vagabond Duchess, pp. 182-8.

[9]Bryan Bevan, Nell Gwyn: Vivacious Mistress of Charles II (New York: Roy Publishers, Inc., 1969), p. 124; Dalrymple, I, App. pp. 341-42, p. 355; Firth, p. 711.

[10]Mengel, II, 169-170, lines 34-35.

Forneron, in his work <u>Louise</u> <u>de</u> <u>Keroualle</u> (pp. 139-40),
as quoted in Mengel, accused Montagu's sister of being a
lesbian.

[11]Lawrence Stone, <u>The</u> <u>Family,</u> <u>Sex</u> <u>and</u> <u>Marriage</u> <u>in</u>
<u>England,</u> <u>1500-1800</u> (Harmondsworth: Penguin Books, Ltd.,
1977), p. 82, pp. 186-87.

[12]<u>Ibid.</u>, p. 82, pp. 186-87.

[13]Antonia Fraser, <u>Royal</u> <u>Charles:</u> <u>Charles</u> <u>II</u> <u>and</u> <u>the</u>
<u>Restoration</u> (New York: Alfred A. Knopf, 1979), p. 284.

[14]John Harold Wilson, <u>Six</u> <u>Restoration</u> <u>Plays</u> (Boston:
Houghton Mifflin Company, 1959), pp. VII-X.

[15]Edward Barrington de Fonblanque, <u>Annals</u> <u>of</u> <u>the</u> <u>House</u>
<u>of</u> <u>Percy:</u> <u>From</u> <u>the</u> <u>Conquest</u> <u>to</u> <u>the</u> <u>Opening</u> <u>of</u> <u>the</u>
<u>Nineteenth</u> <u>Century</u> (London: Richard Clay and sons,
1887), p. 493-94; Falk, p. 125.

[16]de Fonblanque, pp. 493-95; Falk, p. 126.

[17]de Fonblanque, pp. 493-94; Falk, p. 126.

[18]de Fonblanque, p. 495.

[19]de Fonblanque, pp. 496-98; Falk, pp. 127-28.

[20]James J. Cartwright, ed., <u>The</u> <u>Memoirs</u> <u>of</u> <u>Sir</u> <u>John</u>
<u>Reresby</u> <u>of</u> <u>Thrybergh,</u> <u>Bart.,</u> <u>M.P.</u> <u>for</u> <u>York.</u> <u>&c.</u> <u>1634-</u>
<u>1689;</u> <u>Written</u> <u>by</u> <u>Himself</u> (London: Longmans, Green and
Co., 1875), p. 235.

[21]de Fonblanque, p. 497.

[22]Falk, p. 128.

[23]de Fonblanque, p. 501; Falk   p. 128.

[24]Narcissus Luttrell, A Brief Historical Relation of the State of Affairs from September 1678 to April 1713 (Oxford: University Press, 1875), I, 111; Falk, p. 129.

[25]Falk, p. 129.

[26]Ibid., p. 129.

[27]Haley, p. 669; Hotton Correspondence, II, 2-3.

[28]Haley, p. 669.

[29]Haley, p. 682; H.M.C. Ormonde MSS. N.S. VI, 242.

[30]Boyer, Annals, VIII, 371; Gladys S. Thompson, The Russells in Bloomsbury 1669-1771 (London: Jonathan Cape, 1940), p. 66; Falk, p. 129.

[31]Falk, p. 129.

[32]Ibid., pp. 129-30.

[33]J.R. Jones, pp. 13-14.

[34]K.H.D. Haley, p. 568.

35Jones, p. 151.

Jones says: Montagu had always aspired to office, even at times dreaming of becoming Lord Treasurer, Consequently, the ministers hated him far more than any other opponent. Most Whigs wanted to reduce the royal prerogative and hold ministers responsible for their actions. That was bad enough, but Montagu was far more immediately dangerous, he schemed to supplant them, in office. Montagu and his associates were essentially frondeurs, courtiers who were in disfavour; their opposition was to the persons, not the principles of the ministers.

[36]Sidney, Diary, II, 303.

[37]J.P. Kenyon, pp. 70-71; Sidney, Diary II, 185; Ashley, p. 277.

[38]Kenyon, p. 70.

[39]C.J., IX, 695-96; Ashley, p. 277.

40Jones, pp. 61-62.

[41]Jones, p. 62.

42Ibid., p. 62.

Jones states: Montagu, for example, whose ambitions were almost limitless, had expected to become a councillor, and was disgusted that his former colleagues had not insisted on his inclusion before they would accept themselves. From a man of his character this is surprisingly naive.

[43]H.M.C. 7th Report, p. 292, Sidney, Diary, I, 69, Firth, p. 711.

[44]Cal. S.P. Dom. 1682, p. 207; Falk, p. 130.

45M.M.C. Ormonde MSS. N.S. VI, 292, Falk, p. 130.

[46]Ibid., p. 130.

[47]H.C. Foxcroft, A Supplement to Burnet's History of My Own Time (Oxford: Clarendon Press, 1902), p. 227.

[48]Ibid., p. 136.

49Ibid., p. 187, pp. 189-190.

[50]H.C. Foxcroft, A Life of Gilbert Burnet, Bishop of Salisbury (Cambridge: University Press, 1907), pp. 209-10.

[51]Duckett, p. 90; Firth, p. 712.
52Buccleuch MSS. I, 314, 331.

[53]The Court in Mourning, p. 10.

CHAPTER VIII
There Was a Frown Upon Him
at Court

On the Advancement of the King <u>James</u> to the
Throne his Lordship finding there was a frown
upon him at Court, resolv'd to avoid it, by
going to Travel; in the mean time it is
remarkable, that he had let the Earl of
<u>Devonshire</u> [William Cavendish, Third Earl of
Devonshire] reside at his house, generally
called <u>Montague-House</u>....[1]

Although Montagu and his wife spent a pleasant
exile (1683-85) in Paris and Montpelier[2] seemingly
divorced from politics and immersed in the world of
pleasurable entertainment with such luminaries of French
society as Jean de La Fontaine, celebrated French poet
and author famous for his fables, and Charles de
Marguetel de Saint-Denis de Saint-Evremond, French
critic and writer, this did not mean that the newly
`created' Lord was not in the least interested in or
concerned with political happenings in England. Montagu
may have given the impression to those around him that
he was in no hurry to return home to a land which was
considered hostile. Little had changed for him to want
to return; still vivid to his mind was the execution of
the Lord William Russell. But, if the truth were known,
Montagu was anxious to be back in England in the thick
of the political milieu. His desire came to fulfillment
with the death of Charles, February 6, 1685, and the
accession of James to the Throne. Charles' death offered Montagu the prospect of returning home and to the
Court, if only he were careful and could `cause' James

to `love' him as he once boasted he would make Charles do.

It was this possibility of return that prompted him to write Lawrence Hyde, Earl of Rochester, the King's brother-in-law, on April 4th 1685, to congratulate him upon being made Lord Treasurer and to tell him of his intention to attend the new King's coronation. Montagu had not forgotten how to flatter those who could be helpful to him.

I intend, my Lord, to pay my attendence at his Majesty's Coronation. I know not how unfortunate I may be as to lie under his Majesty's displeasure, but I know the generosity of his nature to be such, that Louis Duke of Orleans, when he came to the Crown of France, said it was not for a King of France to remember the quarrels and grudges of a Duke of Orleans, so I hope his Majesty will be pleased to think the King is not to remember any thing that has passed in relation to the Duke of York; for whatever my opinions were when I delivered them, being trusted by the public, they are altered now I am become his subject, knowing myself obliged, by the laws of God and man, to hazard life and fortune in the defense of his sacred person, crown, and dignity. I hope my coming can give no offence, since it is out of no other end but to do my duty and submission, as it is fit for a subject to do, and to enjoy that protection and justice under his Majesty's

Government, which I am confident he will refuse to no man who resolves to be so loyal and respectful to him in all things as I do. I beg of your Lordship, when the occasion offers, to afford me your good offices, which shall always be acknowledged as the greatest obligation in the world.....3

With such humble assurances of loyalty, who could refuse to grant the request?! In due course, therefore, Montagu was allowed to return to England (August 1685).[4] Whether or not Montagu attended the Coronation is not known.

It is not likely that James forgot or forgave Montagu his part in the attempt to exclude him from the Throne, but there must have been some reason, which he kept within the royal breast to cause James to receive Montagu at Court. Perhaps a Montagu 'under eye' was better than a Montagu 'for-afoot.' It was even rumored that Montagu would be employed as Secretary of State in place of Charles, Second Earl of Middleton.[5] However, if Montagu ever hoped to enter into the royal service again he was to be disappointed, for James made no move to advance him.

With no access at Court, Montagu directed his energies to rebuilding his town house which was lost to fire on January 18/19, 1686. When he left for France in voluntary `exile' in 1683, Montagu rented his home to the Earl of Devonshire for five hundred guineas per year.[6] Sending notice ahead of his return to London, Montagu ordered his house to be readied for occupancy. These orders caused him to lose his home to fire due to the carelessness of a servant, producing one of the most spectacular fires in the city since the Great Fire of London in 1666.

> Whitehall, 21st Jan. 1686.
> On Wednesday, at one in the morning, a sad fire happened at Mountague House, in Blooms-bury, occasioned by the steward airing some hangings &c. in expectation of my Lord Mountague's return home, and sending after-wards a woman to see that the fire pans with charcoal were removed, which she told him she had done, though she never came there. The loss that my Lord Mountague has sustained by this accident is estimated at 40,000 l., be-sides 6,000 l. in plate, and my Lord Devon-shire's loss in pictures, hangings, and furniture is considerable.[7]

The fire and its cause found mention in Evelyn's Diary.[8]

The house and its contents were completely destroyed. The loss monetarily was devastating.[9] Montagu lost some very cherished possessions: paintings, sculp-tures, tapestries and furniture--works that he had so lovingly collected over the years. He then sued Devon-shire at the common pleas bar and lost because "the plaintiff was nonsuit" (failure to appear).[10]

Almost immediately, Montagu set about to rebuild the house. The famed architect Pierre Puget (Poughet), sculptor, painter and architect, was brought from Paris to design the second Montagu House.[11] In the redecoration, the walls and ceilings were done by the

French artists: Charles de la Fosse (historical and allegorical themes from Ovid's Metamorphoses), Jacques Rousseau (landscape subjects), Jean Baptiste Monnoyer (floral reliefs) and Jacques Parmentier (feigned sculpture).12

In A New View of London printed in 1708 the house is described:

> Montagu House, is an extraordinary noble and beautiful Palace situated on the N. side of Great Russel Str. near Bloomsbury in the Occupation of his Grace the Lord of Montague. It was erected, i.e. the Shell, in the Year 1677. The building constitutes 3 sides of a Quadrangle, is composed of fine Brick and Stone Rustick work, the Roof covered with Slate, and there is an Acroteria of 4 figures in the Front being the 4 Cardinal Virtues. From the House the Gardens are Nd, where is a Fountain, a noble Tarrass, a Gladiator and several other statues. ... The Inside is richly furnished and beautifully finished; the Floors of most Rooms finnier'd; there are a great variety of noble Paintings, the Stair-case and Cupolo-room particulary curious, being Architecture done in Perspective, & c. and there are many other notable things too numerous to insert here. On the S. side of the Court, opposite to the Mansion-house, is a spacious Piazza adorned with Columns of the Ionick Order, as is the Portal in the middle of a regular and large Frontpiece toward the Str.13

This house was one of the most impressive structures in London and "without comparison the finest building in the whole city of London or county of Middlesex, Hampton Court alone excepted."[14]

Behind the house Montagu planted extensive gardens, and if magnificence was the hallmark of Montagu's home, then the gardens must have been of equal splendor.

> But the garden behind Montagu House, close by, was on a far more elaborate scale that that which lay behind Southampton House, and [John] Strype found it, as he had found the house, much superior to its fellow.
> What Strype chiefly admired in the Montague House garden was its `curious' lay-out. The formal garden was still preferred to the wild garden.... The much rubbed map shows the trees, flower beds and grass plots behind Montagu House arranged with careful formality, in squares, in rectangles and in triangles.[15]

This garden with its planned views of the beauties of nature became famous as a favorite rendezvous for duelling. The garden became known from 1680 onward as the 'Field of the Forty Steps'.[16]

Not too long after the loss of his home to flames Montagu suffered another loss, this time one of a very personal and grievous nature. On February 6, 1687 his son Ralph, whom he idolized, died at Bloomsbury at the age of eight, probably as a result of one of the childhood diseases so prevalent in those days. Unable to withstand the deep grief that the sight of the house evoked, Montagu and his Lady resided awhile with his sister, while his son Winwood, and daughter, Anne, were cared for by their aunt, Lady Rachel Russell, Lady Montagu's sister. After a short while they returned to Bloomsbury. Fearing that Winwood might suffer the same fate as young Ralph, his parents were most anxious about his health and arranged that he be watched at all times, even when going from room to room.[17] In this son reposed all Montagu's hopes for future family greatness.

Meanwhile, the rumor that Montagu might go as ambassador to France or might be made Secretary of State by James proved false.[18] Henry Hyde, the Earl of Clarendon in a letter to the Earl of Rochester on August 3, 1686 remarked:

> Every packet from England brings some entertainment or other, the last, which was of the 27th past, says, (at least I have seen mention of it in two or three letters hither), that my Lord Montague was extraordinarily well received by the King, and that the general opinion was, that he should be secretary of state in the place of Lord Middleton, though it is not said that the Lord is in disgrace, or that he is to be advanced to a higher station: if that should be, I will only say, miracles are not yet ceased.[19]

In 1685, as a further indication of James' displeasures with him, and to dispell any rumors of royal favor, Montagu was relieved of his office as the Master of the Great Wardrobe. His office was then given to Lord Preston, the former Ambassador to the Court of

Louis XIV.20 Since there was little hope of receiving
any office from James, Montagu thought it best to retire
to his country home at Boughton, in Northamptonshire,
and there to live quietly and devote himself to the
running of his estates. Montagu now lived in relative
seclusion removed from the mainstream of politics, and
there is little evidence that he took or sought an
active part in politics during the next three years.
With James as King there was not much hope of acceptance
at Court or advancement there and any political activity
would be closely monitored by James with commensurate
consequences. Therefore, Montagu decided to remain
relatively politically inactive for the time being.

Toward the end of 1688, however, Montagu came out
of his three year political retirement and became
involved in the revolutionary activity that brought the
Protestant Champion, William of Orange, to the English
Throne. While his part in the making of the Glorious
Revolution was not the most significant and the Revolution would have taken place and succeeded without him,
he was one of those who was most vociferous in the House
of Lords debates in demanding that the Throne be
considered vacant and that William be declared the law-
ful king (Dec. 24, 1688).

It was urged, (as I remember, by Lord Paget,)
that the King's withdrawing was demise in law;
and, therefore, he moved, that the Princess of
Orange, might be declared Queen. He was
seconded by the Bishop of London and Lord
North; but the Earls of Pembroke and Nottingham opposed that motion: they spoke with great
moderation and tenderness towards the King, as

did several others. Those who were most bitter and fierce were the Lords Devonshire, Montague, Cornwallis, and Delamere.21

On January 31, 1688/89 Montagu declared in the House of Lords:

...he was so perfectly satisfied that the throne was vacant, that he had a dispensation within him, without the help of one from my Lord Jeffries or Sir Edward Harbert, and therefore did declare, that from this day he looked upon himself to be absolved from all allegiance to King James....22

Montagu had as little love for James as he had had for his brother, Charles II. He especially disliked James for having stripped him of the lucrative office of the Wardrobe and its annual stipend of three thousand pounds. With few pangs of conscience then, he declared that the Throne was vacant and pronounced himself free of any and all allegiance to James. Thus, on December 11, 1688 the very night that James fled into exile, after tossing the Great Seal into the Thames, Montagu met with twenty-eight other Lords of the Realm assembled at Guildhall to take over the governance of the nation until the arrival of William as King of England.23

In the often tumultuous days following James's departure, a variety of ways to secure that `tool called parliament' were canvassed. One alternative, pursued resolutely by James's remaining supporters, was to contrive a summons, in one form or another, under the King's authority. Within hours after James left London on 11 December 1688, the peers in and about the capital were summoned to Guildhall by letters under Archbishop Sancroft's signature. ... But though the loyalists were a majority among the twenty-nine peers who responded, they were not able to dictate the terms of the declaration drawn up at this gathering late on the 11th. Lords Montagu (Danby's accuser in 1676) and Wharton (the leading Nonconformist peer), joined by Viscount Newport and Lord Culpepper, generated enough resistance to Turner's original draft to compel the omission of a key clause that explicitly affirmed James' right to the throne. So, the loyalists had to be satisfied with a statement avowing the peers' readiness to assist William in procuring a 'free parliament.'[24]

Moreover, arguments arose about the legality of calling a Parliament without the direct sanction of the King, especially when he was `absent.' but in the end, twenty-nine of the peers, including Montagu, signed a declaration declaring the Throne to be vacant because of James' absence, pronouncing their legality in convocation and offering the Throne to William, Prince of Orange, and his wife Mary, James' daughter.

Henry Horowitz in his work Revolution Politiks describes the scene:

Lord Paget then rose to propose that the Princess of Orange be declared queen. As soon as she was proclaimed, he pointed out, a parliament could be summoned. His motion was supported by Lord North who declared that the king's withdrawl constituted a `demise in law', while Lord Montagu suggested, instead, that the procedure emobdied in the Exclusion bill to convene the Houses should be adopted. Both these expedients were attacked by Bishop Turner and also by Pembroke [William Herbert, 3rd Earl of Pembroke] who recommended the convoking of a `convention' on precedent of 1660. Clarendon followed by urging that the 184 members who could be returned on those writs which James had issued should assemble and order, in conjunction with the peers, the issue of the remainder. But Mordaunt and Delemere replied by denouncing any who might be chosen in such a fashion. At last Nottingham rose to address the assembly again. He began by opposing the notion to elevate Mary to the throne speaking, so Clarendon reported, `with great moderation and tenderness towards the King'. The kingdom, he argued, `cannot come to have a parliament but by the King', and for this reason he avowed he `would treat with the King'. He then closed, as Halifax cryptically recorded, by calling for 'a Guardian or Regent'.[25]

Although not one of those who officially sent William the formal invitation in June of 1688 to come to England as its King, Montagu felt that he acted in a truly noble manner by joining with the Lords in Conclave at Guildhall. True to the cynical political philosophy of the age, that no deed was done without its price, Montagu requested, once William and Mary were on the Throne, that he be created an Earl for his part in obtaining the English Throne for them. His request was granted and Ralph Montagu, Third Baron of Boughton, was elevated to the rank of Vicount of Monthermer and Earl of Montagu on April 9, 1689.[26] He finally obtained the honor which eluded his father! William also restored him to his seat on the Privy Council on February 14, 1690,[27] and honored him with restoration of the office of the Master of the Great Wardrobe on June 28. He was given this patent for life. Lord Preston, to whom James had given the office on his acession to the Throne, had refused to give it up unless forced to do so by law. Montagu brought suit against Preston and won; receiving thirteen hundred pounds damages.[28] However, in an uncharacteristically altruistic move, he paid the cost of the suit and even allowed Preston to retain the sums he had already received from the office.[29]

March 29th, 1690 brought increased joy to the Montagu household with the birth of another son, John. However, the joy of an heir was offset, when Montagu sustained the tragic loss of his wife, the Lady Montagu, on September 9, 1690.[30]

Some love was certainly present between the couple. Elizabeth remained loyal to him through the years and never gave him any reason for regret. She gave him the children he wanted and never abandoned him in the midst of the scandals his indiscretions caused, especially during the Castlemaine affair, and it is significant that he asked to be buried next to her in the family crypt in Warkton. Even though by her marriage to Montagu she lost the title of Duchess and was forced to take the lower title of Lady Montagu, this did not affect her willingness to marry him and bear his children.[31] (Cf. appendix for the legal ruling of her title.)

After a year's mourning, Montagu entered the mainstream of society once again and began to entertain at his homes in Boughton and London. His lavish dinners were attended by such notables as the King himself, the Duke of Ormonde,(James Butler, 1st Duke of Ormond, Lieutenant-Governor of Ireland), the Earl of Dorset (Charles Sackville, poet and courtier), the Earl of Shrewsbury (Charles Talbot, future Secretary of State under William III), the Earl of Monmouth (Charles Middleton, 2nd Earl of Middleton, titular Earl of Monmouth, Secretary of State to James II), the Earl of Portland (Edward Herbert, former Lord Keeper to Charles II), Lord Newport (former Comptroller to the household of Charles II), Lord Sidney (Henry Sidney, former Master of Robes to Charles II), and Lord Godolphin (Sidney Godolphin, Lord of the Treasury).[32] However, Montagu's entertainments were not mere social convention. He had another purpose in mind. His goal was now a Dukedom for himself and the pathway to this honor lay, he believed, in the cultivation of the `right people at the right time'. Montagu decided to entertain the best of his society with a display of lavishness that would dazzle those who could be of the most help to him. He would court the courtiers.

To accomplish this objective, the `capture' of a Dukedom, it was imperative that Montagu replenish his fortune. The rebuilding of his house in Bloomsbury, with its expensive redecoration and furnishing by the leading artists of the time, and the lavish entertainments given there cost him great sums of money. A further drain on his resources was the cost of the maintainence and enlargement of the family estate at Boughton. Even the annually stipend of six thousand pounds which his dead wife had brought him, combined with the three thousand pounds annual from the office of the Great Wardrobe recently restored, and the revenues from his estates were not enough to meet his expenses. To maintain these buildings in suitable fashion in order to entertain on a proper scale required large amounts of money even for those days. Montagu's taste for the `finer things,' his desire to be accepted in proper society and the hopes he had for great honors from the King required vast sums. Again, the answer to his needs lay in a speedy and very fortunate marriage.

Such considerations caused Montagu to carefully survey the availability of the very rich. While it was taken for granted that he would remarry, none guessed that he was comtemplating marriage with one who was reportedly mad. To everyone's surprise on September 8, 1692, Montagu married the enormously wealthy Duchess of Albemarle, Elizabeth Cavendish, widow of Christopher Monck, the Second Duke of Albemarle, and daughter of the Second Duke of Newcastle.33 The relationship involved in this marriage was rather complicated. She was the sister of the Lord Ogle, the first husband of Montagu's step-daughter, Lady Betty Percy, now Duchess of Somerset. Montagu had married the sister-in-law of his step-daughter.

While he was in France Lord Montagu gained a
considerable reputation for gallantry. Grammont an authority on these matters, declared
him much to be feared in the courts of love
"for his persistence, for his quickness of wit
and for certain other talents." Now, all
passion spent perhaps - and his first wife
dead - Ralph set his cap at the middle-aged
widow of the Duke of Albemarle. Very rich and
quite dotty, the lady had declared she would
give her hand to no one but a crowned head so
Ralph courted her in the guise of Emperor of
China.34

The Duchess had declared that she would marry none
but a `crowned head' so, Montagu, equal to her
declaration, wooed her disguised as the Emperor of
China. A highly eccentric woman, many believed her to
be mad. Hans Sloane, the great naturalist and collector
of the seventeenth century, described her `as of a
wayward and peevish temper'. Her behavior may "....have
afforded an excuse for him [the former Duke of
Albemarle] for closer friendship with the bottle."35
Could her former husband have died of alcoholism?

Montagu's courtship of the Lady would hardly have
been possible, much less successful, were it not for the
`conspiracy' of her guardians: Drs. Hans Sloane and
Barwick and the sisters Wright.36 It was their duty,
presumably, to protect the mad Duchess from unscrupulous
suitors who might seek to take advantage of unfortunate
woman. But it was perhaps also to their financial
advantage to see to it that she was well protected, for
they were probably the administrators of her estates in

her mad condition. Montagu, however evidently must have made it worth their while to lend their support in his suit for the Duchess' hand. Once again, Montagu proved himself equal to the task; he had not forgotten the ways of intrigue he had so skillfully learned as ambassador to Paris in the seventies.

To the end of his days Montagu fostered her illusion that she was the Empress of China and had her attendants look after her in the manner of `slaves,' always serving her on their knees. "Montague wooed and won her in the character of the Emperor of China, and he kept her in a sort of confinement in Montague House, where she was always served upon the knee as Empress of China."37 That Montagu could convince her that he was the Emperor was due, in part, to his own physical build and appearance. He is described as of middle stature, inclined to be fat, and of coarse, dark complextion.38 He may have even dressed the part.

The marriage did little to increase his popularity39 since some tended to be of the opinion that he simply took advantage of this poor mad woman. However, this in no way affected Montagu personally. He cared not that she was no beauty. She was rich, very rich and this was what counted in Montagu's eyes. Perhaps he even enjoyed a sense of exhiliration rather than shame at the marriage. He had outwitted several rivals intent upon the `prized' Duchess. Henry Savile, brother of Lord Halifax, "The Trimmer," sought her hand as did Richard, Lord Ross, who in a fit of pique penned the following lines:

Insulting rival; never boast
Thy conquest lately won;
No wonder if her heart was lost,
Her senses first were gone,

From one that's under Bedlam's laws
What glory can be had?
For love of thee was not the cause;
It proves that she was mad.[40]

Montagu was a very practical person where his advancement was concerned. It was money he needed not beauty. He needed her large income to finance the cost of the beautification of his Northamptonshire home. The marriage was merely one of convenience.

...his Lordship married his second Lady, the Duchess Dowager of Albemarle, of whom it has been said that she had been little seen since, but by his own servants; and that even she has been Dead some years, and great Suits commenc'd thereby betwixt his Lordship and the Earl of Bath, next Heir apparent to the Duchess, but upon Tryal his Lordship prov'd her to be alive. `Tis certain this Lady, who was the greatest Fortune that ever English Nobleman wedded, was Discompos'd in her Mind, and that was the reason his Lordship kept her up in her Chamber, which occasion'd that Report, and even occasions one now at his Death, that the strange Funeral of a Lady in the Strand has some relation thereto, to which several ladies were invited, and had Rings given them, and were desired to touch the

Body, for some intent; all which Ladies came
and went home again surpriz'd at what they had
seen: but this we must leave to time.41

From the very beginning she became his captive;
forced to live in relative obscurity. Montagu succeeded
in keeping her so cut off from society that a rumor
began to circulate that she had died and that Montagu
concealed this fact in order to retain the stipend of
seven thousand pounds a year42 which, upon her death,
reverted to John Grenville, Lord Bath.43 Believing her
dead, relatives demanded that Montagu produce her before
the House of Lords to prove that she was alive. Montagu
complied with the order.

It was inevitable that the courtship and marriage
became the subject of attack in literature by way of
ridicule. Montagu became a `godsend' to comedy. The
satirists found this subject too good to pass up; the
affair was a natural for portrayal on the stage. Nor
were the theatrical audiences slow to recognize the
source of inspiration. Colley Cibber, the playwright,
wittily fastened upon the courtship and placed it on the
theater's boards in his play The Double Gallant or the
Sick Lady's Cure. The dramatist William Burnaby in his
comedy The Ladies Visiting Day portrayed Montagu as a
gallant lover named Courtine, who in the guise of a
Prince of Muscovy, was the wooer of the Lady Lovetoy,
who would have no other than a prince as her lover.44

In the same year as his marriage, 1692, the
Mortlake Tapestry became the property of the Earl of
Montagu. His sister, had gained control of the works

around 1667 and transferred direct control to Ralph in
1674, when he took possession of the `whole estate and
interest in the houses and materials at Mortlake' from
the Earl of Sunderland and Lord Brouncker.45 Montagu
now added another `portion' to his fortune by becoming
the master of the tapestry industry, as these works were
the only producing tapestry works in England at the
time.

Giving every indication of fast becoming a dying
industry, a last desperate effort was made to revive the
craft. Montagu transferred the works to a joint-stock
company in the hopes of saving the works and securing a
profit for himself and the stockholders. On April 12,
1692 the tapestry makers were incorporated by a royal
charter under the name of the Governor and Company of
the Tapestry Makers in England with the Earl of Montagu
appointed the first Governor of the company. To protect
the industry against competition, the importation of
tapestry from abroad was prohibited. However, the
legislation was too little and too late. Much of the
competition to the Mortlake works actually came from
within the country itself. Many of the former weavers
of the Mortlake works had established works of their own
and were in direct competition from their shops in
London and its environs. Besides, it was quite fashionable to buy foreign made tapestry in spite of the
prohibition! This incorporation of tapestry makers and
prohibition of imports proved futile. In 1703, the
works came into the possession of Daniel Harvey, Lady
Harvey's husband, who desired to free himself of the
works, which from the times of Charles II had been
limited solely to the making of tapestry. Eventually,
Queen Anne gave permission for the dissolution of the

company.46 With the death of this company, a bit of the Montagu well-known splendor also died.

Montagu went his way busy with his daily life: estates and family, Tapestry works, the House of Lords. However, he again felt the stirrings of ambition. He believed he had not received the full honors he claimed he deserved for his part in bringing William to the English Throne. He reasoned that his part in the Revolution and his marriage to a Duchess of immense wealth should have brought him the coveted title of Duke. He thought these factors, plus his own position, should have gained him his proper station in the nobility. Therefore, he decided to place his petition for a Dukedom before William. Montagu had no doubt of the justice of his request; the King had only partially paid his debt by granting him an Earldom. On May 18, 1694, he addressed a letter to William in petition for the title of Duke.[47]

The letter is a masterpiece of self-styled import-ance, a letter composed by one convinced of his exaggerated self-worth. Montagu lists the 'rights' by which he had claim to the rank of Duke. Bedford and Shrewsbury (Charles Talbot) had been made Dukes, there-fore, it was only right that he should be given the same honor, since he was head of a family that went back even to the days of York and Lancaster. He himself belonged to the younger branch. He had married a Duchess and such dignity on the female side deserved to be honored by a like dignity on the male side. King William should remember that it was only four votes, his and three others, that gave William the Throne. He had ventured his all for the King's service and could even have lost his life in doing so! Further, he reminded his majesty of his services and of the promise he made in his bed-chamber at St. James before he became King. All his Majesty need do, according to Montagu, was to consult with the Duke of Shrewsbury and he would have confirmation of the sufferings Montagu endured under the Kings Charles and James on behalf of the nation and of the great personal losses he sustained on William's behalf.48 (See Appendix for the full text of the letter.)

Montagu's claims were presumptuous at best and his plea fell on deaf ears. William refused the request. William probably found Montagu's letter of petition shameless and audacious: William was well aware of what Montagu had done on his behalf and how much he had suffered for the cause of the Protestant Prince. Indeed, Montagu's implying that he had taken part in the Rye House Plot was fabricated. He had been most careful to see that he was well removed from any part in it. William must also have known of Montagu's dealings as ambassador with the French Court; William well knew that Montagu was no friend of the Dutch. It is quite reasonable to suspect that William had his spies in Paris and knew of Montagu's `French' activities. Had Montagu been aware of these facts he might well have been somewhat hesitant to present his petition.

While he pursued his elusive goal, Montagu was besieged with other troubles. The marriage he considered such a coup was beginning to cause him some problems. The problems were not of the domestic kind since, given the nature of the person he married and the reasons for the marriage, there was little chance of the two living in close intimacy. The problems were of another's making, namely, John Grenville, the Earl of Bath, and resulted in a long and protracted litigation in the law courts. The source of the difficulty arose out of the title to the Albemarle estates. The right to clear title was complicated by the fact that the Duchess' first husband left two wills: one dated 1675, which favored a Grenville, the first cousin of the Duchess; the other will, dated 1687, favored a Colonel Thomas Monck, the illegitimate elder brother of the testator.49 In the first will the bulk of the estate was left to the Earl of Bath, while in the second, the estate went to the Moncks. The case turned somewhat scandalous: there were charges and counter-charges of perjury, bribery and corruption of witnesses on both sides.50

> The verdict was brought in this morning [May 10, 1679] for the Earl of Bath, and one Harris, a witness for my Lord Montague's, is convicted of perjury, and another, who came to support his testimony, is ordered to be prosecuted for the like crime.51

> The Earl of Bath has brought an information for subornation, and perjury against my Lord Montague's chaplain and solicitor. It is pretended that the Lord of the manor from whence these goodly witnesses came was promised 2,000 l. upon the success of the cause.52

> My Lord Montague's chaplain, who is informed against for suborination, is one Lambert, Stone tells me he is not his domestic now; but

he has lately married the rich widow of a
planter....

And this, Mr. Sloen says, is the charge
against Mr. Lambert and the solicitor, that
they overruled him by their insinuations and
promises of a great match; and that the 2,000
l. was what they undertook my Lord Montague
should lend upon his manor, which lies in the
neighbourhood of the rest of the witnesses.53

Eventually the case came before the House of Lords and
the contestants were persuaded to waive their right of
privilege. However, this did not completely settle the
matter.54

The case seemed interminable--dragging on for almost seven years (1693-1699). In the end it cost both
litigants a good ten thousand pounds apiece and was
settled out of court in 1698 by compromise. At least
four witnesses for Montagu were convicted of perjury.55
The Earl of Bath finally relinquished all claims to the
estate which then came to the Duchess for the remainder
of her life. Perhaps both hoped for her early demise!

To embarrass Montagu further, in 1694, there arose
the possibility that the Duchess was the wife of an
illegitimate first husband. This allegation led to
another challenge to the seven thousand pounds annuity
and estates that Montagu enjoyed as her husband. Anne
Clarges and George Monck, First Duke of Albemarle, were
supposedly never legally married since her first husband, Thomas Radford, was still alive at the time of the
'second' marriage. However, the claim was never

substantiated. The case had all the earmarks of a modern mystery novel: perjury, strange witnesses, mysterious accidents, deaths and even suicides.

...Many queer figures appeared in Court, including Anne Clarges' old neighbours from the Strand, Christopher's nurse, Honour Mills, servants and apprentices. Dark stories came to light. Each side accused the other of perjury, and sometimes with reason. Witnesses died sudden and mysterious deaths, houses fell on others. Even suicide was added to the catastrophes laid at the door of the great lawsuit. But in spite of years of endeavor, the Monck cousins could not substantiate their claim.56

It was first insisted upon by the Earl of Bath's counsel, with whom were joined some counsel for the Earl of Montague (I supposed pro forma to keep up his pretensions), that no proof of bastardy ought to be admitted after the party's decease, but the Court were of the opinion they should proceed. Then it was agreed that the old Duchess had been formerly married to one Radford, a perfumer in Exchange, and that he broke long before '52, and went beyond sea. All that the Earl of Bath's counsel could say to this was, he was never heard of since his first absenting him-self; but Pride produced two old women to swear they saw Radford, and saw him after the year '52; nay, one, went so far as to swear he outlived the Duchess, and was by when she was

put into her coffin, and received a pension
from her as long as she lived, with many other
circumstances that must have carried the point
if she had been believed; but they were both
thought to swear too much, and the verdict was
brought in for my Lord Bath next morning.[57]

[Montagu's] actions during these years bespeak a
man of cynical nature. Montagu's his humble service to
[James II] once he was established on the Throne in
1685, tell of a man who viewed politics with a great
deal of cynicism. His championship of [William III's]
bid to the Throne arose from selfishness. Montagu
championed him because he saw that to do so might
possibly bring him an elevation in the peerage. He
claimed he chose William at great personal risk: What if
James should ever return and remove William, would not
then Montagu and his family be liable to loss of
property and life? He claimed he acted out of
patriotism, but this was patriotism at a price!

It would be totally unfair to say that Montagu
acted entirely from cynical selfishness, he must have
had some stirrings of patriotic sentiments somewhere in
his political dealings. Yet it would also be naive to
believe that he viewed politics as something for the
good of others. To him politics was something of a game
one played for one's own profit. Montagu believed that
altruism was wasted unless it was rewarded. Guided by
this cynicism, he did not hesitate to seek a Dukedom as
a reward for service rendered to his country. Again,
the manner in which he won his second wife, his marriage
and his subsequent treatment of her and his involvement

in a series of long law suits over the possessions of a mad-woman show once more how Montagu viewed people: people, generally, were objects to be manipulated to one's advantage.

CHAPTER VIII

Footnotes

[1] The Court in Mourning, p. 7.

[2] A. Boyer, The History of Queen Anne, Wherein All the Civil and Military Transactions of the Memorable Reign are Faithfully Compiled from the Best Authorities, and Impartially Related (London: T. Woodward, 1735), p. 46.

[3] Samuel Weller Singer, The Correspondence of Henry Hyde, Earl of Clarendon and of His Brother Laurence Hyde, Earl of Rochester: with the Diarys of Lord Clarendon from 1678 to 1690. Containing Minute Particulars of the Events Attending the Revolution: and the Diary of Lord Rochester, During His Embassy to Poland in 1676 (London: Henry Colburn, 1828) I, 114-15. Firth, p. 712.

[4] Singer, I, 522; George Agar Ellis, The Ellis Correspondence: Letters Written During the Years 1686, 1687, 1688 and Addressed to John Ellis, Esq. (London: Henry Colburn, 1829), I, 154-59; Firth, p. 712.

[5] Singer, I, 522; Ellis Correspondence, I, 154-9; Firth, p. 712.

[6] Falk, p. 132; Thomson, The Russells in Bloomsbury, p. 172.

[7] Ellis, II, 25-7; Mengel, IV, 184.

[8] Evelyn, Diary, III, 15-16.

9Luttrell, I, 369-70.

10Ibid., II, 400.

11Manchester, p. 280; Luttrell, I, 397.

12J. Morduant Crook, The British Museum: A Case Study in Architectural Politics (London: Pelican Books, 1972), pp. 56-60; Falk, p. 103.

13
_____, A New View of London; or, An Ample Account of that City, In Two Volumes, of Eight Sections (London: R. Chiswell et al., 1708), I, 627-28; Marjorie Caygill, The Story of the British Museum (London: British Museum Publications Limited, 1981). p. 9; Boyer, Annals, VIII, 371.

14Boyer, Annals, VIII, 371; Firth, p. 712; George Duckett, p. 90.

15Thomson, Russells in Bloomsbury, p. 176.

16Wise, pp. 80-81.

The field is famous through legend:
The story is that two brothers fell in love with the same lady, and agreed to settle their pretensions by that usual court of arbitration, in those days--the duel. They fought so furiously that both were killed, whilst the lady sat by to see the combat.

From that time up to the building over the spot, the footsteps of the two brothers are said to have been indelible, resisting every effort to erase them,

reappearing even after the field had been ploughed.
Hence, the field received the name of the "Field of
Forty Footsteps."

[17]Falk, p. 134.

[18]H.M.C. Downshire MSS. I, Part I, 203; singer, I, 114;
Ellis Correspondence, I, 154-60; Firth, p. 712.

[19]Singer, I, 522.

[20]Luttrell, II, 48; Firth, p. 712.

21Singer, p. 235.

[22]Ibid., p. 257.

[23]S.P. 8/2 Part 2, f. 83; Peter Whalley, The History and
Antiquities of Northamptonshire Compiled from the
Manuscripts of the Late and Learned Antiquary John
Bridges, Esq. (Oxford: Sold by T. Payne, 1791), II, 351;
Duckett, p. 90.

[24]Henry Horowitz, Parliament, Policy and Politics in the
Reign of William III (Manchester: Manchester University
Press, 1977), p. 6.

25
_____, Revolution Politiks: The Career of
Daniel Finch, Second Earl of Nottingham, 1647-1730
(Cambridge: University Press, 1968), p. 68.

26The London Gazette, April 8-11, 1689, Numb. 2443;
Manchester, p. 281; Colbert, VI, 421; The Court in
Mourning, p. 7; Duckett, p. 90; Firth, p. 712.

[27]P.C. 2/73/f. 237; Firth, p. 712.

[28]Luttrell, II, 49; Manchester, p. 280; Mengel, IV, 184-84; Whalley, p. 351.

[29]H.M.C. Rutland MSS. II, 334; Manchester, p. 281.

[30]Luttrell, II, 106; Firth, p. 712.

[31]Longleat MSS., Portland Papers, Vol. XXI, f. 215.

[32]Luttrell, I, 215.

[33]Finch MSS. IV, 457; Boyer, Annals VIII, 372-73; Cockayne, IX, 107; Luttrell, II, 563; Firth, p. 712.

[34]Peter Gorham Webb, Portrait of Northamptonshire (London: Robert Hale, 1977), p. 126; Boyer, Annals, VIII, 372.

[35]E. St. John Brooks, Sir Hans Sloane: The Great Collector and His Circle (London: Batchworth Press, 1954), p. 76; J. Granger, A Bibliographical History of England from Egbert the Great to the Revolution (London: W. Nicholson, 1804), IV, 158; Luttrell, II, 563; Firth, p. 712.

[36]Estelle Frances Ward, Christopher Monck: Duke of Albemarle (London: John Murray, 1915), p. 344.

[37]Sidney, Diary, I. 70.

[38]Granger, Biographical History, II, 37; Ward, p. 344.

[39]Firth, p. 712; Cockayne, IX, 107.

[40]Ward, p. 345.

[41]The Court in Mourning, p. 8.

[42]Webb, p. 126; Boyer, Annals, VIII, 372.

[43]Firth, p. 712.

[44]F.E. Budd, ed., The Dramatic Works of William Burnaby (London: Eric Patridge, 1931), pp. 88-89.

Budd says:

Although this ocurtship sounds both incredible and absurd, it was not beyond the scope of the fashionable ladies and gentlemen of those days; in fact, it is directly based on the actual courtship of Elizabeth, Duchess of Albemarle, by Lord Montagu disguised as the Emperor of China. Burnaby never set out to beat the air.

[45]W.G. Thompson, A History of Tapestry from Earliest Times Until the Present Day (London: Hodder and Stoughton, 1906), pp. 300-01; H. Arthur Doubleday, ed., The Victoria History of the Counties of England: A History of the County of Surrey in 4 Volumes (Westminster: Archibald Constable and Co., n.d.), p. 358.

[46]S.P. Dom./44/236/f, 177. ff/ 186-87; S.P. Dom./44/341/ff. 204-05; Thomson, p. 300; Doubleday, p. 358.

[47]Dalrymple, II, App. 256-58.

[48] bid., p. 258.

[49]Boyer, Annals, VIII, 372; Firth, p. 712.

[50]ADM. 78/4/f. 25, f. 57. f. 61; House of Lords MSS. I, 311-21; II, 253-59; III, 114, 176-78; Luttrell, III, 140, 208, 231, 245-46, 270-73, 389, 437, 465; IV, 78, 336-37, 353-55, 549, 386, 443; Firth, "Montagu," p. 712.

[51]G.P.R. James, ed., James Vernon, Letters Illustrative of the Reign of William III from 1696 to 1708, Addressed to the Duke of Shrewsbury (London: Henry Colburn, Publisher, 1841), III, 240.

[52]Ibid., p. 287.

[53]Ibid., pp. 302-03.

[54]Russell, J. Kerr and Ida coffin Ducan, eds., The Portledge Papers: Being Extracts from the Letters of Richard Lapthrone, Gent., of Hatton Garden London to Richard Coffin Esq. of Portledge, Bideford, Devon from December 10, 1687-August 7th 1697 (London: Jonathan Cape, 1928), p. 242.

[55]James, III, 240, 287, 303; Luttrell, II, 140, IV, 78, 255, 443; Firth, P. 712.

[56] Ward, p. 346.

[57] Robert Sutton, Lord Lexington, The Lexington Papers;
or, Some Account of the Courts of London and Vienna: At
The Conclusion of the Seventeenth Century (London: John
Murray, 1851), pp. 56-57.

CHAPTER IX
To the Great Grief of the Court
and All His Family

...till the beginning of the Month of <u>March</u>, as what time His Grace was stricken with a Distemper that held him till the 9th day, when between the hours of 5 and 6 he Expir'd at his House in <u>Russell- Street</u>, <u>Bloomsbury</u>, in the 71st year of his Age, to the great grief of the Court and all his Family....1

The last years of Montagu's life, 1695-1709, were filled with building, decorating and planting. Before Examining in detail his building at Boughton, Ditton Park (Winwood House) and his lodgings at the Cockpit in Whitehall,2 one must put this building in the perspective of the rebirth of the arts under Charles II and their employment as a means to enoblement. Montagu would attempt to use this penchant for building and decorating as a sort of lever to impress King William from whom he hoped to obtain the coveted title of duke. William might have accepted entertainment at Boughton in October, 1695, but he felt under no obligation to reward Montagu, although he did give him a position as one of the commissioners of Greenwich Hospital in 1695,3 and made him Lord Lieutenant of Northamptonshire in 1697, which post Montagu held until 1702.4

Out of politics, Montagu gave himself over to patronage of the arts. With the Restoration of Charles to the Throne, prospects for the arts appeared to be good. Charles, in imitation of his illustrious cousin,

Louis XIV, felt he had an obligation to foster and protect the arts. He desired that his Court be a font of beauty as well as grace and elegance. It was clear that Charles intended to re-establish court patronage. He returned Nicholas Lanier to his post of Master of the King's Musick, Sir Norbert Howard was given the position of Serjeant-Painter and the positions of the Office of Works (Master Mason and Master Carpenter) were filled with intent to refurbish the royal residences.5

These indications of royal favor, led some artists to entertain excessive expectations. They hoped that, since Charles was a sophisticate and a man of taste and discernment, they would enjoy the King's blessing and patronage almost without limitation. They looked forward to a time of grand resurgence of interest in art at Court and a period of great prosperity. However, these men were doomed to disappointment. The golden age of art, when the monarch was practically the chief source of commissions and funding, had not really returned. In fact, the arts had to endure the fortunes of politics, influence and favor. Many found, to their sadness and expense, that neither one's genius nor service automatically qualified him to enter such an exalted circle, even if one was a musician, artist or architect of considerable talent.6

However, Charles' interest in the arts was partially responsible for the reawakened and lively interest of the nobility in art during the Restoration. His taste in art and his protection of the artist foreshadowed the involvement of the nobility. Good taste and a desire to enjoy painting, architecture and gardening eventually became an essential part of a gentleman's style.7 The desire to become an arbiter of good taste and the protector of the arts spread through the courtly society.

The aristocrats took to the fine arts with a definite enthusiasm. Vying with each other in the fostering of the arts, they came to view themselves as the protectors, helpers and intermediaries between the deserving artists and the Court's fountain of monies and favors. Many possessed a real appreciation and ardently wished to encourage both art and artist and freely gave of their time and money to those they deemed deserving. By this patronage they sought to enhance their reputations, seeking the respect and honor accorded a patron of the arts.8

Among the most prominent of these patrons was Montagu. He busily spent his days in the renovation of his family estate at Boughton. Special attention was given to the creation of the magnificent gardens. These gardens covered about one hundred acres and surrounded a mansion restyled in the architectural style Montagu had come so to love while in France - that of Le Brun, the architect of Versailles. Originally Tudor in style, Boughton House surrounded several courts and was covered by the gorgeous facade added by Montagu. Everything had to be French! In France he found his ideas of building and gardening.

The influence of St. Cloud and Versailles is still strong on the landscapes. Ralph Montagu employed a Dutch gardener called Leonard Van de Neulen to create his formalised layout of canals, fountains and parterres to the west and the north of the house. The highest pool to the south of the house, which is still there, provided the head water piped to the four fountains in the parterre which Stukeley shows in a drawing in 1706. Another source of water was the Grand Etang, now seen in outline to the north-east of the house, and a stream was canalised to frame the west end of the parterre, finally supplying the cascade before resuming its normal course. John, the second Duke, modified the layout from 1720 onwards, adding a great court and a large pond in place of the parterres and fountains. He also added a new network of elm avenues and rides which intersect and border the estate, reputedly of the same mileage as separates Kettering from London.9

John Churchill, the Duke of Marlborough, once complimented Montagu on the magnificent waterworks at Boughton. Montagu replied, most graciously and wittily, that they were nothing compared to the great general's "fireworks",10 an obvious reference to Marlborough's career as a famous general of the army.

Versailles figured greatly in Montagu's plans of establishing a magnificent family seat. Boughton House boasted of spacious and broad avenues and stables attached to the main house. Its rooms were handsomely decorated and furnished. The spacious ceilings were painted by the Frenchman, Louis Cheron, and the Neopolitan painter, Antonio Verrio, brought to England by Charles II, with scenes of mythological deities. The most notable of these ceiling paintings were the works of Verrio: Aurora or the Dawn, the inhabitants of Olympus are depicted in the presence of Zeus; the Healing of the Sick, the spectators depicted wear wigs and some of the personages are recognizable, e.g. Verrio himself and Sir Godfrey Kneller, another great portrait artist of the times.[11]

[Montagu] did not neglect the use of tapestry and paintings in the decoration of his mansion. The tapestries were of singular magnificence, many of them being the product of the [Mortlake works] once owned by the Earl himself. Of especial interest and beauty was the set of eight woven Mortlakes whose subject was Scriptural, was called the Acts of the Apostles. The grouping called Peter and John Healing the Lame Man at the Beautiful Gate of the Temple, Paul Preaching at Athens, and Christ's Charge to Peter, "Feed My Sheep," was of particular beauty.

Included, in Montagu's collection were some fine specimens of Gobelins, and Flemish works as well as tapestriea adapted from the cartoons of Raphael. Many of the paintings that Montagu collected were the works of such prominent artists of the day as Kneller, who painted many members of the Montagu family and Jean Baptiste Monnoyer, the famous French floral painter. Other artists favored by Montagu included Carlo Dolci, Michael Dahl, Gonzales Coques, Michel Corneille, James Moore, Carlo Maratta. While it is not known exactly what artists Montagu collected personally other than [Kneller], [Monnoyer], [La Fosse], and [Jean Rosseau], a judgment can be made on what he would have collected by knowing the dates of these artists and their fame at the time.12

Many of the furnishings of the house were in the French style. Some of the pieces were: a Boulle Cabinet designed by [Charles Le Brun], c.1680 with the arms of

Cardinal Carraresi della Anguilara; a Boulle bracket
clock movement by Vulliamy (London) with Ralph Montagu's
monogram; a Boulle Marriage Casket, Louis XIV; a Centre
table, with the monogram of Ralph Montagu; table and
torcheres by Daniel Marot, c. 1690; pair of torcheres
giltwood and marquetry, by Daniel Marcot, c. 1690.[13]

Also found amongst the furnishings were an ebonized
and metal gilt table and companion mirror with crowned
monogram of Ralph, Duke of Montagu, c. 1684 and a gilt
gesso table by James Moore, with monogram and coronet of
Ralph Montagu, c. 1684. Noteworthy are Montagu's
presumptuous pretentions in having his monograph placed
in Ducal form on the mirror accompanying the ebonized
and metal gilt table. As further proof of this audacity,
Montagu had a bed cover woven at the Mortlake Tapestry
Works with his Ducal coat of arms sometime in the same
year.[14] In doing so, Montagu exhibited a determination
to reach his goal, even to the point of foolhardiness,
since he had not as yet been created an Earl. If
William saw these items on his fifteen-day visit to
Boughton in October 1684, one can only guess what his
thoughts were. Certainly, if he did see them, his
suspicions were probably aroused and he may have
determined to be very careful of any further dealings
with Montagu.

William may have also noticed that Montagu probably
had some interest in astrology or held some supersition
dealing with time as exhibited in the number of days in
a week and a year and the number of weeks and months of
the year. These numbers are expressed in the very
construction of the house: "....view reveals the

extraordinary complexity of the house with its seven
courtyards, twelve entrances, fifty-two chimney-stacks
and three hundred-sixty five windows."15 Why there is
this exactness in numbers is not known. Perhaps it was
merely an expression of the whimsical side of Montagu.

The King was delighted with his visit but confined
his thanks to a simple message of thank-you. There was
no elevation in the peerage or any other office conferred. What must have been particularly irritating to
Montagu at this time was the creation of his old arch
rival, Danby, as the Duke of Leeds on May 4, 1694, 16
and the appointment of his younger cousin, Charles
Montagu, as Chancellor of the Exchequer.17 However, he
was a patient man; he believed he would have his day.

Ever desirous of the title of a Duke, Montagu
endeavored to keep himself in the mainstream of
society, and 'before the eye' of the King, by his
assiduous cultivation of the `cultured.' His homes,
both in London and Northamptonshire, were always ready
to receive and display or be a haven to the learned and
cultured, French as well as English. These gatherings
most likely had the air and structure of the French
salon. Those who gathered were men of affairs, well
informed and of significance in the social strata; the
conversation was pleasurable in its content as well as
form. Probably political matters were for the most part
excluded and the direction of the discussions was guided
towards the production of the social `desire': the
creation of the `gentle-man', a cultivated, well
mannered, socially atuned person.

St. Evremond, the cordial French philosopher, was a frequent guest (1691-1701) and claimed his greatest joy was to partake in the witty and enlightened conversations held at these homes. He considered Montagu to be one of the greatest courtiers of the Restoration, a true patron of the arts, and the genius who created Boughton House and Montagu House. St. Evremond was in Montagu's debt in that Montagu was his benefactor paying him an annuity of a hundred pounds during his residence in England.18 St. Evremond, author of the Comedie des Academistes, a satirical attack on the Academie Francaise, was not the only Frenchman to know the Montagu generosity and hospitality. While envoy in Paris, Montagu became acquainted with La Fontaine, author of Fables choisies mises en vers and Contes et nouvelles en vers. The intimacy between La Fontaine and the Montagus was such that La Fontaine dedicated one of his famous Fables, Le Renard Anglais, to Lady Harvey, who, he said, inspired the story.19

Montagu was a most amiable host, an entertainer par excellence, with a quick and ready wit which made him an excellent conversationalist. St. Evremond considered conversation with Montagu one of his great joys of life. He wrote: "But you will easily guess the greatest of all, and that is being with my Lord Montagu, to enjoy his conversation twice a day, before and after the best cheer in the world."20 Again: "I never desired any thing so earnestly as to go to Boughton, to see my Lord, the good Company and Learning in its full lustre, when Monsieur le Vassor is there...."21 Montagu also hosted the great names of the English theatre. William Congreve, the famous playwright, was Montagu's guest in the summer of 1699. After his visit Congreve wrote the

play (his last comedy) <u>The</u> <u>Way</u> <u>of</u> <u>the</u> <u>World</u> and
dedicated it to Montagu. In the dedication Congreve
claims that if in any part of the play he had gained a
turn of style or an expression more correct than
formerly, he must ascribe this to participating in the
conversation of his Lordship (Montagu) and his friends.

> One who has at any time had the Honour of Your
> Lordship's Conversation, cannot be suppos'd to
> think meanly of that which he wou'd prefer to
> your Perusal....

> Whatever Value may be wanting to this Play
> while it is mine, will be sufficiently made up
> to it, when it is once become Yor Lordship's;
> and it is my Security, that I cannot have
> over-rated it more by my Dedication, than Your
> Lordship will dignifie it by Your Patronage.

> . . .

> If I am not mistaken, Poetry is almost the
> only Art, which has not yet laid Claim to
> your Lordship's Patronage. Architecture, and
> Painting, to the great Honour of our Country,
> have flourish'd under your influence and pro-
> tection. In the mean time, Poetry the eldest
> Sister of all Arts, and Parent of most, seems
> to have resign'd her Birthright, by having
> neglected to pay her duty to your Lordship;
> and by permitting others of a later Extrac-
> tion, to prepossess that Place in Your Esteem,
> to which none can pretend a better Title.
> Poetry, in its Nature, is sacred to the Good

and Great; the Relation between them is recip-
rocal, and they are even propitious to it. It
is the Privilege of Poetry to address to them,
and it is their Prerogative alone to give it
Protection.22

It can hardly be said that Montagu was averse to such
words of praise. Although the dedication is written in
a flowery and almost fawning manner, it does indicate
that Montagu did have a deep appreciation of the arts
and was involved in the cultivation and patronage of art
and artists. Many owed him a great deal both in
commission and protection.

Another visitor to Boughton and Bloomsbury was
Thomas Fuller, author of the famous Worthies, who
received both money and encouragement from Montagu.23
Shrewsbury maintained that the quickest and surest way
of curing the boredom of the times was a week's visit to
Boughton.24 Pierre Slyvestre, a native of Holland, who,
through the offices of Montagu, eventually became
William III's personal physician, was a frequent visitor
to the Montagu home. He became tutor to John, Montagu's
only son and heir after the death of Winwood in 1702.
(Winwood died "coming from Hanover [being] said to be
killed drinking too much in that court.")25 Sylvestre
became the boy's mentor and guide and accompanied him on
his Continental tour through France and Italy.26
Another protege of Montagu was the historian Michael Le
Vassor, a lapsed Catholic, author of a history of Louis
XIII.27

A host that served such distinguished guests would
of necessity serve only the finest of victuals. The
`delicious abundance' as Evremond referred to the food
at Montagu's table included oysters, salmon, heathcocks,
fruit, game pies, mutton, beef, truffles and carp. The
letters of St. Evremond to Sylvestre gave evidence of
the delicacies served at the Montagu table amid palatial
surroundings.[28]

If the poor Duchesse Mazarin, had been yet
alive, she would have had Peaches, of which
she would not have fail'd to give me a share;
she would have had Tuiffles, which I should
have eat with her; not to mention the Carps of
Newhall. I must make up the loss of so many
advantages, by the Sundays and Wednesdays of
Montagu-House.[29]

By such patronage of the men of letters, painters, and
sculptors, Montagu revealed himself to be a champion of
the arts. He himself to be a devoted aristocratic
patron: his purse was always open to writers and
artists of talent. In short, Montagu was a most hospit-
able patron who enjoyed charming surroundings in which
fine furnishings and beautiful paintings were much in
evidence.

Although Montagu alternated his presence between
his home in the country and his town house overseeing
and entertaining, this presence at either greatly
depended upon the sessions of the House of Lords, which
meant that Montagu was in London most of the wintertime.
However,his presence in London was deliberate; attendance at the House of Lords not only kept him in touch

with the happenings in the capital, but also made his presence very obvious to the monarch. The Journal of the House of Lords records his frequent attendance at the sessions of that body between 1685-1709. He was in almost regular attendance sitting on committees and listening to debates.30 Montagu evidently intended to remain in constant contact with the leading figures of the Whig party and thus declare his willingness to serve and advise.

Of course, Montagu's presence in London was often needed, not in any position that influenced the making of policy, but as the Master of the Great Wardrobe. He was responsible for the fitting out, furnishing, and maintainance of the royal households and the supplying of things ceremonial upon state occasions. This office brought him into frequent contact with the King. Mindful of this, Montagu performed his services with exacting care. Here he was directly in the `royal eye!' To be so meant that he had a greater chance of obtaining his Dukedom. He was especially diligent in the performance of his duties upon the death of William in March of 1702 and the Coronation of his successor, Queen Anne.31

Around the year 1703 Montagu seriously began to consider the possibility of an advantageous marriage for his only surviving son, John. He began to search for a suitable bride for him, one who would, of course, bring the largest dowry. Also, with his son's future in mind, he began to consider the possibility of the office of the Great Wardrobe being transferred to John after his death. In order to facilitate the transfer, Montagu arranged to receive a lesser stipend per annum.32

Eventually, a suitable match was decided upon. Montagu desired that his son should marry Mary Churchill, the last of the unmarried daughters of the Duke of Marlborough. Despite an objection due to the girl's age, she was only fourteen,33 she was quite acceptable to Montagu and John needed no coaxing to marry her. He found Mary of a pleasing disposition and of high spirits and fell in love with the girl almost at first sight. Of course, there were other suitors (the Earl of Huntington, Lord Mordaunt), but none survived the period of scrutiny, either on the grounds of Mary's preference or of character flaws.34

The Montagus and the Churchills eventually came to an agreement and a marriage contract was drawn up to the mutual satisfaction of both parties. "A treaty for Marriage is on foot between the Lord Mount Hermon, only son to the Earl of Montague, and the Lady Mary Churchill, daughter of the Duke of Marlborough."35 The contract was then endorsed by Queen Anne herself; Sarah Churchill, Mary's mother, was both a friend and confidant of the Queen.36

The marriage took place on March 20, 1705 in Marlborough's private apartments in St. James. Both the Queen and the Prince were present at the ceremony and as dowry the Queen gave the couple ten thousand pounds. That same day the Queen created Montagu a Duke and granted that the post of Master of the Great Wardrobe should come to his son upon his death.37 Montagu had gained the day! The object of all his exertion and efforts was achieved.

The match was extremely advantageous for both the Montagus and the Churchills. Each could help the other. Marlborough believed that Montagu, with his connections with the leaders of the Whig party, could be of help to him during his absences abroad on the Queen's business. He depended on Montagu to protect him from any combination of Whigs and Tories that might seek to do him in.38 Besides, it was to his great advantage to have a son-in-law who stood next in line to one of the greatest fortunes in all of England. Montagu enjoyed an income of thirty thousand pounds at this time and his estates and revenue were valued at near two hundred thousand pounds.39 This prospect alone was enough to delight the 'aspirations' of his wife Sarah. She was not about to allow her daughter to marry anyone of less wealth or social standing than herself. Further, with such a marriage, Marlborough's daughter would enjoy the advantage of family connections with some of the leading families of the realm: Manchester, Sunderland, Sandwich, Northumberland, Albemarle, Russell, Newcastle.

On the other hand, Montagu was given the insurance of the advocacy of the Duke and Duchess with the Queen directly. There was no end to the honors that he could claim for himself and his family! He lost no time in taking advantage of this. It was probably due to his prodding that: "The Queen has ordered the marchionesse of Mounthermer's wife to be put into the patent for making the marquesse master of the great wardrobe, after the duke of Montague's death, to enjoy it in case she survives her husband."40 The office would remain in his line. It was the beginning of security for his progeny.

And so, on April 20, 1705, Montagu was created the Marquis of Monthermer and the First Duke of Montagu.[41] At long last, he had achieved his goal after many a misadventure that could well have cost him his life. It was now some twenty-seven years since he had betrayed the King and nation with its resultant dishonor, but that was of small matter to him now that he possessed the coveted title. He was now to be known to all as: Ralph, First Duke of Montagu.

His promotion was not without cynical observation on the part of the public. The rhymesters had a field day. That some thought his promotion was far beyond his merits can be gathered from the following lines of Mr. Gwinnett alluding to this creation.

> The Queen, like Heaven, shines equally on all,
> Her favours now without distinction fall.
> Great Read [a physician to the Queen] and
> slender Haines [an occultist] both knighted,
> show
> That none their honours shall to merit owe.
> That popish doctrine is exploited quite,
> Or Ralph had been no Duke, and Read no Knight:
> That none may virtue or their learning plead,
> This has no grace, and that can hardly read.42

True to the maxim that the more one has the more one wants, Montagu was unsatisfied and unfulfilled. Happy though he was with his elevation to the rank of Duke, this was not to be the end of his ambitions. There was still one more brush stroke to be added to finish the portrait of his life. Montagu believed himself worthy of one more honor: the Order of the Garter.

If the Duke of Leeds (Danby) could be granted this honor, then why not he? He was now a Duke and certainly worthy of this honor by his rank. "It is said that the duke of Montague will have the garter of the late duke of Devon...."[43]

If his past actions are any criteria, Montagu went straight to the Duchess of Marlborough to obtain this favor from the Queen. He was counting on family relationship and her intimacy with Anne to win for him that which he had sought from the earliest days of his service as ambassador in France. However, he erred in his calculations and had to face disappointment once more. There was only one Garter to be awarded that year and Anne excused herself on the grounds that with so many applicants pleading past or future services she was forced to put off any conferral until there were more vacancies.[44]

Since he could not gain any honor at this time for himself, Montagu tried another tack. It might be possible to obtain some sort of office for his son and by this means enhance the family honor. Accordingly, he petitioned the Duchess of Marlborough to use her influence with Anne to obtain for her son-in-law a captaincy in the Yeomen of the Guard.[45] This request was also turned down. Anne felt that John Montagu had already been granted enough. Besides, she had created Montagu a Duke and granted the reversion of the Mastership as personal favors to the Montagus because of the marriage of the daughter of her favorite and not through any merit of their own;[46] the present honors and offices sufficed. The Duchess having failed, he now turned to the Electress Sophia of Hanover, in whose domain his son

Winwood had died near the end of William's reign (1702).47 Once again, his efforts proved fruitless.

Although Montagu never was awarded the Garter, he never gave up. He literally died trying. And so:

...the beginning of the Month of March, 1709, at what time his Grace was stricken with a Distemper that held him till the 9th day, when between the hours of 5 and 6 he Expir'd at His House in Russell Street, Bloomsbury, in the 71st year of his Age, to the great grief of the Court and all his Family, he being a loyal Courtier, and a tender Father, and a kind Master....48

Many who knew him could not exactly say they were in 'days' grief over his passing. In fact, there were some who were elated as his passing. In a letter from Ann Hadley to her cousin Abigail Hadley we read:

Here is no lamentations for ye Duke of Montague, but he by departing has given the inquisitive warld ye long desired satisfaction of knowing his Mad Duchess to be alive; they say she will be given to the Duke of New-castel, when a commission of Lunacy is taken out, and whats more will come in for her thirds of her or her pretended husbands Estate for my part I'me apt to think could he have foreseen, or rather believed at what a distance this present world and he would soon have been, he for the wealth and honner sake of his family would discreetly have knockd her

Ladyship in the head in good time.49

His body was carried from St. Giles in the Fields, his London parish and laid to rest next to his first wife in the family church at Warkton, Northamptonshire, March 16, 1709.50 "The duke of Montague, aged 71, is dead and succeeded in honour, estate and place of master of the great wardrobe (worth 3000 L. per ann.) by his son, the marquesse of Monthermer."[51]

Montagu was survived by his wife, `the Mad Duchess', his son, John, his daughter, Anne, Mrs. Alexander Popham.  The `Mad Duchess' survived him by at least twenty years. She died in 1734 and was buried in Westminster Abbey52

Montagu's later years were relatively free from political activity. His truly active participation in the workings of the House of Lords had been limited to voting for the bestowal of the Crown of William and Mary in 1688 and lending his support to the Bill of Rights in 1689 of the Convention Parliament. An examination of the Journal of the House of Lords, XIV (1685) - XVIII 1685-1714, Vol. I, England and Wales, reveals that although Montagu was in attendance in the House of Lords on almost a daily basis, he lent his name to no major bill or piece of legislation. His activities were confined to sitting on committees and listening to the debates.

Montagu's main concern during these years was the contracting of a profitable marriage solely in the interest of obtaining the wealth he needed for the

refurbishing and extension of his estates, the collection of art, the hosting of social gatherings, and in
the prosecution of his law suits for control of his
wife's vast wealth and estates; his concerns were no
longer political but economic and social. His activities
of later life were directed carefully to gaining his
final prize, the coveted Dukedom, and he cultivated only
those who could be of benefit to him in his quest. He
finally did obtain this prize, but only though the
advantageous marriage of his only son, John, with the
daughter of the Queen's confidant.

Montagu used others to gain his objective, but
this did not bother him. It rather proved Montagu was
constant in nature: cool and calculating in dealing with
those around him to his advantage. And so, Ralph, first
Duke of Montagu, died as he had lived, the `Artful
Contriver'.

[1]The Court in Mourning, p. 8; Boyer, Annals, VII, 373; Luttrell, V, 170; Cockayne, IX, 107; Firth, p. 712.

[2]The cockpit was destroyed by fire on Jan. 6, 1697, along with most of Whitehall in an intense conflagration.

The fire at White hall began the 4th instant about 5 in the afternoon and continued till about 7 the next morning, it is said to begin by the carelessness of a servant putting charcoal ashes into a closet; the lord Portland and the earl of Essex's lodgings were saved, but the kings, queens, earl of Montagues, duke Devonshires, the protestant and popish chappells, the guard chamber, duke Shrewsbury's office, Mr. Chancellor Montagues, lord chancellors, and archbishops lodgings, the treasury and council chambers, and the long gallery leading to the Gatehouse, were all burnt: the banqueting house is standing: and in the after noon his majestie took a view of the ruines, and seemed much concerned, he said, if God gave him leave, he would rebuild it much finer than before. (Luttrell, IV, 328-29)

[3]Cockayne, IX, 107.

[4]Ibid., p. 107.

[5]Michael Foss, The Age of Patronage: The Arts in Society, 1660-1750 (London: Hamish Hamilton, 1971), pp. 20-21.

[6]Ibid., p. 21.

[7] Ibid., p. 30.

[8] Ibid., p. 32.

[9] John Steane, The Northamptonshire Landscape: Northamptonshire and the Soke of Peterborough (London: Hodder and Stoughton, 1974), pp. 241-42.

[10] Montagu, I, 280.

[11] Wise, pp. 40-41; J. Alfred Gotch, The Old Halls and Manor-Houses of Northamptonshire (London: B.T. Batsford, 1936), p. 48; John Cornforth, Boughton House, Northamptonshire, Written in six parts and reprinted from Country Life issued September 3rd, 10th, and 17th, 1970; February 28th, March 4th and 11th, 1971.

[12] Pamphlet entitled Boughton House; Northamptonshire Home of the Dukes of Buccleuch and Queensbury (Montagu Douglas Scott), pp. 2-3; Brochure: Boughton House: State Rooms and High Pavilion, pp. 2-3.

[13] Brochure: Boughton House, pp. 2-3.

[14] Ibid., p. 2.

[15] Pamphlet: Boughton House, p. 2.

[16] Lee, "Osbourne", pp. 1195.

[17]George F.R. Barker, "Montagu, Charles, Earl of Halifax, 1661-1715," Dictionary of National Biography, VIII, 670.

[18]John Hayward. Letters of St. Evremond (London: George Routledge and Sons, Ltd., 1930), p. 295.

[19]Anges Ethel Mackay, La Fontaine and His Friends: A Biography (London: Garnstone Press, 1972), p. 155.

[20]Hayward, p. 356.

21Ibid., p. 354.

[22]Montague Summers, ed., The Complete Works of William Congreve (New York: Russell and Russell and Co., Inc., 1964), pp. 9-11.

23Foss, p. 235.

[24]Falk, p. 145.

25Cockayne, IX, 108.

[26]Hayward, p. 304.

27Ibid., p. 354.

[28]Ibid., p. 354.

29Ibid., pp. 355-57.

[30]Robert Steele, A Bibliography of Royal Proclamations of the Tudor and Stuart Sovereigns and of Others Published Under Authority, 1485-1714 (New York: Burt Franklin, 1967), p. 473.

[31]Ibid., p. 514.

[32]Boyer, The History of Queen Anne, p. 46.

[33]Edward Gregg, Queen Anne (London: Routledge and Kegan Paul, 1980), p. 195.

Gregg comments:
In a corrupt age, Ralph, Earl of Montagu, had acquired a singular reputation of profitable dishonour; his construction of Montagu House in Bloomsbury (the site of the present British Museum) showed that he was one of the wealthiest peers of the realm. When, in May 1703, Montagu had proposed the marriage of his son and heir Viscount Monthermer to Lady Mary, Marlborough had objected that the proposed partners were only fourteen. 'I am confident', he told the Duchess, 'when you shall see the young man and Miss Mary together, you will think she is too much a woman for him.' When Bradford's grandson was mentioned as a possible husband a month later, the queen seconded Marlborough's advice to Sarah that they should wait.

[34]Falk, p. 148.

[35]Luttrell, V, 315; Firth, p. 712.

36Boyer, The History of Queen Anne, p. 46.

[37] Boyer, Annals, VIII, 373; Luttrell, V. 537; Whalley, p. 352; London Gazette, April 2-12-16, 1705, Number 4114; Cockayne, IX, 107; Firth, p. 712.

A description of the duties of the office of Master of the Great Wardrobe is found in The New State of England, Under Our Present Monarch William III. (London: Printed by R.J. for H. Mortlock, et al., 1701), p. 156.

The Master of the Great Wardrobe, whose salary is 21000 L. per annum. His Office is kept in York-Buildings, since the Fire; and he has under him several Officers, and Sworn Servants to the King. Peculiarly a Deputy whose salary is 200 L. and a Clerk, whose Place is worth 300 L. a year. This is the Office which furnishes the Court and forein Ambassadors Houses at their first Arrival here, with Beds, Hangings, and other Necessaries; that provides Presents for forein Princes and Ambassadors, Canopies and other Furniture for the Lord Lieutenant of Ireland, and all His Majesties Ambassadors abroad; all robes for forein Knights of the Garter, for the Officers of the Garter, Coats for the King's Heralds, and Porsuivants of Arms, and Liveries for His Majesties Servants.

Luttrell, V, 531 - states the marriage took place on the 17th of March but he does not agree to the date that Montagu was created a Duke. He further states that the queen granted the reversion of the office of the Great Wardrobe on the 22nd and not on the 20th as Gregg (Queen Anne) claims.

[38] A.T. Thomson, Memoirs of Sarah, Duchess of Marlborough and of the Court of Queen Anne (London: H. Colburn, 1839), II, 9-16; Firth, p. 712.

[39] The Court in Mourning, p. 1.

[40] Luttrell, V. 537.

[41]Boyer, Annals, VIII, 373; Cockayne, IX, 107; Firth, p. 712.

[42]John Gough Nichols, ed., The Topographer and Genealogist (London: John Bowyer Nichols and Sons, 1858), III, 154; Cockayne, IX, 107; Falk, p. 149.

43Luttrell, VI, 210.

[44]Falk, p. 149.

[45]B.H. Add. MSS. 61450 ff. 196-96, 198-200; Buccleuch MSS. I, 520.

[46]Buccleuch MSS. I, 520, Boyer, The History of Queen Anne, p. 46.

[47]Falk, p. 50.

[48]The Court in Mourning, p. 8; Boyer, Annals, VIII, 373.

49Ward, pp. 349-50.

[50]Cockayne, IX, 107; Firth, p. 712.

51Luttrell, VI, 416.

[52]Cockayne, IX, 107-108; Firth, p. 712.p. 20

Once the Duke was dead a controversy arose amongst the Duchess's relatives as to who should be her guardian.

The dispute arose from the fact that her guardians would receive a hamdsome stipend for their services. To settle the matter a Lunacy commission was set up and on March 31, 1709 it declared "the Duchess Dowager of Montagu is a lunatic and not in her right mind understanding and does not enjoy lucid intervals and is therefore not capable of the Government of herself and her estate." John, Duke of Newcastle, Thomas, Earl of Thanet, and Charles, Earl of Sunderland, who were married to her two sisters, were appointed her guardians. (Ward, p. 350. See also Luttrell, VI, 420, 425.)

CONCLUSION

Achilles' Choice

My Divine Mother, Thetis of the
Silver Feet, says that Destiny
has left two courses open to me
on my journey to the grave. If
I stay here and play my part in
the siege of Troy, there is no
homecoming for me, though I
shall win undying fame. But if
I go home to my own country, my
good name will be lost, though
I shall have long life, and
shall be spared an early death.
(E.V. Rieu, Trans., The Iliad
by Homer (London: The Folio
Society, 1975), p. 135).

Achilles was given a choice by his mother--the
choice of immortality conditioned upon the doing of
his duty or the gift of a long life accompanied by
the loss of fame. Like Achilles, Montagu, due to a
number of decisions, created the manner of his
remembrance. He had all that could be desired to
make him remembered: family, wealth and education,
all that could have assisted him to become a
statesman and have his country indebted to him for
generations.

Montagu's political life spanned the years of
the Restoration of Charles II to the Throne, the
rise of the Whig party and the event of the

Glorious Revolution. On the domestic scene, he witnessed the constant struggle between the King and his Parliament, Court versus Parliament, which gave birth to the political party system in English politics. At the same time he was drawn into European politics through the `tug-of-war' between the King with his pro-French and pro-Catholic foreign policy and the Parliament with its anti-French and pro-Protestant policy and entered into the secret dealings between the two monarchs for subsidies which, if revealed, would have cost Charles his crown and Montagu his head. Montagu later became a member of Parliament, with Louis XIV's blessing, in an attempt to destroy the Lord Treasurer because of an imagined affront (not being chosen Secretary of State) and afterwards was a constant source of irritation to the French in his quest for payment of the money he thought was his due for his part in Danby's destruction. He took part in the exclusion crisis dealing with James II and went into exile in France for his troubles. His last major venture into the political arena was his advocacy of the Glorious Revolution with its enthronement of William III and Mary as the Protestant rulers of the nation. For this effort he reckoned he deserved a Dukedom but had to wait almost ten years before his cherished dream came true.

Montagu often did not see beyond his own self-gratification. Yet in his concern for the garnering of a title, must not one consider that he wished to bequeath this title to his progeny and to be remembered by posterity by the creation of a ducal line and by the homes---nay palaces--that he built for them to inhabit? In this he showed a certain growth--a growth that indicated that he could, at times, go beyond himself and think of others. On the other hand, he was never overly loyal to his country, something that his contemporary John Churchill, Duke of Marlborough, could be accused of also. Perhaps the fervent patriotism inspired by nineteenth-twentieth century nationalism was foreign to this generation. Working with a different sense of morality, Montagu did not concern himself with future evaluations of his political activities.

Montagu was a pure opportunist in public life as well as in private life; when he saw an advantage he was not loath to seize it. Early in his life he had determined to pursue wealth and a title. He was willing to use any means to attain his goal. Service at Court appeared to be the way to rise in the world, hence his willingness to serve his king. Montagu then used this service as a means to enrich and advance himself, but at the expense of both king and country without qualms of conscience. All this reveals a not uncommon cynical view of his world and of the people who populated it.

Montagu may have been a planner but he was not a man of vision. He really did not look beyond his own life span. He desired a title for himself and a position of honor for his family, but beyond that he did not appear concerned about the judgment of posterity. He did not consider the immediate ramifications and repercussions of his traitorous actions for his part in the Danby affair nor the far-reaching negative effects upon the government he served. His dealings with the Whig party in its attempt to exclude James II from the Throne and his part in its Glorious Revolution reveal him as a man willing to parade his shameless conduct of betrayal under the guise of patriotism.

One must stop here and remember unfortunately, there are many gaps in Montagu's life for which no information is available and what we do possess is somewhat sketchy. There is a paucity information to be had, for example, concerning his youth, especially his days at Westminster school other than his attendance there. Nor is there any infor- mation available as to his actual program of studies or his deportment. What information we have concerning such instanaces in his life is derived from negative evidence or from secondary sources. In some cases the events and Montagu's action or reaction had to be reconstructed from such sketchy material. Sadly, much material dealing with the Montagu family was destroyed in the bombings of London in the Second World War.

Until the death of his father (1683) he was prevented from entering the ranks of the nobility. Realizing that while his father was alive he could not enjoy either the privileges or the honors due to one of noble rank, Montagu sought other signs of royal favor. He openly sought the conferral of the Order of the Garter for his services as ambassador to France. When this was denied him, he decided to `enter' the nobility by way of assimilation, a tactic often used by those of lower degree who desired noble rank but knew they could never obtain it.1 He would become `ennobled' by assumption or assimilation of the aristocratic culture. Montagu mimicked the culture of the aristocracy.2

In this action Montagu was representative not only of his countrymen, but even of Seventeenth Century Europe. He believed that he could aspire to the nobility through culture and eventually be assimilated into the Court. The best road to this assimilation was to imitate the nobility in patronizing the arts and the artists. By fostering and protecting the arts--painting, sculpture, architecture, theater and the garden--Montagu intended to achieve his goal. He would earn a `pedigree of nobility' by his patronizing of great artists-- Verrio, Monnoyer, Kneller; the performing arts-- Congreve; the entertaining of the best of society-- La Fontaine, St. Evremond; and grandiose buildings--his houses in London and Boughton; the laying out of formal gardens at his homes in London and Boughton.3 Even the garden became a medium of aesthetic appreciation for these `aspiring nobles.' "Since ancient days the garden has served Western man as a mirror of paradise to measure his temporal state."4

These works of art were the material manifestations of an aristocratic culture. They were for Montagu the open declaration and expression of its assimilation, and they indicated a culture of grace, the aesthetic and the sensuous.5 Art not only became an ornament expressing good taste but also became a source of value. It became a source of value, not only in itself, but also as a measure of the support given by the person to "the temple of art as a surrogate form of assimilation" into the aristocratic life.[6] Art was seen as expressing the ideals of the noble society and bringing grace to the individual.[7] The measure of one's patronage was the measure of assimilation into aristocratic life.

What Carl Schorske says in his work Fin De Siecle Vienna of the importance of art in the scale of the bourgeois values at the end of the nine-teenth century was equally true of those desiring assimilation into the aristocracy of the seven-teenth century:

> Direct social assimilation to the aristocracy occured rarely in Austria. Even those who won a patent of nobility were not admitted, even in Germany, to the life of the imperial court. But assimilation could be purchased along another, more open road: that of culture.[8]

His patronage of the arts; the lending of his name and the offering of monetary support to the painters, sculptors and playwrights of his time, was perhaps the most laudable thing that Montagu ever did. That he loved good conversation, the company of intellectuals, good food and fine surroundings there is ample proof in the fine homes he built and the great people he entertained. But even here his actions were not without purpose; Montagu hoped that these would make him known, appreciated, respected, and, perhaps, even remembered in a historical sense.

Further, he employed his taste for the finer things in the cultivation of influential people, not with a view to be of service, but to enlist their influence with the monarch to gain the long sought Dukedom. Careful in speech and action, he directed all his efforts to attaining this goal and he admitted of no contradiction between what he thought his right and the means of achieving his end. If at times his actions were immoral, the morality of his efforts was not a factor he considered.

The public and personal life of Montagu reflect the attitudes of the times in which he lived. His life is, then, a prism through which the standards of the day are refracted. He lived his life in accordance with the morality of the day and he became recognized as one most successful for his times. He attained almost all he sought from life and died, in the world's view, successful, wealthy and honored.

Achilles chose immortality. Ralph Montagu, in contrast, earned a dubious, and at best tangential immortality; one derived from Coffee-House pamphlets, satirical plays, polemical poetry and association with men of substance. Consequently, Ralph Montagu, First Duke of Montagu, as an historical figure remains only a footnote of history,(even though in his contriving way he had some brief influence on the European stage of politics and life).

CONCLUSION
Footnotes

1Carl F. Schorske, Fin de Siecle Vienna: Politics and Culture (New York; Alfred Knopf, 1980), p. 7.

2Ibid., p. 8

3Ibid., p. 8.

4Ibid., p. 280.

5Ibid., p. 10.

6Ibid., p. 10.

7Ibid., p. 297.

8Ibid., p. 7.

APPENDICES

Appendix A Latin poem written by the schoolboy Ralph Montagu.

Appendix B Three letters dealing with the death of Henriette Anne, Charles II's sister.

Appendix C Account of Bishop Burnet of Danby's impeachment, the subsidy for Charles II and Montagu's involvement with the Duchess of Cleveland.

Appendix D Excerpt from a letter dealing with 'troubles' of Ralph Montagu with the Duchess of Cleveland.

Appendix E Lady Montagu's (Elizabeth, Countess of Northumberland) letter to Sir William Coventry on her husband's behalf after his flight from London.

Appendix F Ralph Montagu's speech before the House of Commons calling for the banishment of 'papists' and the calling of frequent Parliaments.

Appendix G Legal ruling concerning the dignity and title of the Countess of Northumberland (Lady Montagu).

Appendix H A description of the office and duties of the Master of the Great Wardrobe.

Appendix I Ralph, Earl of Montagu's letter to William III petitioning him for a Dukedom.

Appendix J A description of the gardens and water works of Boughton House, Northamptonshire (1712).

Poem of the young Ralph Montagu written upon
the death of Henry, Lord Hastings and published in
the school magazine <u>Lachrymae</u> <u>Musarum</u> (1649)

Nobilium pueris bulla olim insignia; Morbi
   Nos insignivit plurima bulla notis,
Me nuper languente, infecit pustual corpus;
   Iam menten affecit, Te moriente, meam.
Morbi itermum videor tecum sentire dolores;
   Quam leve ferre meos, quam grave ferre tuos!
Partior ipse tuis languores corporis: O si
   Virtutes animae partiar ipse Tuae!

> Radulphus Mountague,
> Edwardi Mountague Baronis de
> Boughton, Filius natu minor,
> ex Schola Wesmonast.

At one time the golden "blister" was the badge
   of nobility for boys;

> A much greater blister of disease has marked
>   us with its brand,

Not long ago I was sick and a pustule infected
   my body;

> And now since you are dying, it has
>   affected my spirit.

I seem once again to be experiencing with you
   the pain of disease;

> How easily I seem to bear my pains; how
>   grievously do I bear yours!

I share the ill-health of your body: O if only

I could share the virtues of your soul!

Ralph Montague
Younger   son   of   Edward
    Mountague
Baron of Boughton
at Westminster School

APPENDIX B

Three Letters "From a Person of Quality being actually upon the spot, give a particular Relation of the Death of Madam." as quoted in: The Right Honourable the Earl of Arlington's Letters to Sir W. Temple, Bar. From July 1665. All Printed from the Originals and never before Publish'd. (London: Printed by W.N., 1701), pp. 438-39, 443-45, 447.

Paris, June 30, 1670
Four in the Morning

My Lord,
I am sorry to be obliged, by my Employment, to give you an Account of the saddest Story in the World, and which I have hardly the courage to write. Madam, on Sunday the 29th. of this instant, being at St. Clou, with a great deal of Company, about Five a Clock in the Afternoon, called for a Glass of Cichory water, that was prescribed her to drink, she having, for two or three Days after Bathing, found her self indisposed, she had no sooner drunk this, but she cryed out she was Dead, and fell into Madam Mascbourgh's Arms, and desired to be put to Bed, and have a Consellor. She continued in the greatest Tortures imaginable till Three a Clock in the Morning; when she dyed: The King, the Queen, and all the Court being there till about an hour before.

God send the King our Master Patience and Constancy to bear so great an Affliction. Madam, declared she had no reluctancy to die, but out of the Grief, she thought, it would be to the King her Brother; and when she was in any ease, from the Torture she was in, which the Physician called Cohick Bileuse, she asked for me, and it was to charge me to say all the kind things from her to her Brothers, the King and Duke. I did not leave

her till she expired, and happened to come to St.
Clou an Hour after she fell ill. Never any Body
died with that Piety and Resolution, and kept her
Senses to the last. Excuse this imperfect Relation
for the Grief I am in. I am sure all, that had the
Honour to know her, will have their share for so
great and general a loss. I am, my Lord,

Yours &c.

To the KING

Paris, July 15, 1670.

Sir,
I ought to begin with begging your Majesty's
Pardon for saying any thing to you upon so sad a
Subject, and where I had the misfortune to be a
Witness of the cruelest, and most generous End any
Person in the World ever made. I had the Honour,
on the Saturday, which was the day before Madam
dy'd, to entertain her a great while; the most of
her discourse being concerning Monsieur, and how
impossible she saw it was for her to live happily
with him, for he was fallen out with her worse than
ever, because that, two days before she had been
at Versailles, and there he found her talking
privately with the King, about affairs which were
not fit to be communicated to him. She told me
your Majesty and the King here were both resolved
upon a War with Holland, as soon as you could be
agreed on the manner of it; These were the last
Words I had the Honour to have from her till she
fell ill, for Monsieur came in and interrupted her,
and I returned to Paris the next day. When she
fell ill, she called for me two or three times;
Madam de Mechelburgh sent for me; as soon as I came
in, she told me, you see the sad condition I am in;
I am going to die, how I pity the King my Brother!
For, I am sure, he loses the Person in the World

that loves him best. A little while after she called me again, bidding me be sure to say all the kind things in the World from her to the King her Brother, and thank him for all his Kindness and Care of me. Then she asked me if I remembred what she had said to me, the night before, of your Majesty's Intentions to joyn with France against Holland; I told her yes; pray then, said she, tell my Brother I never perswaded him to it, out of my own Interest, or to be more considered in this Countrey; but because I thought it was for his Honour and Advantage. For I always lov'd him above all things in the World, and have no regret to leave it, but because I leave him. She called to me several times to be sure to say this to you, and spoke to me in English. I ask'd her then, if she believ'd her self Poison'd: Her Confessor that was by, understood that Word, and told her, Madam, you must accuse no Body, but offer up your Death to God as a Sacrifice; so she would never answer me to that Question, tho I asked her several times, but would only shrink up her Shoulders. I asked her for her Casket, where all her Letters were, to send them to your Majesty; she bid me take it from Madam de Borde; but she was swounding and dying to see her Mistress in that Condition, and, before she came to her self, Monsieur had seized on them. She recommended to you to help, as much as you could, all her poor Servants; She bid me write to my Lord Arlington, to put you in mind of it (and tell the King my Brother) I hope he will for my sake, do for him what he promised; Car c'est un home qui l'ayme, & qui le sert bien, For he is a person that both loves him, and serves him faithfully. She spoke afterwards a great deal in French aloud, bemoaning and lamenting the condition she knew your Majesty would be in when You heard the News of her Death. I humbly again beg your Majesty's pardon for having been the unfortunate teller of so sad News; there being none of your Servants, that wishes your Content and Happiness with more Zeal and Truth, than Sir,

Your Majesties, &c.

My Lord,
     I Am not well able to write you in my own Hand,
being so Lame, with a fall I had in coming, that, I
can very hardly stir either Hand or Arm; however, I
hope in a day or two to go to St. Germains.
     This is only to give your Lordship an
account, of what I believe you know
already, of the Chevalier de Lorain's
being permitted to come to Court, and to
serve in the Army, as a Marshall de Camp
to the King.

     If Madam were Poisoned, as few People doubt,
he is look'd upon, by all France, to have done it;
and it is wonder'd at, by all France; That that
King should have so little regard to the King of
England our Master, considering how insolently he
always carried himself to her when she was alive,
as to permit his return. It is my Duty to let you
know this, to tell His Majesty; and, if he thinks
fit to speak to the French Ambassador of it, to do
it vigorously; for I assure you it reflects here
much upon him to suffer it.

APPENDIX C

Bishop Burnet's account of Danby's opposition in
the Parliament of 1678, his ordering Montagu to
seek a subsidy for Charles II, the intrigue between
Montagu and the Duchess of Cleveland. (Bishop
Burnet's History of His Own Time: With Notes by the
Earls of Dartmouth and Hardwicke, Speaker Onslow,
and Dean Swift, 2nd ed. 6 vols. (Oxford: University
Press, 1823), II, 139-141).

... representing to the king the ill effects of his
not hearkening to their address the former year
with relation to foreign affairs; and desiring him
to change his ministry, and to dismiss all those
that had advised the prorogation at that time, and
his delaying so long to assist the allies. This
was carried only by a small majority of two or
three. So Lord Danby brought up all his creatures,
the aged and infirm not excepted: and then the
majority lay the other way: and by short
adjournments the parliament was sitting til
Midsummer. Once lord Danby, thinking he had a
clear majority, got the king to send a message to
the house, desiring an additional revenue of
300,000 l. during life. This set the house all in
a flame. It was said, here was no demand for a
war, but for a revenue, which would furnish the
court so well, that there would be no more need of
parliaments. The court party thought such a gift
as this would make them useless. So the thing was
upon one debate rejected without a division. Lord
Danby was much censured for this rash attempt,
which discovered the designs of the court too bare-
facedly. At the same time he ordered Mountague to
treat with the court of France for a peace, in case
they would engage to pay the king 300,000 l. a year
for three years. So, when that came afterwards to

be known, it was then generally believed, that the
design was to keep up and model the army now
raised, reckoning there would be money enough to
pay them till the nation should be brought under a
military government. And the opinion of this prevailed so, that lord Danby became the most hated
minister that had ever been about the king. All
people said now, they saw the secret of that high
favour he had been so long in, and the black
designs that he was contriving. At this time
expresses went very quick between England and
France: and the state of foreign affairs varied
every post. So that it was visible we were in a
secret negotiation: of which Temple has given so
particular an account, that I refer my reader
wholly to him. But I shall add one particular,
that he has not mentioned: Mountague, who was a man
of pleasure, was in an intrigue with the duchess of
Cleveland, who was quite cast off by the king, and
was then at Paris. The king had ordered him to
find out an astrologer, of whom it was no wonder he
had a good opinion; for he had, long before his
restoration, foretold he should enter London on the
29th of May, 60. He was yet alive, and Mountague
found him; and saw he was capable of being
corrupted. So he resolved to prompt him, to send
the king such hints as should serve his own ends.
And he was so bewitched with the duchess of
Cleveland, that he trusted her with this secret.
But she, growing jealous of a new amour, took all
the ways she could think on to ruin him, reserving
this of the astrologer for her last shift. And by
it she compassed her ends: for [the King looked
upon this as a piece of treachery and folly, that]
Mountague was entirely lost upon it with the king,
and came over without being recalled. The earl of
Sunderland was sent ambassador in his room.

APPENDIX D

Excerpt from a letter dated 1678, July 13. relating the `troubles' of Ralph Montagu with the Duchess of Cleveland. (H.M.C. Manuscripts of the Marquess of Ormonde, n.s., Vol. IV, 443-44).

Yesterday his Majesty, in Council, did order Mr. Montagu's name to be struck out of the Council-books, and I think it was the only reason why the Council met, since both Houses were to sit the same afternoon. Thus the badges of honour drop away; for the Embassy of France is granted to Lord Sunderland, and the more material things are already in the general rumour diposed of, namely, the Wardrobe to the Earl of Plymouth, and the Mastership of the Horse to the Lord Latimore--some say to the Lord Dunblany. His Majesty did, as it were casually, meet at my Lord Treasurer's with Mr. Montagu, who, beginning to enter on the story of my Lady Cleveland, His Majesty told him he knew already too much of that, and bade him declare what affair of state it was that made him quit France without leave. In which point, having nothing to answer, he was thenceforth forbidden His Majesty's presence and the Court. And he is loaded by the women to have done many heinous things--as not only without order to have proposed a match between the Dauphin and Mademoiselle, the King's niece, but to have spoken treason to the Duchess of Cleveland, and contemptuously to have acted His Majesty in ridicule among the French. But where the women engage there is no bounds to wrath, and, therefore, as he himself tells the story, it is thus: That long time past my Lord Treasurer did, by the King's command, commit to his care and industry the compassing a match between the Lord Northumberland and Lady Percy. That the Lady Cleveland was herein

ordered to act her part by more complacency and
visiting of his Lady, which at length improved into
a sort of friendship. But his Lady (on a visit to
the Duchess) forbid admission because Monsieur
Chattillean was with her, she returned in high
resentment, so that he, seeing the designed
marriage in danger, took on him to expostulate very
roundly with the Duchess for her licentious course
of life with the said Monsieur, which the whole
town and country rung of, and brought disgrace to
the children His Majesty had by her. The Duchess
not enduring this doctrine, and from such a hand,
returned all upon him with rage and contempt, and
'twas his only care to get well home. The war
being thus begun and Mr. Montagu contriving how to
get some witnesses to speak for him, did so prevail
with a nun who conveyed all the amorous letters
between the Monsieur and her Grace that he got six
of them into his hands, whereof some abounded with
gross and unseemly things in the trade of love;
some with disrespect to His Majesty, and some of a
project to marry the Dauphin unto Mademoiselle. By
some chink or other the Duke of Orleans had a hint
of this project, and to purge himself from any part
therein came to remonstrate his innocence to his
brother the King, who, it seems, till that time had
not heard thereof, and left fall such expressions
on the news as coming to Mr. Montagu's ears
persuaded him also to a compurgation of himself.
And so he went to assure his Most Christian Majesty
that he was not the author of that intrigue, but
had discovered it in the letters aforesaid, which
His Majesty desiring to see he gave him copies,
having (as he said) sent the originals into
England. And this, he says is the whole scope of
the affair, and that his service was here first
approved when he sent over the letters and informed
of the industries used by him to reclaim the
Duchess from the liberty she took. And as to any
foul play between him and the Lady Sussex, he says
that at her coming to Paris the Duchess imparted to
him her condition, which was so bad in point of
disease that he found out both the chirurgeon and

the doctor that took her into cure, and she was so
sensible of his respects that she refused to take
part in the following war that her mother made
against him. And to prevent her mother's severity
hereupon she resolved to remove unto another
convent, unto which removal he gave his humble
assistance and that was all.

APPENDIX E

Montagu was ordered to appear before the Privy
Council to answer charges of possible treason. He
fled London to avoid appearance before the Council
and for his safety until the Parliament of February
1679 should meet and give him Parliamentary
protection to escape the hand of Danby. The
following is a letter from Elizabeth, Countess of
Northumberland, to the Secretary of State, William
Coventry, on Montagu's behalf written by the Lady
either in January or February 1678/79. (The letter
is not dated).

"Sunday morning

Sir
      your letter to Mr. Mountague being sent and
missing of him he being gone from the place before
it came. They sent it backe to me and I opening of
it and finding it to be an order from his Majst for
him to appeare, I thought it fitte to let you know
I did not know where he was or I would have sent it
after him, all the accounte I can give you of Mr.
Mountague is, that the last time I saw him he told
me that he did intend to goe into the country and
that he had noe thought of returning till the
Parlement meette, having been informed that my
Lord Treasurer lay in waite for his life which made
him being in towne very uneasie being always

obliged to goe abroade with a great many servants
Armed this is all the acount can be given you by,

Yr humble Servant
E. Northumberland"

Longleat MSS., Coventry Papers, Vol. II. ff. 153-
154.

APPENDIX F

Ralph Montagu's speech to the House of Commons
(December 15, 1680) calling for the banishment of
`papists' and for the securing of the calling of
frequent Parliaments as found in: A Collection of
the Parliamentary Debates in England from the Year
A.D. LXVIII, to the Present Time. I. 1668-1680.
(London: John Torbuck, 1741), I, 435-37.

    Sir, Great things are expected from this day's
debate; and we could not well have entered into it
sooner; it now comes more seasonable than it would
have done before, because of the opportunities we
have had to feel the pulse of affairs since the
beginning of the session; and the time we have
spent in asserting the right of petitioning, by
which the essence of Parliaments, and the
foundation of the people's liberties were struck
at. And the trial of my Lord Stafford, and the
disinheriting bill could not possibly have been
avoided. And as our labour hath not been lost in
all, so I hope that at last we shall have some
benefit of that spent about the succession-bill.
For as it was said at the passing of the bill, that
there were a loyal party that would never acquiesce
in it; so I do believe, there is a true protestant
party that will never acquiesce in any thing less,
than what may be sufficient for the security of
their religion; which, I am apt to believe, will
end in that bill. But in the meantime, that we may
shew that we are not humorists, let us try what
strength we can muster up to oppose these great
enemies by some other laws; as when a house is on
fire, we make use of buckets and tubs for casting
of water, until the great engines can be got. But
I would move you to be cautious what you do; for I
am afraid that the design of putting you upon

finding out expedients, is not in order to have any
thing done that may be effectual against popery;
but in order to have you offer at something that
may purchase a disrepute on the house, and give
your enemies an advantage to pursue their designs
of breaking us, by alledging that you aim at laws
that will overturn the government. For my part, I
am fully persuaded, that this is the design of
those that have put the King so often to declare
against altering the succession, and to recommend
other ways; and that offer at what you will, if it
be any thing that is like to prove strong enough to
secure us against popery, that you will see the
house put off before it comes to any perfection;
and that in time it will be made use of to arraign
the proceedings of Parliament, and to persuade the
people, that this house did attempt to alter the
government by such and such bills; and so by
degrees possess the people, that Parliaments are
either dangerous, or inconsistent with the
government, that, if possible, they may be well
content to be without them. Sir, I am afraid that
the popish party are more serious in this design
than we are aware of; and that, next to the great
endeavors they have used for many years to keep up
our divisions in points of religion; the next great
artifice which they depend on is, the infusing into
the people the dislike of Parliaments; for they
well know, that popery can never be established in
this nation, as long as Parliaments are permitted
to sit and act. Therefore, though I know it is
below a house of Commons to mind every little
discourse; yet I think, if we conclude, that this
powerful party, amongst their many designs, have
this for one, that we ought to countermine it as
much as we can. We cannot well comprehend what a
bill of association will be before it be drawn up,
nor what difficulties may be found in the
contriving of it; and therefore I think no great
debate will be necessary about it, before such a
bill be brought in. And I believe it will be found
more likely to be serviceable, in case the papists
be banished; and therefore I conceive, A bill for

<u>banishment</u> <u>of</u> <u>all</u> <u>the</u> <u>considerable</u> <u>papists</u> <u>out</u> <u>of</u>
England, may be very necessary: And if at the same
time that we endeavour to secure our selves against
popery, we do not also do something to prevent
arbitrary power, it will be to little purpose; for
the one will be sure to have a hand to bring in the
other; and I think nothing can prevent that, or
rather both, better than frequent Parliaments. And
therefore I humbly move you, that a <u>bill</u> <u>for</u>
<u>securing</u> <u>frequent</u> <u>Parliaments</u> may be taken into
your consideration.

APPENDIX G

The legal ruling concerning the dignity of the Countess of Northumberland resulting from her marrying Ralph Montagu, then not a peer; and of the Duchess of Albermarle marrying one of a lesser rank in the nobility: Ralph, Earl of Montagu.

The Dutchess of Albemarle being married to the Earl of Montague.

The question is whether she remains Dutchess notwithstanding her marriage, and whether this case differs from that of the Countess of Northumberland's marriage with the Lord Montagu before he was a peer.

We find it often said in our law books that a Dutchess marrying an Earl or any other Peer retains her name and dignity; not having lessen'd herself by marrying one who is noble, But the Countess of Northumberland marrying the Lord Montagu not then a Peer entirely lost her title, and can now only partake of her husband's honour, but cannot be rais'd to her former ranke.

Signed J. Sommers Attorney
Gent.
Theo Trevor Sol.
Gent.

Copy by the Earl of Karendon, son to the Chancellor

APPENDIX H

A description of the Office and duties of the
Master of the Great Wardrobe as found in: The Laws
of Honour: Or, a Compendious Account of the Ancient
Derivation of all Titles, Dignities,; Offices, &c.
As Well Spiritual as Temporal, Civil, or Military
(London: Printed for R. Gosling, 1714), pp. 426-27.

Of the Master of the Great Wardrobe.

Is an Office of gret Antiquity and Dignity
upon whom King Henry VI. confer'd many high
Privileges and Immunities, which were confirm'd by
his Successors, King James I. enlarg'd the same,
and ordain'd, That this great Office shou'd be an
Incorporation, or Body Politick for ever.

This office is to make Provision for
Coronations, Marriages, or Funerals of the Royal
Family; to furnish the Court with Beds, Hangings,
Clothes of Estate, Carpets, and other Necessaries;
likewise to furnish Ambassadors Houses at their
first arrival, Presents for Foreign Princes and
Ambassadors, Cloths of Estate, and other Furniture
for the Lord Lieutenant of Ireland, and all Her
Majesty's Ambassadors Abroad. To provide all Robes,
for Foreign Knights of the Garter, and Knights of
the Garter at Home, and all other Furniture for the
Officers of the Garter: Coats for Kings, Heralds,
and Pursuivants at Arms; Robes for the Lord
Treasurer, under Treasurer and Chancellor of the
Exchequer, &c. Livery the Lord Chamberlain, Grooms
of the Privy Chamber, Officers of the Robes, and
several other of the Household Servants: Rich
Liveries for the Two Lord Chief Justices, all the
Barons of Exchequer, and several other Officers in
those Courts; all Liveries for the King, (or

Queens) Servants, as the Yeomen of the Guard,
Warders of the Tower, Trumpeters, Kettle Drummers,
&c. the Messengers and all belonging to the
Stables, as Coachmen, Footmen, Littermen,
Postillions, Grooms &c. All Coaches, Chariots,
Harnesses, Saddles, Bitts, Bridles, &c. The King
(or Queens) Watermen, Gamekeepers, &c. All Linnen
and Laces for the Prince's Person, &c. Likewise
all rich Embroider'd Tilts, and other Furniture for
the Barges, Furniture for Royal Yatches when the
Soverign goes Aboard; Furniture for Courts on
Arraignment of Peers, with many other Services.

He has under him a Deputy, Clerk of the Ward-
robe, who with the Master of the Office, had
anciently their Dwelling-Houses in an House
Assign'd for them at Puddle-Wharf, but since the
Fire of London this Office has been kept in the
York-Buildings. Belonging to this Office are also
Two Clerks acting above Stairs; and to the Number
of about Sixty Trademen and Artifficers all Sworn
Servants to the Crown.

APPENDIX I

Ralph Montagu's (then Earl of Montagu) letter of
May 18th, 1694, to William III asking that a
Dukedom be conferred upon him for the numerous
services rendered to William in obtain the Crown of
England. (S.P. Domestic/8/15/ff,33-351 (No. 55);
State Papers, Dom. - 1694, p. 138; Dalrymple, II,
App. Bk. VI 256-58).

London, May the 18th, 1694

Sir,
       I did not think it very good manners to
trouble your Majesty in the middle of so great
affairs as you had at your going away, else I
should have made it my humble request that you
would have been so gracious as to have done my
family the same honour you have done to my Lord
Clare, Bedford, and others. This request had been
made to you by the old Duke of Schomberg, who
thought himself under some obligation to me for the
encouragement I gave him to attend you in your
expedition into England, but that I did not think
it reasonable to ask that being put over the Duke
of Shromsberge's head; but now, Sir, that you have
given him that rank which the greatness of his
family and personal merit has deserved, I may, by
your Majesty's grace and favour, pretend to the
same dignity as well as any of the families you
have promoted, being myself the head of a family
that many ages ago had great honours and dignities,
when I am sure these had none; and we have lost
them by the civil wars between York and Lancaster,
I am now below the two younger branches, my Lords
Manchester and Sandwich. I have to add to my
pretension the having married the Duke of
Newcastle's eldest daughter; and it has been the

practice of all your predecessors, whenever they
were so gracious to keep up the honour of a family
by the female line, to bestow it upon those who
married the eldest, without there were some
personal prejudice to the person who had that
claim. I may add, Sir, another pretension, which
is the fame for which you have given a Dukedom to
the Bedford family; the having been one of the
first, and held out till the last, in that cause
which, for the happiness of England, brought you to
the crown. I hope it will not be thought a less
merit to be alive and ready on all occasions to
venture all again for your service, than if I had
lost my head when my Lord Russel did. I could not
then have had the opportunity of doing the nation
the service I did, when there was such opposition
made by the Jacobite party, in bringing my Lord
Huntington, the bishop of Durham, and my Lord
Ashley, to vote against the Regency, and for your
having the crown; which was carried by those three
voices and my own. I should not put you in mind of
this, but hoping that so fortunate and so seasonable a service as this, may supply all my other
wants of merit; and which,since you were pleased to
promise me in your bed-chamber at St. James's,
before you were King, never to forget, you will not
now that are so great and so gracious a one. The
Duke of Shrewsbury can further satisfy you what
persecution I suffered, and what losses I sustained
in the two last reigns, which must make the mortif-
ication greater if his humble suit be refused to,
&c.

APPENDIX J

A description of the gardens and water works at
Boughton House, Northamptonshire, as described in
John Morton's The Natural History of Northamptonshire with Some Accounts of the Antiquities. To
Which is Annexed a Transcript of Doomsday-Book so
far as it relates to That County. (London: Printed
for R. Knoplock and R. Wilkin, 1712) pp. 491-92.

The Seat at Boughton is particularly
observable for its spacious, elegant, and
delightful Gardens, and for its sumptuous Water-
works. Below the Western Front of the House are
Three more remarkable Parterres: The Parterre of
Statues, the Parterre of Basins, and the Water
Parterre; wherein is an Octagon Basin whose Circum-
ference is 216 Yards, which in the middle of it has
a Jet d' Eau whose Height is above 50 Feet,
surrounded with other smaller Jets d'Eau. On the
North Side of the Parterre-Garden is a small
Wilderness which is call'd the Wilderness of
Apartments, an exceeding delightful Place, and
nobly adorn'd with Basins, Jets d'Eau, Statues,
with the Platanus, Lime-Tree, Beech, Bayes, &c. all
in exquisite Form and Order. To the Southward of
the lower part of the Parterre-Garden, is a larger
Wilderness of a different Figure, having Ten
equidistant Walks concentring in a round Area, and
adorn'd also with Statues. In one of the Quarters
is a fine Pheasantery. The larger Trees upon the
Sides of the Walks have Eglantine and Woodbind
climbing up and clasping about the Bodies of them.
The Canal at the Bottom of all, is about 1500 Yards
in length in Four Lines falling into each other at
Right Angles. At the lower end of it is a very
Nobel Cascade. The Walls, on each side of the
Cascade at the Head of the Basin that it falls
into, are adorn'd with Vases and Statues. The

Cascade has Five Falls. The Perpendicular about
Seven Feet. A Line or Range of Jets d'Eau in
number Thirteen, are placed at the Head of the
Cascade, and possess the Interval where the Water
enters upon its first Fall. These throw up their
Water, as that of the Canal descends: A very
agreeable and charming Entertainment both to the
Eye and Ear, and a lovely Refreshment to the
Standers-by, in a hot and sultry Air. There are
also several Jets d'Eau in the Basin underneath.
Also the Knot of regularly-figur'd Islets beset
with Aquatick Plants, There call'd the <u>Decoy</u>, is
extremely handsome and pleasant.

PLATE 1

A Plan of the Gardens at Boughton in Northampton Shire containing 110 Acres. One of the Seats of the most Noble John Duke of Montagu, Earl of Montagu, Vicount Mount Herman & Baron Montagu of Boughton Ld. Lieutenant of the County of Northampton and Custos Rotolorum & Ld. Lieutenant of the County of Warwick. Captain of Gentlemen Pensioners. Ld. Proprietor and Cap. General of the Isles of St. Vincent and St. Luce. Knight of the most noble Order of the Garter & Knight & Grand Master of the most noble order of Bath & F.R.S. (British Museum-Maps - K TOP XXXII 16.1)

This plate shows the Gardens of Boughton at the time of John, 2nd Duke of Montagu, Ralph's only surviving son, and dates from 1715. Ralph Montagu must have certainly laid out the original gardens upon which these are built.

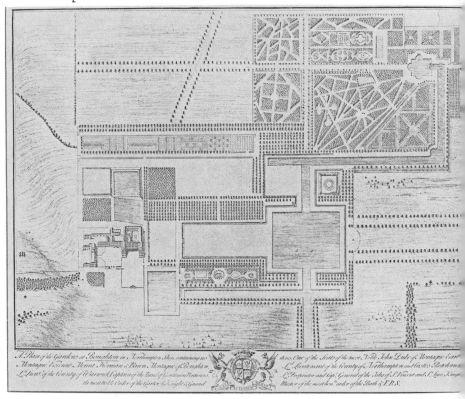

APPENDIX K

Two letters from St. Evremond to Monsieur Sylvestre
describing "the good life" of fine food and good
conversation to be enjoyed at Boughton House,
Northamptonshire family seat of the Montagus.
(John Hayward, ed. Letters of St. Evremond (London:
George Routledge and Sons, Ltd., 1930), pp. 354-
57).

[1700]
TO MONSIEUR SYLVESTRE
    Be satisfied, Sir, with your merit of
Inspector, and don't encroach upon mine. I leave
you your Architecture and Painting; but pray don't
disturb me upon the Geography of Good Eating.
However I must confess, that your Heath-Cocks, your
Oysters, your Salmon, your Fruits, and the rest of
that delicious abundance which you mention to me,
give you some right to insult me, and leave me no
relief, but in attributing all your advantages to
the direction and magnificence of my Lord. Let but
a thing please my Lord Montagu, and don't trouble
your head any further: whatever expense is to be
made; whatever care, whatever industry is to be
employed to have it, you will be sure not to go
without it. These are the very words of the late
Duchesse Mazarin, which are as good as Oracles, and
which were never more just than on this occasion.
I never desired any thing so earnestly as to go to
Boughton, to see my Lord, the good Company and
Learning in its full lustre, when Monsieur le
Vassor is there: I do not look upon my self as any
thing, because I don't understand Greek.

[1700-1701]
TO MONSIEUR SYLVESTRE
    If my new infirmities, or rather my old ones

which are very much grown upon me, had not hindered
me from going to Boughton, I should have been as
happy as a man almost a hundred years of age can
be. I lose a thousand pleasures which are all to
my taste. That of seeing the fine House, the fine
Water-Works, the fine Ducks, would have pleased me
extreamly, altho' I be but an indifferent
Inspector. But you will easily guess the greatest
of all, and that is being with my Lord Montagu, to
enjoy his conversation twice a day, before and
after the best cheer in the world. No Person ever
merited to be more magnificently receiv'd, and more
handsomly entertain'd, than my Lady Sandwich; no
man was ever more proper to receive and entertain
her well, than my Lord Montagu. I hope the Cascade,
the Octogon, the Water-Sheafs, and the Water-
Spouts, shall have made my Lady Sandwich forget
France. And as my Lord is very happy in inspiring
his taste and his designs as to Buildings and
Gardens, I don't question but she will soon
undertake some new work at Hinchinbrooke, which
will not be behind those of Boughton, in any
respect. It is impossible for any one to be more
sensible than I am of the honour of her
remembrance. There was nothing wanting to perfect
my grief, for not having seen Boughton and the
Master of the place, but my not having seen
Hinchinbrooke, and its Mistress, who is the
greatest ornament of all the places where she is.

If the poor Duchesse Mazarin, had yet been
alive, she would have had Peaches, of which she
would not have fail'd to give me a share; she would
have had Truffles, which I should have eat with
her; not to mention the Carps of Newhall. I must
make up the loss of so many advantages, by the
Sundays and Wednesdays of Montagu-House.

PLATE 2

GENEALOGY

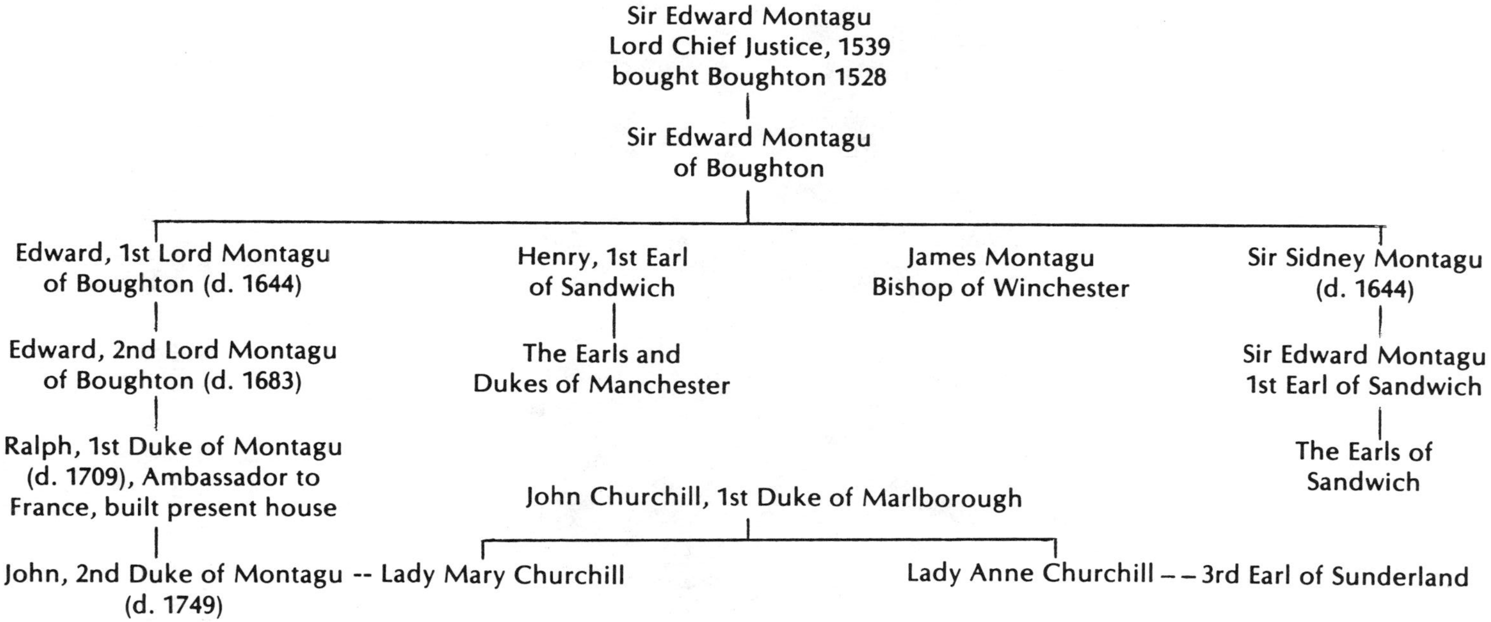

Sir Edward Montagu
Lord Chief Justice, 1539
bought Boughton 1528

Sir Edward Montagu
of Boughton

Henry, 1st Earl
of Sandwich

The Earls and
Dukes of Manchester

James Montagu
Bishop of Winchester

Sir Sidney Montagu
(d. 1644)

Sir Edward Montagu
1st Earl of Sandwich

The Earls of
Sandwich

Edward, 1st Lord Montagu
of Boughton (d. 1644)

Edward, 2nd Lord Montagu
of Boughton (d. 1683)

Ralph, 1st Duke of Montagu
(d. 1709), Ambassador to
France, built present house

John Churchill, 1st Duke of Marlborough

Lady Mary Churchill

Lady Anne Churchill -- 3rd Earl of Sunderland

John, 2nd Duke of Montagu -- Lady Mary Churchill
(d. 1749)

PLATE 3

Mountague House in Great Russel Street. Houlbourn.

A rear view of the magnificent structure of Mountague (Montagu) House (London) rebuilt out of the shell of the original (which was destroyed by fire in 1686) by Ralph, then Lord Montagu, Second Baron of Boughton, after the French design of the architect Puget. (British Museum Folder - 243).

PLATE 4

A front view of Mountague (Montagu) House (London)
including Courtyard, built to replace the original home destroyed by fire
in 1686. The house was designed and built in the French style by the French
architect Puget (British Museum Folder -243—.

BIBLIOGRAPHY

Primary Sources

I.   Manuscripts

Bodleian Library, Oxford University, Oxford,
Oxfordshire, England:

Bodl. MSS. Autographs. b.7 - warrant regarding
Great Wardrobe.

Bodl. MSS. English Miscellaenous. b.31 -
documents regarding Great Wardrobe.

Bodl. MSS. Locke. b.4 - Miscellaenous papers.

Bodl. MSS. Montagu. d.17 - Letters from
Richard Addison.

Bodl. MSS. Rawl. A. 255 - Instructions and
additional instructions to Ralph Montagu as
Ambassador Extraordinary to France, August-
September, 1676.

     Credentials of Ralph Montagu as
Ambassador Extraordinary - September, 1676.

     Credentials of Ralph Montagu as
Ambassador Extraordinary - France, February,
1668/9.

Bodl. MSS. Rawl. A. 268 - Recall of Montagu
from France as Ambassador Extraordinary, July,
1678.

Bodl. MSS. Rawl. C. 172 - Credentials of
Ralph Montagu as Ambassador Extraordinary to
France, February, 1668/9.

Revocation of Credentials of Ralph Montagu as Ambassador Extraordinary to France, March, 1672.

Bodl. MSS. Rawl. C. 421 - Miscellaenous Papers, 1601-1701.

Bodl. MSS. Rawl. D. 809 - Paper relating to London and Westminster.

Bodl. MSS. D. 204 - Letters of Sir J. Reresby to Osborne, 1674-78.

Bodl. MSS. D. 1070 - Two letters of Ralph Montagu (copies), 1678.

British Museum, London, England:

B.M. Add. Mss. 4201; 4205 - Letters to Lord Arlington, 1669-72, Copies (Montagu's embassy to Court of France).

B.M. Add. MSS 4060 - Letters to Sir Henry Sloane from R. Montagu.

B.M. Add. MSS. 5750 - Warrant addressed to Ralph Montagu, 1680.

B.M. Add. MSS. 5751; 5754 - Ralph Duke of Montagu, Master of the Great Wardrobe - receipts signed by him - 1678.

B.M. Add. MSS. 7121 - Letter to Lord Halifax from Ralph, Duke of Montagu, 26 April, 1706.

B.M. Add. MSS 10115 - A collection of papers relative to the projected war with France, formed by Sir Joseph Williamson, Secretary of State, and including some of his dispatches &c.

B.M. Add. MSS. 15,892 - Letters to the Earl of
Rochester, 1685.

B.M. Add. MSS. 21,505 - Royal Autographs.

B.M. Add. MSS. 23,894 - Letters to Lord
Arlington and others from R. Montagu, 1669-
1671.

B.M. Add. MSS. 25,119 - Instructions and
Official Letters to the Ambassadors at
Nimeguen.

B.M. Add. MSS. 25,124 - Extraordinary
Correspondence of Henry Coventry, Secretary of
State.

B.M. Add. MSS. 28,044 - Memorandum of Mr.
Baker concerning Mr. Montagu.

B.M. Add. MSS. 28,054 - Thomas, 1st Duke of
Leeds-Official Correspondence.

B.M. Add. MSS. 28,549 - Letters to Lord Hatton
from Ralph Montagu, 1688-89.

B.M. Add. MSS. 28,972 - Letters to Ch. Hedges,
1702 - Ellis Papers.

B.M. Add. MSS. 31,947; 31,948 - Letters to
Duke of Richmond from Ralph Montagu, 1670-71.

B.M. Add. MSS. 32,094 - State Papers and
Historical Documents.

B.M. Add. MSS. 32,094 - Instructions for Ralph
Montagu, Ambassador to France Feb. 22, 1699
(formerly Malet MSS.) - State Papers.

B.M. Add. MSS. 32,095 - Warrant for Ralph
Montagu's arrest, 1678.

B.M. Add. MSS. 32,680 - Correspondence from

Henry Sidney, Earl of Romney, 1674-1691.

B.M. Add. MSS. 32,476 - Letters and Papers, 1602 - (circa) 1711.

B.M. Add. MSS. 32,680; 32,681 - Letters to Col. H. Sydney from Ralph Montagu, 1678-81.

B.M. Add. MSS. 34,348 - Correspondence of Montagu, Ambassador Extraordinary to France.

B.M. Add. MSS. 36,116 - Suit of Ralph, Earl of Montagu against Lord Bath, 1698.

B.M. Add. MSS. 36,116 - Legal papers of Lord Somers.

B.M. Add. MSS. 36,913 - Earl of Montagu - Privy Council letters to Lord Rivers, 1696.

B.M. Add. MSS. 38,140 - Warrant to Ralph Montagu, 1680.

B.M. Add. MSS. 39,757 - Letters to Lord Danby, Charles II, Hon. C. Bertie from Ralph Montagu 1677-78 - Morrision Collection.

B.M. Add. MSS. 38,849 - Correspondence with Lord Danby - from Ralph Montagu, 1678.

B.M. Add. MSS. 38,849 - Two letters from Mr. Montagu to the Lord Treasurer: One of the 11th, the other of the 18th of Jan., 1678/9, Which were Read in the House of Commons Together with the Lord Treasurer's Speech in the House of Peers, upon an Impeachment of High Treason, &c. Brought Up Against His Lordship by the House of Commons, Dec. 23, 1678.

Some Reflections Upon the Earl of Danby, In Relation to the Murther of Sir Edmondury Godfrey. In a Letter to a Friend. 1679. (ff.

249-50).

An Examination of the Impartial State of
the Case of the Earl of Danby In a Letter to a
Member of the House of Commons. 1680. (ff.
262-80).

A Letter to a Friend in the Country.
Being a Vindication of the Parliaments Whole
Proceedings this Last Session with the State
of the Plot, and the Manner of Its Discovery.
(ff. 281-84).

An Account at Large of the Right
Honourable, The Earl of Danby's Arguments at
the Courts of the King's Bench at Westminster
Upon His Lordship's Motion for Bail, the 27th
Day of May, Term Pasch. 1682. Together with
the Judges Answers and the Earl's Replyes as
They Were Truly Taken. 1682. (ff. 383-97).

B.M. Add. MSS. 61,450; 61,451 - Marlborough
Collection, Letters of Duchess Marlborough to
Mary Montagu; Greenbook of Duchess of
Marlborough.

B.M. Egerton 3326 - Leeds Papers, Vol. III,
(Letters of Ralph Montagu).

B.M. Harley 1518 - State Papers Concerning the
Treaty of Nimeguen.

B.M. Sloane 4060 - Letters to Sir Hans Sloane,
vol. XXV.

B.M. Stowe 195 - Letters to Lord Arlington
1670 (copy)-State Papers.

Longleat House, Warminster, Wiltshire,
England:

Coventry Papers Vol. II, Appendix, III, XXXIII, XXXIV, XXXVI, LXXXVI, LXXXIII, LXXXVII, XCIII, Box One, Item 3 - Letters to and from Ralph Montagu and Henry Coventry, Secretary of State, 1671, pp. 676-78.

Portland Papers, Volume XXI - Letters from Ralph Montagu as Ambassador of France relating to the death of the Duchess Orleans, 1670.

Prior Papers Volumes XIII and VII - letters from Ralph Montagu to Lord Godolphin, 1708/9.

Thyne Papers, Volume LXXV, Box XXVIII - letters from Ralph Montagu as Ambassador to France to Lord Arlington, 1669-70.

Northamptonshire Record Office, Delapre Abbey, Northampton, Northamptonshire, England:

Buccleuch and Queensbury Manuscripts.

Montagu Family Papers:

Letters to the Montagu Family, Volume I - 1336-1741.

Letters to the Montagu Family, Volume III - 1560-1746 (Autographs).

Letters to the Montagu Family, Volume II - 1678-1735.

Letters to the Montagu Family, volume V - 1638-1689.

Letters to the Montagu Family, Volume III - 1560-1746 (Autographs).

Letters to Lord Montagu from Various Persons, Volume II - 1661-1699.

Book of Accounts: Boughton 1690--1889;
Barnwell, 1700-1889.

Accounts of Boughton Estate, 1690-1775,
1690-1709.

Old Box 18 - leases and rentals.

Old Box 27 - deeds.

Old Box 110 - debts.

Old Box 112 - mortgages and conveyances.

Old Box 114 - deeds and papers relating to the
affairs of Lady Harvey (Old Box M7).

- papers relating to Lady Anne Montagu
(Old Box M8).

- law papers of Lord and Lady
Hinchingbrook (Old Box 11).
Old Box 115 - Law Papers - Duke of Montagu vs.
Thornhill and others (Old Box M9, 10, 12, 13).

Box Nos. x8801, x8802, x8791, x8789, x8798-
Law Papers.

A 33 Montagu Papers found at Boughton House (b
2 52).

C 66 Misc. State Papers 1689-97, Vol. XXII-
Letters of Brown to Earl of Montagu.

C 67 Misc. State Papers 1685-1705, Vol. XXIII
- A Description of King Charles.

Public Record Office, Chancery Lane, London,
England:

P.R.O./Adm. 78/4 Admiralty Papers. Greenwich

Hospital News Letter, Nov. 27, 1690- Dec. 12, 1691.

P.R.O./Ind:/6819 Admiralty Index - Signet Office Documents.

P.R.O. Chancery Proceedings before 1714 - C 6/215/70 Elizabeth, Countess of Northumberland vs. ·Pierpoint, Wm., 1674.

P.R.O. Chancery Proceedings before 1714 - C 6/250/66 Elizabeth, Countess of Northumberland vs. Peterborough, Wm., 1684.

P.R.O. Chancery Proceedings before 1714 - C 6/228/2 R. Montagu and Elizabeth, Duchess of Albermarle vs. Earl of Bath.

P.R.O. Chancery Proceedings before 1714 - C 7/231/25. Ralph Montagu and Elizabeth, Duchess of Albemarle vs. Earl of Bath.

P.R.O. C8 586/13 - Bath and Creswell, 1698.

P.R.O. C8 456/19 - Creswell, 1698.

P.R.O. C8 603/8 Christopher Monck's estate vs. Cheney, Wm., 1702.

P.R.O. C10 Bundle 113/77 - Montagu vs. Brend, Dame Frances, 1673.

P.R.O. C10 Bundle 147/52 - Montagu suit over Bewley Manor, 1683.

P.R.O. C10 Bundle 282/46 - Montagu vs. Barney, John, 1691.

P.R.O. C10 Bundle 300/38 - Montagu vs. Cheynes, Wm. Lord, 1703.

P.R.O. C10 Bundle 303/47 - Montagu vs. Charges, Sir Thomas, 1706.

P.R.O. C10 Bundle 303/49 - Montagu vs. Charges, Dame Elizabeth, 1706.

P.R.O. C10 Bundle 303/46 - Montagu vs. Charges, Dame Elizabeth, 1707.

P.R.O. C10 Bundle 305/47 - Montagu vs. Bath, Wm. Henry, et. al., 1707.

P.R.O. C10 Bundle 307/52 - Montagu vs. Bath, Wm., Earl, et. al., 1708.

P.R.O. C10 Bundle 317/17 - Montagu vs. Harris, Francis, 1704.

P.R.O. C10 Bundle 377/25 - Montagu vs. Chenyes, Wm., Lord et al., 1706.

P.R.O. C10 Bundle 383/39 - Montagu vs. Montague, Edward, Richard Essex, et al., 1708.

P.R.O. C10 Bundle 390/36 - Montagu vs. Rolfe, Edward, et al., 1710.

P.R.O. C22 Bundle 546/14 - Montague vs. Bath - Wm. 3rd.

P.R.O. Indentures:

P.R.O. C 54/4351 (11) 1672.

P.R.O. C 54/4777 (17) Recognizances 1676 (Pt. 24).

P.R.O. C 54/4839 (18) Montagu, Comes Rudalphus et Bennet, Jr., et al., 1689.

P.R.O. C 54/4939 Montagu, Ralph, Earl, et Dummer, Tho., 1704.

P.R.O. C 54/4989 (16) - Montagu, Rudalphus et

Browley, Wm., et al., 1708.

Lord Chamberlain's Books:

P.R.O.- LC 5/185 - 1663-64.

P.R.O.- LC 5/186 - 1664-68 - Petitions.

P.R.O.- LC 5/187 - 1668-70 - Petitions.

P.R.O.- LC 5/188 - 1670-71 - Petitions.

P.R.O.- LC 5/189 - 1671-73 - Petitions.

P.R.O.- LC 5/190 - 1673-77 - Petitions.

P.R.O.- LC 5/191 - 1677-85 - Petitions.

P.R.O.- LC 5/192 - 1689-97 - Petitions.

P.R.O.- LC 5/194 - Anne to Geo. IV - Patents.

P.R.O.- LC 5/195 - 1685-88; 1695-97 - Orders to removing Wardrobe, orders to messengers.

P.R.O.- LC 5/196 - 1697 (Chas. II - Jas. II) Orders for lodgings, household regulations.

P.R.O.- LC 5/200 - 1625-84 - Precedent Books.

P.R.O.- LC 5/201 - 1660-87 - Precedent Books.

P.R.O.- LC 5/202 - 1697-1739 - Precedent Books.

P.R.O.- LS 13/197 - Lord Steward's Books.

P.R.O.- LS 13/252 - Lord Steward's Books.

P.R.O. Privy Council Registers:

P.R.O.   P.C. 2/63 - May 1671 - April 1673.

P.R.O.   P.C. 2/64 - April 1673 - Sept. 1675.

P.R.O.   P.C. 2/65 - Oct. 1675 - April 1677.

P.R.O.   P.C. 2/66 - May 1667 - Dec. 1678.

P.R.O.   P.C. 2/71 - Feb. 1685 - March 1687.

P.R.O.   P.C. 2/72 - April 1687 - Dec. 1688.

P.R.O.   P.C. 2/73 - Feb. 1688 - Aug. 1690.

P.R.O.   P.C. 2/74 - Sept. 1690 - Sept. 1692.

P.R.O.   P.C. 2/75 - Oct. 1692 - Aug. 1694.

P.R.O.   P.C. 2/76 - Dec. 1694 - April 1697.

P.R.O.   P.C. 2/77 - May 1697 - Dec. 1699.

P.R.O.   P.C. 2/78 - April 1700-1701.

P.R.O.   P.C. 2/79 - March 1701/2 - Jan. 1703/4.

P.R.O.   P.C. 2/80 - Jan. 1703/4 - Sept. 1705.

P.R.O.   P.C. 2/81 - March 1702 - Jan. 1704/5 (Anne).

P.R.O.   P.C. 2/82 - March 1708 - May 1710.

P.R.O. Signet Office Docket Books - 1660-1737 - Warrants.

P.R.O. Signet Office Letter Books - S.O. 1/9, 10, 13, 14.

P.R.O./S.P./8/1 - State Papers, Domestic - King William's Chest.

P.R.O./S.P./8/1/1pt. - State Papers, Domestic - King William's Chest.

P.R.O./S.P./8/2 - State Papers, Domestic - King William's Chest.

P.R.O./S.P./3 - State Papers, Domestic - King William's Chest.

P.R.O./S.P./7 - State Papers, Domestic - King William's Chest.

P.R.O./S.P./13 - State Papers, Domestic - King William's Chest.

P.R.O./S.P./14 - State Papers, Domestic - King William's Chest.

P.R.O./S.P./15 - State Papers, Domestic - King William's Chest.

P.R.O./S.P./257 - State Papers, Domestic - Charles II.

P.R.O./S.P./259 - State Papers, Domestic - Charles II.

P.R.O./S.P./29/291 - State Papers, Domestic - Charles II.

P.R.O./S.P./29/292 - State Papers, Domestic - Charles II.

P.R.O./S.P./29/294 - State Papers, Domestic - Charles II.

P.R.O./S.P./29/302 - State Papers, Domestic - Charles II.

P.R.O./S.P./29/303 - State Papers, Domestic - Charles II.

P.R.O./S.P./29/309 - State Papers, Domestic -
Charles II.

P.R.O./S.P./29/310- State   Papers, Domestic   -
Charles II.

P.R.O./S.P./29/335 - State Papers, Domestic -
Charles II.

P.R.O./S.P./29/338- State   Papers, Domestic   -
Charles II.

P.R.O./S.P./29/361 - State Papers, Domestic   -
Charles II.

P.R.O./S.P./29/366 - State Papers, Domestic -
Charles II.

P.R.O./S.P./29/376- State Papers, Domestic   -
Charles II.

P.R.O./S.P./29/417 - State Papers, Domestic -
Charles II.

P.R.O./S.P./30/Case G - State Papers, Domestic -
Charles II, Political Papers.

An Impartial State of the Case of the
Earl of Danby, In a Letter to a Member of the House
of Commons.   London: 1679.

An Explanation of the Lord Treasurer's
Letter to Mr. Montagu, The King's Late Ambassador
in France, March 25th 1678. Together with the said
Letter; and The Two Letters of Mr. Montagu, Which
were Read in the Commons.   London: 1679.

P.R.O./S.P./32/4 - State Papers, Domestic - William
and Mary.

P.R.O./S.P./32/6 - State Papers, Domestic - William
and Mary.

P.R.O./S.P./32/7 - State Papers, Domestic - William and Mary.

P.R.O./S.P./32/8 - State Papers, Domestic - William and Mary.

P.R.O./S.P./32/9 - State Papers, Domestic - William and Mary.

P.R.O./S.P./32/10 - State Papers, Domestic - William and Mary.

P.R.O./S.P./32/14 - State Papers, Domestic - William and Mary.

P.R.O./S.P./32/15 - State Papers, Domestic - William and Mary.

P.R.O./S.P./44/55 - State Papers, Domestic - Entry Book 55.

P.R.O./S.P./44/57 - State Papers, Domestic - Ecclesiastical Entry Book 75.

P.R.O./S.P./44/99 - State Papers, Domestic - Entry Book 99.

P.R.O./S.P./44/100 - State Papers, Domestic - Secretary's Letter Book 1694-1701 - Entry Book 100.

P.R.O./S.P./44/102 - State Papers, Domestic - H.D. Letter Book 1701-1702 - Entry Book 102.

P.R.O./S.P./44/275 - State Papers, Domestic - Whitehall Lords Justice Correspondence Entry Book 275.

P.R.O./S.P./44/341 - State Papers, Domestic - Warrant Book, 1690-93.

P.R.O./S.P./44/345 - State Papers, Domestic - Warrant Book, 1697-1702, Book 345.

P.R.O./S.P./44/347 - State Papers, Domestic - Entry Book 347.

P.R.O./S.P./44/348 - State Papers, Domestic - Duke of Shrewsbury, J. Vernon - State Papers Office, 1826.

P.R.O./S.P./63/334 - State Papers, Domestic - Elizabeth - George II Letters and Papers.

P.R.O./S.P./78/126 - State Papers, Foreign - France - 1669, Jan.-June.

P.R.O./S.P./78/127 - State Papers, Foreign - France - 1669, July-Oct.

P.R.O./S.P./78/128 - State Papers, Foreign - France - 1669, Nov.-Dec.

P.R.O./S.P./78/129 - State Papers, Foreign - France - 1670, Jan.-June.

P.R.O./S.P./78/130 - State Papers, Foreign - France - 1670 - July-Dec.

P.R.O./S.P./78/131 - State Papers, Foreign - France - 1671, Jan.-Aug.

P.R.O./S.P./78/132 - State Papers, Foreign - France - 1671, Sept.-Dec.

P.R.O./S.P./78/133 - State Papers, Foreign - France - 1672, Jan.-April.

P.R.O./S.P./78/135 - State Papers, Foreign - France - 1672, Sept.-Dec.

P.R.O./S.P./78/142 - State Papers, Foreign - France - 1677-78.

P.R.O./S.P./78/186 - State Papers, Foreign - France - 1678-80 - Secretary's Letter Book.

P.R.O./S.P./101/17 - State Papers, Foreign - News Letters, France.

P.R.O./S.P./101/18 - State Papers, Foreign - News Letters, France.

P.R.O./S.P./105/29 - State Papers, Foreign - France - Prior Papers.

P.R.O./S.P.104/176 - State Papers, Foreign - Entry Books, 1667, Nov.-1672, June.

P.R.O./S.P./104/179 - State Papers, Foreign - Entry Books, 1676, Jan.-1677, Nov.

P.R.O./S.P./104/180 - State Papers, Foreign - Entry Books, 1676, Aug.-1698, Aug.

P.R.O./S.P./104/185 - State Papers, Foreign - Misc. France, Secretary's Letter Book.

P.R.O./S.P./104/186 - State Papers,Foreign - Misc. France, Secretary's Letter Book.

P.R.O./C/219/51-54 - Parliament and Council records.

P.R.O./W./O./94/135-37 - Tower Prisoners.

P.R.O./Prob. 11/509 - Last Will and Testament of Ralph, 1st Duke of Montagu.

P.R.O./30/24/7/580 - The Institution of the 2nd forme att Westinster Schoole.

Baschet Transcripts - copies of correspondence of Ambassador Barrillon to Louis XIV. Originals are in Ministere des Affaires Estrangeres, Quai d'Orsay, Paris. 1678-1683.

P.R.O./31/3/138 - Vol. 127.

P.R.O./31/3/139 - Vol. 128.

P.R.O./31/3/140 - Vol. 130.

Baschet Transcripts of Ambassador's Correspondence from France to England - Henry VIII to George I - 1509-1714.

P.R.O./31/3/141 - Vol. 132.

P.R.O./31/3/142 - Vol. 133.

P.R.O./31/3/143 - Vol. 136.

P.R.O./31/3/144 - Vol. 138.

P.R.O./31/3/145 - Vol. 138.

P.R.O./31/3/146 - Vol. 139.

P.R.O./31/3/147 - Vol. 140.

P.R.O./31/3/148 - Vol. 142.

P.R.O./31/3/149 - Vol. 142.

P.R.O./31/3/150 - Vol. 143.

P.R.O./31/3/151 - Vol. 146.

P.R.O./31/3/152 - Vol. 147.

P.R.O./31/3/155 - Vol. 150.

Westminster Palace, Westminster, London, England:

House of Lords Manuscripts:

Appointments Books - 1690-1861 - names of Committee members, times and places of meetings.

Calendars of the Journals:
Set I 1510 - 1728 (5 vols.)
Set III 1510-1880 (5 vols.)

Committee for Petitions - 1660-95.

Committee of Privileges - 1661-1880, Peerage claims, proceedings in cases of claims.

Committee on the Popish Plot - 1678-81.

Committee Proceedings to 1837; Minutes of Proceedings at Committees on Private Bills and other Matters, 1661-1837.

House of Lords Record Office - House of Commons - Carol 2 Journal - Oct. 21-Dec. 30, 1678.

House of Lords Record Office - Journal.

Lord Braye's Draft Journals: The Journals, Minutes and Committee Books of the House of Lords.

Manuscript Minute Books - 1661-1827 - speeches in Council, opinions of Judges.

Minutes of Joint Committee "Concerning the Trial of the Lords in the Tower" - 1679-95.

Minutes of Proceedings - 1661-1913 - series of committee Books.

Protest Books - Lords' Protests: A Collection of All the Protestations Entered in the Journal of the House of Lords.

Orders and Judgments -
        No. 5 - Feb. 1676-Nov. 1678.
        No. 6 - Nov. - Dec. 1678.
        No. 7 - March 1678 - March 1681.

Speaker Bromley's Precedent Books - 1547-1731.

Witnesses, 1678, 1679, 1680.

Westminster School, London, England:

D 4 AE1 John Sargeannt - 1542-55. The
Headmaster Nowell, according to Strype - the
reading of Terence and the better learning in the
pure Roman style.

J. Box 4 c 9 - Extracts from Queen Elizabeth
statutes.

MSS. Dulwich. Coll. 2nd Series XXIX - Reg. of
Accounts 1680-1744/5 "The 3rd book" (under letter
W) - The Hor. of Westminister School.

Two letters to Mr. Keeley dated July 12, 1975
regarding the course of studies pursued at
Westminister School in its early days.

Yale University - Osborn Collection: Lachrymae
Musarum - London, 1649- poem of R. Montagu.

Yale University - Beinecke Collection: forty-eight
items - Popish Plot documents, letters and
impeachment of Lord Danby.

Ministere des Affaires Estrangeres, Quai d'Orsay,
Paris, France: Correspondence Politique:
Angleterre, - The correspondence of French
Ambassador Barrillon to Louis, to Courtin,
Pomponne, Croissy, Louvois.

II. Printed Manuscript Sources

Blanchare, Rae, ed. The Correspondence of
Richard Steele. London: Oxford University Press,
1941.

Cole, Christian, ed. Historical and Political
Memoirs, containing Letters written by Sovereign
Princes, from Almost all the Courts in Europe.
Beginning with Decrees, Resolutions,

Representations, Speeches, Answers, Instructions for Ambassadors, and the most important Transactions of each Nation in that Time. London: J. Milan, 1735.

Coxe, William. _Private and Original Correspondence of Charles Talbot, Duke of Shrewsbury, with King William, the leaders of the Whig Party, and other distinguished Statesmen: Illustrated with Narratives Historical and Biographical: from Family Papers in the possession of Her Grace the Duchess of Buccleuch never before published._ London: Hurst, Rees, Orme, and Brown, 1821.

Hardwicke, Philip Yorke, Second Earl of. _Miscellaenous State Papers From 1501 to 1726 in two volumes._ 2 vols. London: W. Strahan & T. Cadell, 1778.

Hodges, John C., ed., _William Congreve Letters & Documents._ New York: Harcourt, Brace & World, Inc., 1964.

Murray, George, ed. _The Letters and Dispatches of John Churchill, First Duke of Marlborough from 1702 to 1712._ 5 vols. London: John Murray, 1845.

Scott, J.F., ed. _The Correspondence of Isaac Newton._ 4 vols. Cambridge University Press for the Royal Society, 1960-1967.

Thompson, Edward Manunde, ed. _Correspondence of the Family Hatton being chiefly letters addressed to Christopher First Vicount Hatton A.D. 1601-1704._ 2 vols. Westminster: Nicholas and Sons, 1878 (Camden Society Publications, New Series 2, Vol. 23).

Williams, ed. _The correspondence of Jonathan Swift._ 5 vols. Oxford: Clarencon Press, 1963-1965.

III. Government Printed Manuscript Sources

Calendar of State Papers, Domestic Series, of the Reign of Charles II, 1660-1661, Green, Anne E., ed. Nendeln/Liechtenstein: Kraus Reprint Limited, 1968.

Calendar of State Papers, Domestic Series, of the Reign of Charles II, 1661-1662, Green, Anne E., ed. Nendeln/Liechtenstein: Kraus Reprint Limited, 1968.

Calendar of State Papers, Domestic Series, of the Reign of Charles II, 1663-1664, Green, Anne E., ed. Nendeln/Liechtenstein: Kraus Reprint Limited, 1968.

Calendar of State Papers, Domestic Series, of the Reign of Charles II, 1664-1665, Green, Anne E., ed., Nendeln/Liechtenstein: Kraus Reprint Limited, 1968.

Calendar of State Papers, Domestic Series, of the Reign of Charles II, 1665-1666, Green, Anne E., ed. Nendeln/Liechtenstein: Kraus Reprint Limited, 1968.

Calendar of State Papers, Domestic Series, of the Reign of Charles II, 1667-1668, Green, Anne E., ed. Nendeln/Liechtenstein: Kraus Reprint Limited, 1968.

Calendar of State Papers, Domestic Series, of the Reign of Charles II, 1668-1669, Green, Anne E., ed. Nendeln/Liechtenstein: Kraus Reprint Limited, 1968.

Calendar of State Papers, Domestic Series, of the Reign of Charles II, 1670, with Addenda - 1660 to 1670, Green, Anne E., ed. Nendeln/Liechtenstein: Kraus Reprint Limited, 1968.

Calendar of State Papers, Domestic Series, of the Reign of Charles II, December, 1671 to May, 1672, Daniell, F.H. Blackburne, ed. Nendeln/- Liechtenstein: Kraus Reprint Limited, 1968.

Calendar of State Papers, Domestic Series, of Charles II, May 18 to September 30, 1672, Daniell, F.H. Blackburne, ed. Nendeln/Liechtenstein: Kraus Reprint Limited, 1968.

Calendar of State Papers, Domestic Series, of the Reign of Charles II, October, 1672 to February, 1673, Daniell, F.H. Blackburne, ed. Nendeln/ Liechtenstein: Kraus Reprint Limited, 1968.

Calendar of State Papers, Domestic Series, of the Reign of Charles II, March 1st, to October 3rd, 1673, Daniell, F.H. Blackburne, ed. Nendeln/ Liechtenstein: Kraus Reprint Limited, 1968.

Calendar of State Papers, Domestic Series, of the Reign of Charles II, November 1st, to February 28th, 1675, Daniell, F.H. Blackburne, ed. Nandeln/ Liechtenstein: Kraus Reprint Limited, 1968.

Calendar of State Papers, Domestic Series, of the Reign of Charles II, March 1st, 1675, to February 29th, 1676, Daniell, F.H. Blackburne, ed. Nendeln/Liechtenstein: Kraus Reprint Limited, 1968.

Calendar of State Papers, Domestic Series, of the Reign of Charles II, March 1st, 1676, to February 28, 1677, Daniell, F.H. Blackburne, ed. Nendeln/Liechtenstein: Kraus Reprint Limited, 1968.

Calendar of State Papers, Domestic Series, of the Reign of Charles II, March 1st, 1677, to February 28th, 1678, Daniell, F.H. Blackburne, ed. Nendeln/Liechtenstein: Kraus Reprint Limited, 1968.

Calendar of State Papers, Domestic Series, of the Reign of Charles II, March 1st, 1678, to December 31st, 1678, Daniell, F.H. Blackburne, ed.

Nendeln/Liechtenstein: Kraus Reprint Limited, 1968.

Calendar of State Papers, Domestic Series, of the Reign of Charles II, January 1st, 1679, to August 31st, 1680, Daniell, F.H. Blackburne, ed. Nendeln/Liechtenstein: Kraus Reprint Limited, 1968.

Calendar of State Papers, Domestic Series, of the Reign of Charles II, September 1st, 1680, to December 31st, 1681, Daniell, F.H. Blackburne, ed. Nendeln/Liechtenstein: Kraus Reprint Limited, 1968.

Calendar of State Papers, Domestic Series, of the Reign of Charles II, January 1st,to December 31st, 1682, Daniell, F.H. Blackburne, ed. Nendeln/ Liechtenstein: Kraus Reprint Limited, 1968.

Calendar of State Papers, Domestic Series, of the Reign of Charles II, January 1st, to June 30th, 1683, Daniell, F.H. Blackburne, ed., Nendeln/ Liechtenstein: Kraus Reprint Limited, 1968.

Calendar of State Papers, Domestic Series, of the Reign of Charles II, July 1st, to September 30th, 1683, Daniell, F.H. Blackburne and Francis Bickley, eds. Nendeln/Liechtenstein: Kraus Reprint Limited, 1968.

Calendar of State Papers, Domestic Series, of the Reign of Charles II, October 1st, 1683 - April 31st, 1684, Daniell, F.H. Blackburne and Francis Bickley, eds. Nendeln/Liechtenstein: Kraus Reprint Limited, 1968.

Calendar of State Papers, Domestic Series, of the Reign of Charles II, May 1st, 1684 - February 5th, 1685, Daniell, F.H. Blackburne and Francis Bickley, eds. Nendeln/Liechtenstein: Kraus Reprint Limited, 1968.

Calendar of State Papers, Domestic Series, Addenda, Daniell, F.H. Blackburne and Francis Bickley, eds. Nendeln/Liechtenstein: Kraus Reprint

Limited, 1968.

Calendar of State Papers, Domestic Series, of the Reign of William and Mary, May, 1690-October 1691, Hardy, William John, ed. Nendeln/ Liechtenstein: Kraus Reprint Limited, 1968.

Calendar of State Papers, Domestic Series, of the Reign of William and Mary, 13th Feb., 1689- April, 1690, Hardy, William John, ed. Nendeln/ Liechtenstein: Kraus Reprint Limited, 1968.

Calendar of State Papers, Domestic Series, of the Reign of William and Mary, 1st November, 1691- End of 1692, Hardy, William John, ed. Nendeln/ Liechtenstein: Kraus Reprint Limited, 1969.

Calendar of State Papers, Domestic Series, of the Reign of William III, July 1 - December, 1965, and Addenda 1689-1695, Hardy, William John ed. Nendeln/Liechtenstein: Kraus Reprint Limited, 1969.

Calendar of State Papers, Domestic Series, of the Reign of William III, 1st January, - 31st December, 1696, Hardy, William John, ed., London: H.M. Stationery Office, 1913.

Calendar of State Papers, Domestic Series, of the Reign of William III, 1st January, - 31st December, 1697, Hardy, William John, ed. London: H.M. Stationery Office, 1927.

Calendar of State Papers, Domestic Series, of the Reign of William III, 1st January, - 31st December, 1698, Bateson, Edward, ed. London: H.M. Stationery Office, 1933.

Calendar of State Papers, Domestic Series, of the Reign of William III, 1st January, 1699-31st March, 1700, Bateson, Edward, ed. London: H.M. Stationery Office, 1935.

Calendar of State Papers, Domestic Series, of
the Reign of William III, 1st April, 1700 - 8th
March 1702, Bateson, Edward, ed. London: H.M.
Stationery Office, 1937.

Calendar of State Papers, Domestic series, of
the Reign of Anne, 1702-1703, Mahaffy, Robert
Pentland, ed. London: H.M. Stationery Office, 1916.

Calendar of State Papers, Domestic Series, of
the Reign of Anne, 1703-1704, Manhaffy, Robert
Pentland, ed. London: H.M. Stationery Office, 1924.

Calendar of State Papers and Manuscripts,
Relating to English Affairs existing in the
Archives and Collections of Venice, and in other
Libraries of Northern Italy, 1666-1668. Vol.XXXV.
Hinds, Allen B. ed. London: His Majesty's
Stationery Office, 1935.

Calendar of State Papers and Manuscripts,
Relating to English Affairs existing in the
Archives and Collections of Venice, and in other
Libraries in Northern Italy, 1669-1670. Vol.
XXXVI. Hinds, Allen B. ed. London: His Majesty's
Stationery Office, 1937.

Calendar of State Papers and Manuscripts,
Relating to English Affairs existing in the
Archives and Collections of Venice, and in other
Libraries of Northern Italy, 1671-72, Vol. XXXVII.
Hinds, Allen B., ed. London: His Majesty's
Stationery Office, 1939.

Calendar of Treasury Books, 1667-1668.
Preserved in the Public Record Office. Shaw,
William A., ed. London: H.M. Stationery Office,
1904.

Calendar of Treasury Books, 1667-1668.
Preserved in the Public Record Office. Shaw,
William A., ed. London: H.M. Stationery Office,
1905.

Calendar of Treasury Books, 1669-1672.
Preserved in the Public Record Office. Vol. III,
Part I. Shaw, William A., ed. London: H.M.
Stationery Office, 1908.

Calendar of Treasury Books, 1672-1675.
Preserved in the Public Record Office. Shaw,
William A., ed. London: H.M. Stationery Office,
1909.

Calendar of Treasury Books, 1676-1679.
Preserved in the Public Record Office. Vol. V.
Part I. Shaw, William A., ed. London: H.M.
Stationery Office, 1911.

Calendar of Treasury Books, 1679-80.
Preserved in the Public Record Office. Vol. VI.
Shaw, William A., ed. London: H.M. Stationery
Office, 1913.

Calendar of Treasury Books, 1681-1685.
Preserved in the Public Record Office. Vol. VII.
Part I. Shaw, William A., ed London: H.M.
Stationery Office, 1916.

Calendar of Treasury Books, 1685-1689.
Preserved in the Public Record Office. Vol. VIII.
Part I. Shaw, William A., ed. London: H.M.
Stationery Office, 1923.

Calendar of Treasury Books, 1685-1689.
Preserved in the Public Record Office. Vol. III,
Part II. Shaw, William A., ed. London: H.M.
Stationery Office, 1923.

Calendar of Treasury Books, 1689-1692.
Preserved in the Public Record Office. Vol. IX.
Part I. Shaw, William A., ed. London: H.M.
Stationery Office, 1931.

Calendar of Treasury Books, 1689-1692.
Preserved in the Public Record Office. Vol. IX.
Part II. Shaw, William A., ed. London: H.M.

Stationery Office, 1931.

Calendar of Treasury Books, Preserved in the Public Record Office. Introduction to Vols. XI-XVII Covering the Years 1695-1702. Shaw, William A., ed. London: H.M. Stationery Office, 1934.

Calendar of Treasury Books, April-September, 1697. Preserved in the Public Record Office. Vol. XII. Shaw, William A., ed. London: H.M. Stationery Office, 1933.

Calendar of Treasury Books, October, 1697 to August, 1698. Preserved in the Public Record Office. Vol. XIII. Shaw, William A., ed. London: H.M. Stationery Office, 1933.

Calendar of Treasury Books, September, 1698 to 31 July, 1699. Preserved in the Public Record Office. Vol. XIV. Shaw, William A., ed. London: H.M Stationery Office, 1934.

Calendar of Treasury Books, August, 1699 to September, 1700. Preserved in the Public Record Office. Vol. XV. Shaw, William A., ed. London: H.M. Stationery Office, 1933.

Calendar of Treasury Books, 1 October, 1700 to 31 December, 1701. Preserved in the Public Record Office. Vol. XVI. Shaw, William A., ed. London: H.M. Stationery Office, 1938.

Calendar of Treasury Books, 1702. Preserved in the Public Record Office. Vol. XVII. Part I. Shaw, William A., ed. London: H.M. Stationery Office, 1939.

Calendar of Treasury Books, 1703. Preserved in the Public Record Office. Vol. XVIII. Shaw, William A., ed. London: H.M. Stationery Office, 1936.

Calendar of Treasury Books, January, 1704 to

March, 1705. Preserved in the Public Record
Office. Vol. XIX. Shaw, William A., ed. London:
H.M. Stationery Office, 1938.

Calendar of Treasury Books, April, 1705 to
September, 1706. Preserved in the Public Record
Office with Introductory Matters and Accounts for
the Year 1706. Vol. XX. Part I. Introduction.
Shaw, William A., ed. London: H.M. Stationery
Office, 1952.

Calendar of Treasury Books, October, 1706 to
December, 1707. Preserved in the Public Record
Office with Introductory Matters and Accounts for
the Year 1706. Vol. XXI. Part I, Introduction,
Etc. Shaw, William A., ed. London: H.M. Stationery
Office, 1952.

Calendar of Treasury Books 1708. Preserved in
the Public Record Office. Vol. XXII. Part I.
Introduction. Etc. Shaw, William A., ed. London:
H.M. Stationery Office, 1952.

Calendar of Treasury Books 1709. Preserved in
the Public Record Office. Vol. XXIII. Part I.
Introduction. Shaw, William A., ed. London: H.M.
Stationery Office, 1952.

Calendar of Treasury Books Jan-Dec. 1710.
Preserved in the Public Record Office. Vol. XXIV.
Part I. Introduction. Shaw, 1952.

Great Britain. Historical Manuscripts Commission:

_____. Calendar of the Manuscripts
of the Marquis of Bath Preserved at Longleat,
Wiltshire. Presented to both Houses of Parliament
by Command of His Majesty. Vol. II. Dublin: John
Falconer, 1907.

_____. Calendar of the Manuscripts
of the Marquess of Ormonde, K.P. Preserved at

Kilkenny Castle. Presented to Parliament by Command of His Majesty. n.s. Vol. IV. London: Ben Johnson & Co., 1906.

_____. Calendar of the Manuscripts of the Marquess of Ormonde, K.P. Preserved at Kilkenny Castle. Presented to Parliament by Command of His Majesty. n.s. Vol. VI. London: Published by His Majesty's Stationery Office, 1911.

_____. Calendar of the Manuscripts of the Marquess of Ormonde, K.P. Preserved at Kilkenny Castle. Presented to Parliament by Command of His Majesty. n.s. Vol. VIII. London: Published by His Majesty's Stationery Office, 1920.

_____. Eighteenth Report of the Royal Commission on Historical Manuscripts. Presented to Parliament by Command of His Majesty. London: Published by His Majesty's Stationery Office, 1917.

_____. Eighth Report of the Royal Commission on Historical Manuscripts. Presented to both Houses of Parliament by Command of Her Majesty. Pt. I. London: Geo. E. Eyre and Wm. Spottiswoode, 1881.

_____. Eleventh Report. Appendix, Part VII. The Manuscripts of the Duke of Leeds, the Bridgewater Trust, Reading Corporation, the Inner Temple, &c. Presented to both Houses of Parliament by Command of Her Majesty. London: Geo. E. Eyre and Wm. Spottiswoode, 1888.

_____. Fifteenth Report, Appendix, Part VII. The Manuscripts of the Duke of Somerset, the Marquis of Ailesbury, and the Rev. Sir. T.H.G. Puleston, Bart. Presented to both Houses of Parliament by Command of Her Majesty. London: Eyre and Spottiswoode, 1898.

_____. Fifteenth Report, Appendix,
Part II. The Manuscripts of J. Eliot Hodgkin,
Esq., F.S.A. of Richmond, Surrey. Presented to
both Houses of Parliament by Command of Her
Majesty. London: Eyre and Spottiswoode, 1897.

_____. Fifteenth Report of the
Royal Commission on Historical Manuscripts.
Presented to both Houses of Parliament by Command
of Her Majesty. Norwich: The "Norfold Chronicle"
Company, Ltd., 1898.

_____. Fifth Report of the Royal
Commission on Historical Manuscripts. Presented to
both Houses of Parliament by Command of Her
Majesty. Pt. I. London: Geo. E. Eyre and Wm.
Spottiswoode, 1876.

_____. First Report of the Royal
Commission on Historical Manuscripts. Presented to
both Houses of Parliament by Command of Her
Majesty. London: Geo. E. Eyre and Wm.
spottiswoode, 1870.

_____. Fourteenth Report, Appendix,
Part IV. The Manuscripts of Lord Kenyon.
Presented to both Houses of Parliament by Command
of Her Majesty. London: Eyre and Spottiswoode,
1894.

_____. Fourteenth Report, Appendix,
Part IX. The Manuscripts of the Earl of
Buckinghamshire, the Earl of Lindsey, the Earl of
Onslow, Lord Emly, Theodore J. Hare, Esq. and James
Round, Esq., M.P. Presented to both Houses of
Parliament by Command of Her Majesty.. London:
Eyre and Spottiswoode, 1895.

_____. Fourteenth Report, Appendix,
Part VI. The Manuscripts of the House of Lords,
1592-1693. Presented to both Houses of Parliament
by Command of Her Majesty. London: Eyre and
Spottiswoode, 1894.

_____. Fourth Report of the Royal
Commission on Historical Manuscripts. Presented to
both Houses of Parliament by Command of Her
Majesty. Pt. I. London: Geo. E. Eyre and Wm.
Spottiswoode, 1874.

_____. The Manuscripts of the House
of Lords, 1702-1704, In Continuation of the Volumes
issued under the authority of the Historical
Manuscripts Commission. n.s. 5. London: Eyre and
Spottiswoode, 1910.

_____. The Manuscripts of the House
of Lords, 1704-1708, In Continuation of the
Volumes issued under the authority of the
Historical Manuscripts Commission. n.s. 6.
London: Eyre and Spottiswoode, 1921.

_____. The Manuscripts of the House
of Lords, 1695-1697, In Continuation of the Volumes
issued under the authority of the Historical
Manuscripts Commission. n.s. 2. London: Eyre and
Spottiswoode, 1903.

_____. The Manuscripts of the House
of Lords In Continuation of the Volumes issued
under the authority of the Historical Manuscripts
Commission. n.s.3. London: Eyre and Spottiswoode,
1905.

_____. The Manuscripts of the House
of Lords, 1699-1702, With an Appendix, the Journal
of the Protectorate House of Lords, from the
original Manuscripts in the possession of Lady
Tangye, In Continuation of the Volumes issued under
the authority of the Historical Commission..
n.s.4. London: Eyre and Spottiswoode, 1908.

_____. Report on Manuscripts in
Various Collections. The Manuscripts of Sir George
Wombwell, the Duke of Norfolk, Lord Edmund Talbot,
Miss Buxton, Mrs. Harford and Mrs. Wentworth of
Woolley. Presented to Parliament by Command of His

Majesty. London: Mackie & Co., 1903.

_____ . Report on the Manuscripts of His Grace the Duke of Portland, K.G. preserved at Welbeck Abbey. Vol. VI. Presented to both Houses of Parliament by Command of His Majesty. London: Mackie & Co., Ltd., 1901.

_____ . Report on the Manuscripts of the Duke of Buccleuch and Queensberry, K.G., K.T., Preserved at Montagu House, Whitehall. Presented to Parliament by Command of Her Majesty. Vol. I. London: Eyre and Spottiswoode, 1899..

_____ . Report on the Manuscripts of the Duke of Buccleuch & Queensbury, K.G., K.T., preserved at Montagu House, Whitehall. Presented to Parliament by Command of Her Majesty. Vol. II, Pt. 1. London: Mackie & Co., 1908.

_____ . Report on the Manuscripts of the Earl of Egmont. Presented to Parliament by Command of His Majesty. Vol. II. Dublin: John Falconer, 1909.

_____ . Report on the Manuscripts of the Late Allan George Finch, Esq., of Burley-On-The-Hill, Rutland. Vol. II. London: Published by His Majesty's Stationery Office, 1922.

_____ . Report on the Manuscripts of the Late Allan George Finch, Esq., of Burley-On-The-Hill, Rutland. A.D. 1692. Vol. IV. Francis Bickley, ed. London: Her Majesty's Stationery Office, 1965.

_____ . Report on the Manuscripts of the Late Reginald Rawdon Hastings, Esq., on the Manor House, Ashby-De-La-Zouche. Vol. II. Francis Bickley, ed. London: Published by His Majesty's Stationery Office, 1930.

_____. Report on the Manuscripts of
Lord Montagu of Beaulieu. Presented to Parliament
by Command of Her Majesty. London: Mackie & Co.,
1900.

_____. Report on the Manuscripts of
the Marquess of Downshire. Preserved at
Easthampstead Park, Berks. Papers of Sir William
Trumbull. Vol. I. Pt. 1. London: Published by
His Majesty's Stationery Office, 1924.

_____. Report on the Manuscripts of
Mrs. Frankland-Russell-Ashley, of Chequers Court,
Bucks. Presented to both Houses of Parliament by
Command of Her Majesty. London: Mackie & Co.,
1900.

_____. Report on the Manuscripts of
the Right Honourable Viscount de L'Isle, V.C.
preserved at Penhurst Place, Kent. Sidney Papers,
1626-1698. Vol. VI. G. Dyfnallt Owen, ed.
London: Her Majesty's Stationery Office, 1868.

_____. Seventh Report of the Royal
Commission on Historical Manuscripts. Presented to
both Houses of Parliament by Command of Her
Majesty. Pt. I. London: Geo. E. Eyre and Wm.
Spottiswoode, 1879.

_____. Sixteenth Report of the
Royal Commission on Historical Manuscripts.
Presented to Parliament by Command of His Majesty.
London: Ben Johnson & Co., 1904.

_____. Sixth Report of the Royal
Commission on Historical Manuscripts. Presented to
both Houses of Parliament by Command of Her
Majesty. Pt. I. London: Geo. E. Eyre and Wm.
Spottiswoode, 1877.

_____. Supplementary Report on the
Manuscripts of the Late Montagu Bertie, Twelfth

Earl of Lindsey, formerly preserved at Uffington
House, Stamford, Lincolnshire A.D. 1660-1702.
C.G.O. Bridgeman and J.C. Walker, eds. London: His
Majesty's Stationery Office, 1942.

_____. Tenth Report, Appendix, Part
IV. The Manuscripts of the Earl of Westmorland,
Captain Stewart, Lord Stafford, Lord Muncaster, and
Others. Presented to both Houses of Parliament by
Command of Her Majesty. London: Eyre and
Spottiswoode, 1885.

_____. Third Report of the Royal
Commission on Historical Manuscripts. Presented to
both Houses of Parliament by Command of Her royal
Majesty. London: Geo. E. Eyre and Wm.
Spottiswoode, 1872.

_____. Thirteenth Report, Appendix,
Part VI. The Manuscripts of Sir William
Fitzherbert, Bart., and Others. Presented to both
Houses of Parliament by Command of Her Majesty.
London: Eyre and Spottiswoode, 1893.

_____. Twelfth Report, Appendix,
Part IX. The Manuscripts of the Duke of Beaufort,
K.G., the Earl of Donoughmore, and Others.
Presented to both Houses of Parliament by Command
of Her Majesty. London: Eyre and Spottiswoode,
1891.

Journal of the House of Commons. Vols. IX-XVIII.
Printed by Order of the House of Commons.

Journal of the House of Lords. Vols. XIV-XX.

The Statutes of the Realm, printed by command
of His Majesty King George the Third in pursuance
of an address of the House of Commons of Great
Britain from Original Records and Authentic
Manuscripts. 9 vols. and Index. London: Record
Commission, 1810-1828.

IV.   Contemporary Newspapers.

Dawk's News-Letter.   London: twice weekly, 1688-1709.

The English Poet.   London: twice weekly, 1688-1709.

The London Gazette.   London: twice weekly, 1666-1709.

The Lover.   London: Feb.-May, 1714.

V.   Primary Printed sources - Books.

An Account of the Principal Officers, Civil and Military, of England in the Year 1697.   London: Abel Roper, 1697. (A broadsheet).

    Barker, G.F. Russell, Memoir of Richard Busby, D.D. (1605-95) with Some Account of the Westminster School in the Seventeenth Century.   London: Lawrence and Bullen, 1895.

    Barker, G.F., Alan H. Stemming. Records of Old Westminster. A Biographical List of all Those Who are Known to Have been Educated At Westminster School from Earliest Time to 1927.   2 vols. London: Cheswick Press, 1928.

    Bebington, Tho.   The Rt. Honourable the Earl of Arlington's Letters to Sir W. Temple, Bar. from July 1665.   London: Printed by W.N., 1701.

    Blencowe, R.W.   ed., Diary of the Times of Charles the Second by the Honourable Henry Sideny (Afterwards Earl of Romney) Including His Correspondence with the Countess of Sunderland and Other Distinguished Persons at the English Court to Which Are Added Letters Illustrative of the Times of James II. and William III.   2 vols. London: Henry Colburn, 1843.

Bohn's Extra Volume. Count Grammont's Memoirs of the Court of Charles the Second and the Boscobel Narratives Probably published in London: Henry Bohn, 1846.

Boyer, Abel. The History of the Reign of Queen Anne Digested into Annals. 10 vols. London: Printed for T. Ward, 1710.

_____. The History of Queen Anne. London: T. Woodward, 1735.

Browning, Andrew. Memoirs of Sir John Reresby. The Complete Text and a Selection from His Letters. Glasgow: Jackson & Son, & Co., 1936.

_____. Thomas Osborne, Earl of Danby and Duke of Leeds. 3 vols. Glasgow: Jackson & Son, and Co., 1951.

Budd, F.E., ed. The Dramatic Works of William Burnaby. London: Eric Partridge, 1931.

Burnet, Gilbert. History of His Own Time. 4 vols. London: A. Millar, 1753.

_____. Bishop Burnet's History of His Own Time: With Notes By the Earls of Dartmouth and Hardwicke, Speaker Onslow, and Dean Swift to Which are Added Other Annotations. 6 vols. 2nd ed. Oxford: University Press, 1883.

Cartwright, James J., ed. The Memoirs of Sir John Reresby by Thrybergh Bart., M.P. for York, & c. 1634-1689; Written by Himself. London: Longmans, Green, and Co., 1875.

Chamberlayne, Edward. Angliae Notitia: Or the Present State of England: Together With Divers Reflections Upon the Ancient State thereof. London: (Savoy) Printed by T.N. for John Martyn, 1669.

_____. Angliae Notitia: Or The
Present State of England, The First Part. Together
with Divers Reflections Upon the Ancient State
thereof. London: (Savoy) Printed by T.N. for J.
Martyn, 1679.

_____. Angliae Notitia: Or The
Present State of England, With Divers Remarks Upon
the Ancient State thereof. In Three Parts.
London: Printed by T. Hodgkin for R. Chiswell, et
al., 1700.

_____. Angliae Notitia: Or The
Present State of England, With Divers Remarks Upon
the Ancient State thereof. In Three Parts.
London: Printed by T.H. for S. Smith, et al., 1702.

_____. Angliae Notitia: Or The
Present State of England, With Divers Remarks Upon
the Ancient State thereof. In Three Parts.
London: Printed by T.H. for S. Smith, et al., 1704.

_____. Angliae Notitia: Or The
Present State of England, With Divers Remarks Upon
the Ancient State thereof. In Three Parts.
London: Printed for S. Smith, et al., 1707.

Christie, William D., ed. Letters Addressed
From London to Sir Joseph Williamson While
Plenipotentiary At the Congress of Cologne in the
Years 1673 and 1674. 2 vols. Westminster: The
Camden Society, 1874.

Clark, Andrew. The Life and Times of Anthony
Wood, Antiquary, of Oxford, 1632-1695, described by
Himself. 3 vols. Oxford: Clarendon Press, 1892.

Cobbert, W. Parliamentary History of England
from the Norman Conquest in 1066 to the Year 1803.
36 vols. London: R. Bagshaw, 1809.

Cockayne, George Edward, Alexander Fry, eds.
Calendar of Marriage Licenses Issued by the Faculty

Office - 1632-1714. 33 vols. London: British
Record Society, Ltd., 1905.

Cockayne, George Edward. The Complete
Peerage. Revised eds., eds. H.A. Doubleday and
Lord Howard de Walden. 13 vols. London: St.
Catherine Press, 1936.

A Collection of the Parliamentary Debates in
England from the Year 1668, to the Present Time.
21 vols. Dublin and London: John Torbuck, 1741.

The Court in Mourning. Being the Life and
Worthy Actions of Ralph, Duke of Mountague, Master
of the Great Wardrobe to Queen Anne, Who Dyed at
his House in Russell-street in Bloomsbury, on
Wednesday the 9th of March 1708/9. Containing His
Travels Abroad, his Marriages, Children and other
Actions at Home: With his Death, Sickness and
Character. Licensed according to order. London:
Printed for J. Smith in Cornhill, 1709.

Crawford, James L. A Bibliography of Royal
Proclamations of the Tudor and Stuart Sovereigns
and of Others Published Under Authority 1485-1714
with an Historical Essay on Their Origin and Use.
4 vols. in 3. New York: Burt Franklin, 1967.

Dalrymple, John. Memoirs of Great Britain and
Ireland from the Dissolution of the Last Parliament
of Charles II till the Capture of the French and
Spanish Fleets in Vigo. 3 vols. London: A.
Strahan and T. Cadell, 1790.

Danby, Earl of. Copies and Extracts of Some
Letters Written to and from the Earl of Danby (Now
Duke of Leeds) in the Years 1676, 1677, and 1678.
With particular Remarks Upon some of them. London:
Published by his Grace's Direction, 1710.

_____. Memoirs Relating to the
Impeachment of Thomas, Earl of Danby (Now Duke of

Leeds) in the Year 1678. Wherein Some Affairs of those Times are Represented in a Juster Light than has hitherto appear'd. London: Printed for John Morpher, 1710.

Davis, Herbert, ed. Jonathan Swift: Miscellaneous and Autobiographical Pieces, Fragments and Marginalia. 14 vols. Oxford: Basil Blackwell, 1969.

De Beer, E.S., ed. The Diary of John Evelyn: Kalendarium 1673-1689. 5 vols., Oxford: Clarencon Press, 1955.

de Fonblanque, Edward Barrington. Annals of the House of Percy: From the Conquest to the Opening of the Nineteenth Century. 2 vols. London: Richard Clay and Sons, 1887.

Dixon, Thomas, ed. Reports of Cases in Law and Equity from 1670 to 1706. With Tables of the Names of the Cases and Principal Matters by the Honourable Richard Freeman, Esq. Late Lord Chancellor of Ireland. London: Thomas Dixon, 1742.

_____. The Dramatic Works of Colley Cibber, Esq. in Five Volumes London: Printed for J. Rivington and Sons, et al., 1777.

Duckett, Sir George. Penal Laws and Test Acts. Questions Touching Their Repeal Propounded in 1687-8 by James II. London: Printed for Subscribers only, 1883.

Durant-Cooper, William. Savile Correspondence. Letters To and From Henry Savile, Esq. Envoy at Paris, and Vice Chamberlain to Charles II. and James II. Including Letters From His Brother, George Marquess of Halifax. Printed for the Camden Society, 1858.

An Exact Collection of the Debates of the House of Commons Held at Westminster. 12 vols. London: Printed for R. Baldwin, 1689.

Ellis, George Agar. The Ellis Correspondence: Letters Written During the Years 1686, 1687, 1689 and Addressed to John Ellis, Esq. 2 vols. London: Henry Colburn, 1829.

Farresley, Thomas. Modern Cases Argued and Adjudged in the Court of King's Bench at Westminster in the Reign of Her Late Majesty Queen Anne in the Time When Sir John Holt Sat Chief-Justice There. London: J. Nutt, 1716.

Foxcroft, H.C. The Life and Letters of Sir George Savile, Bart. First Marquis of Halifax &c. 2 vols. London: Longmans, Green and Co., 1898.

Granger, J. A Biographical History of England from Egbert the Great to the Revolution. 7 vols. London: W. Nicholson, 1804.

Grey, Amchitell. Debates of the House of Commons: From the the Year 1617 to the Year 1694. 10 vols. London: T. Becket & P.A. De Hondt, 1769.

Grey, Lord Ford. The Secret History of the Rye House Plot: And of Monmouth's Rebellion. London: Printed for Andrew Millar, 1754.

Hayward, John, ed. Letters of St. Evremond. London: George Routledge and Sons, Ltd., 1930.

_____. The History and Proceedings of the House of Lords, From the Restoration in 1660, To The Present Time. 7 vols. London: Printed for Ebenezer Timberland, 1742.

_____. The History of England During the Reigns of K. William, Q. Anne, and K. George I. With An Introductory Review of the Reigns of the Royal Brothers, Charles and James; In Which Are To

Be Found the Seeds of the Revolution. London: Printed by Daniel Browne, 1744.

_____ The History of England, During the Reigns of the Royal House of Stuart, Wherein the Errors of Late Histories are Discover'd and Corrected: With Proper Reflections, and Several Original Letters from King Charles II. James II. Oliver Cromwell, & c. As also The Lord Saville's Famous Forg'd Letter of Invitation, brought the Scots into England in the Year 1640, and gave Occasion to the Beginning of the Civil Wars. London: Printed for John Pemberton, et al., 1730.

_____ Inventaire Sommaire Des Archives Du Department Des Affaires Estrangeres - Correspondence Politique. 2 vols. Paris: Impririe Nationale, 1903.

James, C.P.R., ed. Letters Illustrative of the Reign of William III, From 1696 to 1708. Addressed to the Duke of Shrewsbury, By James Vernon, Esq. Secretary of State. 3 vols. London: Henry Colburn, 1841.

Jusserand, J.J., ed. Receuil Des Instructions Donnes Aux Ambassadeurs Revolution Francaise: Angleterre. 2 vols. Paris: Anciennes Maisons Thorin et Fontemoing, 1929.

Kenyon, John Phillip. Robert Spencer, Earl of Sunderland, 1641-1702. London: Longmans, Green and Co., 1958.

Kerr, Russell J., Ida Coffin Duncan, eds. The Portledge Papers being extracts from the letters of Richard Lapthorne, Gent., of Hatton Garden London to Richard Coffin Esq. of Portledge, Bideford, Devon from December 10th 1678 - August 7th 1679. London: Jonathan Cape, 1928.

_____ The Laws of Honour: Or, A
Compendious Account Of the Ancient Derivation of
All Titles, Dignitaries, Offices, &c. As Well As
Spiritual, Temporal, Civil, or Military. London:
Printed for R. Gosling, 1714.

    Lee, Matthew Henry, ed. Diaries and Letters
of Philip Henry. London: Kegan Paul, 1882.

_____ Letters of Lady Rachel Russell
from the Manuscripts in the Library of Woburn
Abbey. London: J. McCreery, 1809.

    Longe, Julia G. Martha Lady Giffard: Her
Life and Correspondence (1664-1722), A Sequel to
the Letters of Dorothy Osborne. London: George
Allen and Sons, 1911.

    Lough, John,   ed. Locke's Travels in France,
1675-1679.   As related in his Journals,
Correspondence and Other Papers. Cambridge:
University Press, 1953.

    Luttrell, Narcissus. A Brief Historical
Relation of the State of Affairs from September,
1678 to April 1714. 6 vols. Oxford: University
Press, 1857.

    MacCaulay, Thomas Babington. The History of
England from the Accession of James the Second. 6
vols. London: Macmillan and Co., 1915.

    Mackey, John. Memoirs of the Secret Service
of John Mackey, Esq., During the Reigns of King
William, Queen Anne and King George I. London:
1732.

    Macpherson, James. Original Papers:
containing the secret history of Great Britain,
from the restoration to the accession of the House
of Hanover. To which are prefixed extracts from
the life of James II, as written by himself. The
whole arranged and published by James Macpherson,

esq. 2 vols. London: W. Strahan and T. Cadell, 1775.

Maitland, F.W., ed. The Constitutional History of England by A.L. Fisher. Cambridge: University Press, 1968.

Mignet, M. Negociations Relatives A La Succession D'Espagne Sous Louis XIV. 4 vols. Paris: Imprimerie royale, 1842.

Montagu, William Drogo. Court and Society from Elizabeth to Anne: Edited from the Papers at Kimbolton by the Duke of Manchester. 2 vols. London: Hurst and Blacket, 1864.

Morton, John. The Natural History of Hamptonshire With Some Accounts of the Antiquities. To which is Annexed A Transcript of Doomsday Book so far as it related to That County. London: Printed for R. Knoplock and R. Wilkin, 1712.

Murray, George, ed. The Letters and Dispatches of John Churchill First Duke of Marlborough from 1702-1712. London: John Murray, 1845.

_____ A New View of London: Or, An ample Account of that City, In Two Volumes, or Eight Sections. 2 vols. London: Printed for R. Chiswell, et al., 1708.

Oldmixon, John. The History of England during the Reigns of the Royal House of Stuart. London: Printed for John Pemberton, et al., 1730.

Powney, Richard. The State Letters of Henry Earl of Clarendon Lord Lieutenant of Ireland During the Reign of K. James the Second And His Lordship's Diary For The Years 1687, 1688, 1689, and 1690. 2 vols. Oxford: Clarendon Press, 1765.

Petitor, A. et Mommerque. Collection Des Memoires Relative A L'Histoire De France Depuis L'Avenement De Henri IV Jusqu'a La Paix De Paris Conclue En 1763. 73 vols. Paris: Foucault Librarie, 1828.

Quennell. Peter, trans. Memoirs of the Court of Charles II by Count de Gramont. London: George Routledge and Sons, Ltd., 1910.

_____. Memoirs of the Comte de Gramont by Anthony Hamilton. New York: E.P. Dutton and Company, 1930.

Reid, Stuart Johnson. John and Sarah: Duke and Duchess of Marlborough - 1660-1744. Based Upon Unpublished Letters and Documents at Blenheim Palace. London: John Murray, 1914.

_____ Returns of Members of Parliament. 2 vols. London: Henry Hansard and Son, 1878.

Robin, Henry W., Walter Adams, etc. The Diary of Robert Hooke. London: Wykeham Publications, Ltd., 1968.

Roger, James E. Thorold. A complete Collection of the Protests of the Lords. 3 vols. Oxford: Clarendon Press, 1885.

Sainty, J. Christopher. Divisions in the House of Lords. An Analytical List - 1686-1875. London: Her Majesty's Stationery Office, 1976.

Salmon, Mr. The Chronological Historian: Containing a Regular Account of all Material Transactions and Occurrences Ecclesiastical, Civil, and Military Relating to the English Affairs from the Invasion of the Romans to the Fourteenth Year of King George II. 2 vols., 2nd ed., London: Printed for T. Ware, et al., 1747.

Salzman, L.F., ed. The Victoria History of the County of Northampton. 4 vols. London: Oxford University Press, 1937.

Scott, A.F. Every One A Witness: The Stuart Age. New York: Thomas Y. Crowell Company, 1974.

Shelmerdine, J.M., trans. The Secret History of Henrietta, Princess of England, First Wife of Phillipe, Duc d'Orleans by Madame de La Fayette. London: George Routledge, 1929.

Singer, Samuel Weller. The Correspondence of Henry Hyde, Earl of Clarendon and of His Brother, Laurence Earl of Rochester: With The Diary of Lord Clarendon From 1678 to 1690, Containing Minute Particulars of The Events Attending the Revolution: And The Diary of Lord Rochester During His Embassy To Poland in 1676. 2 vols. London: Henry Colburn, 1828.

Snyder, Henry L., ed. The Marlborough-Godolphin Correspondence. 2 vols. Oxford: Clarendon Press, 1975.

Stanhope, Philip Henry. History of England comprising the Reign of Queen Anne until the Peace of Utrecht, 1701-1713. London: John Murray, 1870.

Strype, John. Survey of the Cities of London and Westminster: Containing the Original, Antiquity, Increase, Modern Estate and Government of Those cities. 2 vols. London: Printed for A. Churchill, et al., 1720.

Summers, Montague, ed. The Complete Works of William Congreve. 4 vols. New York: Russell and Russell, Inc. 1964.

Sutton, H. Manners, ed. The Lexington Papers, Or some Account of the Courts of London and Vienna: At the Conclusion of the Seventeenth Century. London: John Murray, 1851.

Temple, William. Letters Written by Sir
William Temple, Bar. and Other Ministers of State,
Both Home and Abroad. Containing an Account of the
Most Important Transactions that pass'd in
Christendom from 1665-1672. London: Printed for J.
Round, et al., 1731.

_____. Memoirs of What Past in
Christendom from the War, Begun 1672 to the Peace
Concluded 1679. London: Roc. Shifwell, 1700.

_____. The Third Part of the
Present State of England. London: Printed for R.M.
by Y. Passinger, 1683.

Thomson, A.T. Memoirs of Sarah, Duchess of
Marlborough, and of the Court of Queen Anne. 2
vols. London: H. Colburn, 1839.

Tindal, N., trans. The History of England
Written in French by Mr. Rapin de Thoyras. 2 vols.
London: Printed for James, John, and Paul Knapton,
1751.

_____. A True Copy of the
Journal-Book of the Last Parliament, Begun at
Westminister the sixth day of March 1678/79.
London: 1680.

Turnbull, H.W. The Correspondence of Isaac
Newton. 7 vols. Cambridge: University Press, 1960.

Turner, Edward Raymond, Gaudence Megaro. The
Cabinet Council of England in the Seventeenth and
Eighteenth Centuries 1622-1784. 2 vols.
Baltimore: Johns Hopkins Press, 1932.

Walford, Edward. Old and New London: A
Narrative of Its History, Its People and Its
Places. 6 vols. London: Cassell Petter and
Galpin, n.d.

Welch, Joseph, ed. List of Scholars of St.

Peter's College, Westminster As They Were Elected
to Christ Church, Oxford and Trinity College,
Cambridge from the Foundation of Queen Elizabeth
MDLXI to the Present Time. London: J. Nichols,
1788.

Westergaard, Waldemar. The First Triple
Alliance: The Letters of Christopher Lindenov,
Danish Envoy to London 1668-1672. New Haven: Yale
University Press, 1947.

Whalley, Peter, Rev. The History and
Antiquities of Northamptonshire Compiled from the
Manuscripts of the Late and Learned Antiquary John
Bridges, Esq. 2 vols. Oxford: Sold by T. Payne,
1791.

Wheatley, Henry B., ed. The Diary of John Evelyn,
Esq. F.R.S. To Which Are Added A Selection From His
Familiar Letters and The Private Correspondence
Between King Charles I. and Sir Edward Nicholas and
Between Sir Edward Hyde (Afterwards Earl of
Clarendon) and Sir Richard Browne. 4 vols.
London: Bickers and Son, 1906.

_____. The Diary of Samuel
Pepys. 8 vols. London: George Bell and Sons,
1905.

_____. London, Past and
Present. Its History, Associations and Traditions.
London: John Murray, 1891.

Williams, William, Speaker, Votes of the
House of Commons: The Debates in the House of
Commons Assembled at Oxford 21 March 1680. London:
John Bill, et al., 1680.

VI. Secondary Sources - Books

Airy, Osmund, ed. Burnet's History of My Own
Time: Part I - The Reign of Charles II. 2 vols.

Oxford: Clarendon Press, 1897.

Aitken, George A. The Life of Richard Steele. 2 vols. New York: Haskell House Publishers, 1968.

Ashley, Maurice. Charles II. Frogmore: Panther Books, 1971.

Baxter, Stephen B. William III and the Defense of European Liberty, 1650-1702. 1st Am. ed. New York: Harcourt, Brace and World, 1966.

Bevan, Bryan. Charles the Second's French Mistress: A Biography of Louise De Keroualle, Duchess of Portsmouth, 1649-1734. London: Robert Hale, 1972.

Blazer, Phyllis Gene. "The Life of Sir Thomas Chaloner: Tudor Soldier, Courtier, Poet and Diplomat - 1521-1565." Diss. State University of New York at Buffalo, 1978.

Borer, Mary Cathcart. The City of London - A History. New York: David McKay Company, Inc., 1977.

Brett, A.C.A. Charles II and His Court. New York: G.P. Putnam's Sons, 1910.

Brooks, Eric St. John. Sir Hans Sloane. London: The Batchworth Press, 1954.

Bryant, Arthur. The England of Charles II. London: Longmans, Green and Co., 1935.

Campbell, Kathleen. Sarah: Duchess of Marlborough. London: Thornton Butterworth Ltd., 1932.

Carlisle, Nicholas. A Concise Description of the Endowed Grammar Schools in England and Wales. 2 vols. London: Baldwin, Cradock and Joy, 1818.

Carleton, John J. Westminster School, A History. London: Rupert Hart Davis, 1965.

Cartwright, Julia. Madame: A Life of Henrietta, Daughter of Charles I. And Duchess of Orleans. New York: E.P. Dutton and Co., 1901.

Cargill, Marjorie. The Story of the British Museum. London: British Museum Publications Limited, 1981.

Chapman, Hester. Great Villiers: A Study of George Villiers, Second Duke of Buckingham - 1628-87. London: Secker and Warburg, 1949.

Churchill, Winston S. Marlborough: His Life and His Times. 4 vols. London: George G. Harrap & Co. Ltd., 1933.

Clinch, George. English Costume - From Prehistoric Times to the End of the 18th Century. East Ardsley: EP Publishing Limited, 1975.

Coate, Mary. Social Life in Stuart England. 2nd ed. London: Methuen and Co. Ltd., 1924.

Coleman, Donald C. The Economy of England, 1450-1750. Oxford: Oxford University Press, 1977.

Cook, J. Mordaunt. The British Museum: A Case-Study in Architectural Politics. Hammondsworth: Penquin Books, Ltd., 1972.

Cope, Esther S. The Life of a Public Man - Edward, First Baron Montagu of Boughton, 1562-1644. Philadelphia: The American Philosophical society, 1981.

Courtney, Thomas Peregrine. Memoirs of the Life, Works, and Correspondence of Sir William Temple, Bart. 2 vols. London: Longman, Rees, Orme, Brow, Green, and Longman, 1836.

Crawford, G.M., trans. Louise De Keroualle, Duchess of Portsmouth, 1649-1734 or, How the Duke of Richmond Gained His Pension, Compiled From State Papers in the Archives of the French Foreign Office by H. Forneron. New York: Schribner and Welford, 1888.

Davis, Eliza Jefferies. The University Site, Bloomsbury. Vol. XVII of London Topographical Record. London: 1939.

Dutton, Ralph. English Court Life - From Henry VII to George II. London: B.T. Batsford Ltd., 1963.

Elsworth, Joseph Woodfall, ed. The Bagford Ballads: Illustrating the Last Years of the Stuarts. 8 vols. Hertford: Printed for the Ballad Society by Stephen Austin and Sons, 1878.

_____. The Rorburghe Ballads. 8 vols. Hertford: Printed for the Ballad Society by Stephen Austin and Sons, 1881.

Falk, Bernard. The Way of the Montagues. London: Hutchinson and Co., Ltd., 1947.

Feiling, Keith. British Foreign Policy 1669-1672. London: Macmillan and Co., Ltd., 1930.

Firth, C.H., S.C. Loomis. Notes on the Diplomatic Relations of England and France - 1603-1688. Oxford: B.H. Blackwell, 1906.

Foss, Michael. The Age of Patronage: The Arts in Society (1660-1750). London: Hamish Hamilton, 1971.

Foxcroft, H.D., ed.. A Life of Gilbert Burnet, Bishop of Salisbury. Cambridge: University Press, 1907.

_____. A Supplement to
Burnet's History of My Own Time. Oxford: Clarendon
Press, 1902.

_____. Some Unpublished
Letters of Gilbert Burnet, The Historian. London:
Royal Historical Society, 1907.

Francis, Alan David. The Wine Trade. London:
Adam & Charles Black, 1972.

Fraser, Antonia. Royal Charles - Charles II
and the Restoration. New York: Alfred A. Knopf,
1979.

Fraser, Peter. The Intelligence of the
Secretaries of State and Their Monopoly of Licensed
News - 1660-88. Cambridge: University Press, 1956.

Girouard, Mark. Life in the English Country
House: A Social and Architectural History. New
Haven: Yale University Press, 1978.

Gotch, J. Alfred. The Old Halls and Manor
Houses of Northamptonshire - An Illustrated Review.
London: B.T. Batsford, Ltd., 1936.

Graham, James. The Letters of Joseph Addison.
Oxford: Clarendon Press, 1941.

Gregg, Edward. Queen Anne. London: Routledge
& Kegan Paul, 1980.

Grego, Joseph. A History of Parliamentary
Elections and Electioneering from the Stuarts to
Queen Victoria. Piccadilly: Chatto and Windus,
1892.

_____. Guide to an Exhibition
of Tapestries, Carpets and Furniture Lent by the
Earl of Dalkeith (March to May 1914). London:
Victoria and Albert Museum Publications (no. 95),
1914.

Haley, K.H.D. The First Earl of Shaftesbury. Oxford: Clarendon Press, 1968.

Hartmann, Cyril Hughes. Charles II and Madame. London: William Heinemann Ltd., 1934.

_____. The King My Brother. London: William Heinemann Ltd., 1954.

Harris, William. An Historical and Critical Account of the Lives and Writings of James I. and Charles I. and of the Lives of Oliver Cromwell and Charles II. After the Manner of Mr. Boyle from Original and State Papers. 5 vols. London: Printed for F.C. and J. Rivington, et al., 1814.

Hatton, Edward. A New View of London, or an Ample Account of That City. 2 vols. London: R. Chipwell, J. Churchill, etc., 1708.

Hatton, Ragnhild, ed. Louis XIV and Europe. London: the Macmillan Press Ltd., 1976.

Henderson, T.F., ed. The History of England from the Accession of James the Second by Lord Macaulay. London: George Routledge and Sons, Ltd., 1907.

Heltzel, Virgil, ed. The Complete Gentleman, The Truth of Our Times and The Art of Living in London by Henry Peacham. Ithaca: Cornell University Press, 1962.

Higson, C.W.J., ed. Supplement to the Sources for the History of Education. London: The Library Association, 1976.

Hill, Christopher. The World Turned Upside Down; Radical Ideas During the English Revolution. Hammondsworth: Penguin Books, Ltd., 1972.

Holdworth, W.S. A History of English Law. 17 vols. London: Methuen and Co., 1924.

Horn, D.B. The British Diplomatic Service, 1689-1789 Oxford: The Clarendon Press, 1961.

Horwitz, Henry. Parliament, policy and politics in the reign of William III. Manchester: Manchester University Press, 1977.

_____. Revolution Politiks: The Career of Daniel Finch, Second Earl of Nottingham - 1647-1730. Cambridge: University Press, 1968.

Ireson, Tony. Northamptoshire. London: Robert Hale and Company, 1974.

Jack, Sybil M. Trade and Industry in Tudor and Stuart England. London: George Allen and Unwin, Ltd., 1977.

Jenkis, Frank. Architect and Patron - A Survey of Professional Relations and Practice in England from the Sixteenth Century to the Present Day. London: Oxford University Press, 1961.

Jones, James R. Britain and Europe in the Seventeenth Century. New York: W.W. Norton and Co., Inc., 1966.

_____. Country and Court: England 1658-1714. Vol V of The New History of England. London: Edward Arnold, 1978.

_____. The First Whigs: the Politics of the Exclusion Crisis 1678-83. London: Oxford University Press, 1961.

Kenyon, J.P. The Stuart Constitution, 1603-1688. Cambridge: Cambridge University Press, 1966.

_____. The Stuarts: A Study in Kingship. London: Fontana/Collins, 1958.

_____. Stuart England. Vol.
V I   of   The   Pelican   History   of   England.
Hammondsworth: Penguin Books, Ltd., 1978.

Lacks, Phyllis. "The Diplomatic Corps Under
Charles II and James II." Diss. Bryn Mawr Univ.,
1963.

Leahigh, James F. "Diplomatic Relations
Between Charles II and Louis XIV - 1668-78." Diss.
Georgetown Univ.. 1934.

Lee, Maurice. The Cabal. Urbana: University
of Illinois Press, 1965.

Linsday, Ann trans. The Life and Times of the
Duchess of Portsmouth by Jeanine Delpech. London:
Elek Books, 1953.

Lindgard, John. The History of England from
the First Invasion of the Romans to the Accession
of William and Mary in 1688. 10 vols. London:
Charles Dolman, 1855.

Lockyer, Roger. Tudor & Stuart Britain -
1471-1714. London: Longman, 1964.

Love, Harold. Congreve. Oxford: Basil
Blackwell, 1974.

Mackay, Angie Ethel. La Fontaine and his
friends - A Biography. London: Garnstone Press,
1972.

Maland, David. Culture and Society in
Seventeenth-Century France. London: B.T. Batsford
Ltd., 1970.

Masters, Brian. The Mistresses of Charles II.
London: Blond & Briggs, 1979.

McConica, James Kelsey. English Humanists and
Reformation Politics Under Henry VIII and Edward

VI. Oxford: Clarendon Press, 1965.

Melville, Lewis. Nell Gwyn: The Story of Her Life. New York: George H. Doran Company, 1924.

_____. The Windsor Beauties. Boston: Houghton Mifflin Co., 1928.

Mengel, Elias F., ed. Poems on Affairs of State: Augustan Satirical Verse - 1660-1714. 7 vols. New Haven: Yale University Press, 1965.

Montagu, Edward (Lord Montagu of Beaulieu). More Equal Than Others: The Changing Fortunes of the British and European Aristocracies. London: Michael Joseph Ltd., 1970.

Newton, The Lady (Evelyn Leah). Lyme Letters. London: William Heinemann Ltd., 1925.

Nichols, John Gough. The Topographer and the Genealogist. 3 vols. London: John Bowyer Nichols and Sons, 1858.

O'Connell, N.J. "Charles Montagu, Earl of Halifax, A Biography." Diss. University of Georgia, 1971.

Ogg, David. England in the Reign of Charles II. 2 vols. London: Oxford University Press, 1963.

Oman, Carola. Henrietta Maria. London, Sydney and Toronto: White Lion Publishers Limited, 1936.

Peel, J.H.B. An Englishman's Home. London: David & Charles, 1972.

Petherick, Maurice. Restoration Rogues. London: Hollis and Carter, 1951.

Pettit, Philip A.J. The Royal Forests of Northamptonshire. A Study in Their Economy - 1558-1714. Gateshead: Northumberland Press, 1968.

Pinchbeck, Ivy, Margaret Hewitt. Children in English Society: Volume I - From Tudor Times to the Eighteenth Century. 2 vols. London: Routledge and Kegan Paul, 1969.

Plumb, J.H. The Originals of Political Stability, England, 1675-1725. Boston: Houghton Mifflin Company, 1967.

Pollock, Sir John. The Popish Plot. A Study in the History of the Reign of Charles II. London: Duckworth and Co., 1903.

Reynolds, Ernest. Northamptonshire Treasures: A Personal Selection. Emberton: Ruth Bean, 1972.

Ronalds, Francis Spring. The Attempted Whig Revolution of 1678-81. Urbana: University of Illinois, Press 1937.

Ronalds, Harris Philip. The Reading Room. Nottingham: Oxley Press, 1979.

Schorske, Carl E. Fin-De-Siecle: Vienna - Politics and Culture. New York: Alfred A. Knopf, 1980.

Sergeant, Philip. My Lady Castlemaine: Being a Life of Barbara Villiers, Countess of Castlemaine, afterwards the Duchess of Cleveland. London: Hutchinson and Co., 1912.

Simms, V.H. "Organization of the Whig Party During the Exclusion Crisis (1678-1681)." Diss. London University, 1934.

Steane, John. The Northamptonshire Landscape: Northamptonshire and the Soke of Peterborough. London: Hodden and Stoghton, 1974.

Stillwell, Sir George. _The First Whig: An Account of the Parliamentary Career of Wm. Sacheverell; The Origin of the Great Political Parties and the Events Which Led Up to the Revolution of 1688._ Scarborough: Printed by the author at his private press, 1894.

Stone, Lawrence. _The Crisis of the Aristocracy, 1558-1641._ Oxford: Clarendon Press, 1965.

_____. _Family and Fortune: Studies in Aristocratic Finance in the Sixteenth and Seventeenth Centuries._ Oxford: Clarendon Press, 1973.

_____. _The Family, Sex, and Marriage in England 1500-1800._ Harmondsworth: Penguin Books Ltd., 1977.

_____. ed. _Schooling and Society - Studies in the History of Education._ Baltimore: The John Hopkins University Press, 1976.

Stuart, Dorothy Margaret. _The Boy Through The Ages._ London: George G. Harrap, 1926.

Thomas, F.S. _Historical Notes - 1603-1714._ 2 vols. London: Geo. Edward Eyre and Wm. Spottiswoode, 1856.

Thompson, Gladys Scott. _The Russells in Bloomsbury - 1669-1771._ London: Jonathan Cape, 1940.

Thompson, Roger. _Women in Stuart England and America: A Comparative Study._ London: Routledge & Kegan Paul, 1974.

Thompson, Wm. _The History of Tapestry from Earliest Times to the Present Day._ London: Hodder and Slaughter, 1906.

Timbs, John. Curiosities of London: Exhibiting The Most Rare and Remarkable Objects of Interest in the Metropolis. London: Virtue and Co., Ltd., 1876.

Trevelyan, George Maculay. English Social History - A Survey of Six Centuries from Chaucer to Queen Victoria. London: Longman Group Limited, 1978.

Trevor-Roper, Hugh. Princes and Artists: Patronage and Ideology at Four Hapsburg Courts, 1517-1633. New York: Harper & Row, Publishers, 1976.

von Ranke, Leopold. A History of England. 6 vols. Oxford: Clarendon Press, 1875.

Ward, A.W., A.R. Waller, eds. The Cambridge History of Literature - Volume II: The Age of Dryden. Cambridge: University Press, 1912.

Ward, Estelle Frances. Christopher Monck: Duke of Albemarle. London: John Murray, 1915.

Webb, Peter Gorham. Portrait of Northamptonshire. London: Robert Hale, 1977.

Wedgwood, C.V. Seventeenth-Century English Literature. London: Oxford University Press, 1970.

Williams, Neville. The Royal Residences of Great Britain - A Social History. New York: The Macmillan Company, 1960.

Wilson, Charles. England's Apprenticeship - 1603-1763. London: Longman, 1965.

Wilson, John Harold, ed. Six Restoration Plays. Boston: Houghton Mifflin Company, 1969.

Wise, C. The Montagus of Boughton and Their Northamptonshire Houses. Kettering: W.E. and J. Gross, 1888.

VII. Pamphlets

Boughton House. Northamptonshire home of the Dukes of Buccleuch and Queensbury (Montagu Douglas Scott). St. Ives: Huntington: Photo Precision Limited.

Boughton House State Rooms and High Pavilion. Kettering: Dalkeith Press Ltd.

VIII. Secondary Sources - Articles

Adair, E.R. "The Privy Council Registers." English Historical Review. 30 (Oct. 1975), 698-704.

Airy, Osmund. "Bennet, Henry, Earl of Arlington (1618-1685)." Dictionary of National Biography, 1, 230-233.

Ashley, Maurice. "Ordinary People in Stuart England." History Today, 14 (March 1964), 192-201.

Barbour, Violet. "Consular Service in the Reign of Charles II." The American Historical Review, 33 (Oct. 1927 - July 1928), 533-578.

Barker, George Fisher R. "Montagu, Charles, Earl of Halifax, 1661-1715." Dictionary of National Biography, 13, 665-670.

Barnes, A.S. "Religion of Charles II in Relation to the Politics of His Reign." Dublin Review, 142 (Jan. 1908), 44-63.

Bevan, B. "Henriette, Duchess of Orleans." Contemporary Review, 185 (Feb. 1954), 107-111.

Clay, Christopher. "Property Settlements, Financial Provision for the Family, and Sale of Land by the Greater Landowners, 1660-1790." Journal of British Studies, 21 (Fall 1981), 18-38.

Cooper, Thompson. "Montagu, Walter (1603-1677)." Dictionary of National Biography, 13, 717-19.

Cornforth, John. "Boughton House, Northamptonshire - I." Country Life, 148 (Sept. 3, 1970), No. 3828, 564-568.

_____. "Boughton House, Northamptonshire - II." Country Life, 148 (Sept. 10, 1970), No. 3829, 624-628.

_____. "Boughton House, Northamptonshire - III." Country Life, 148 (Sept. 17, 1970), No. 3830, 684-687.

_____. "Boughton House, Northamptonshire - IV." Country Life, 149 (Feb. 25, 1971), No. 3846, 420-423.

_____. "Boughton House, Northamptonshire - V." Country Life, 149 (March 4, 1971), No. 3847, 476-480.

_____. "The Making of the Boughton Landscape." Country Life, 149 (March 11, 1971), No. 3848, 536-539.

_____. "Houses Newly Open to the Public - II." Country Life, 159 (April 15, 1976), No. 4111, 962-965.

Cust, Lionel H. "Verrio, Antonio (1639?-1707)." Dictionary of National Biography, 20, 284-85.

Feiling, Keith. "Henrietta Stuart, Duchess of Orleans, and the Origins of the Treaty of Dover."

English Historical Review, 47 (Oct. 1932), 642-645.

_____. "Two Unprinted Letters of Henrietta Stuart, Duchess of Orleans." English Historical Review, 43 (July 1928), 394-398.

Firth, Charles H. "Montagu, Ralph, Duke of Montagu (1638-1709)." Dictionary of National Biography 13, 710-713.

Grose, Clyde. "Charles II of England." American Historical Review, 43 (April 1938), 533-541.

_____. "Louis XIV's Financial Relations with Charles II and the English Parliament." The Journal of Modern History, 1 (June 1929), No. 2, 177-204.

Haley, K.H.D. "Anglo-Dutch Rapprochement of 1677." English Historical Review, 73 (Oct. 1958), 614-648.

Haskell, Francis. "Patronage." Encyclopedia of World Art, 11. 118-132.

Hayes, J. "British Patrons and Landscape Painting in the Seventeenth Century." Apollo, n.s. 82 (July 1965), 38-45.

Hunt, William. "Montagu or Mountague, James (1568?-1618)." Dictionary of National Biography, 13, 698-699.

Hurtsfield, J. "Political Morality of the Early Stuart Statesman." History, 56 (June 1971), 235-43.

Lancaster, Osbert. "Royal Patronage." Architectural Review, 77 (June 1935), 235-40.

Lee, Sidney. "Osborne, Sir Thomas, Earl of Danby and Duke of Leeds (1631-1712)." Dictionary of National Biography 14, 1189-1197.

_____. "Winwood, Sir Ralph
(1563?-1617)." Dictionary of National Biography,
21, 704-707.

Mitchell, A.A. "Charles II, King of Great
Britain, and the Treaty of Dover, 1670." History
Today, 17 (Oct. 1967), 674-682.

Moriarty, Gerald Patrick. "Montagu, or more
properly Mountagu, Edward, first Earl of Sandwich
(1625-1672)." Dictionary of National Biography,
13, 679-684.

Notes and Queries a Medium of Inter-
Communication for Literary Men, Artists,
Antiquaries, Geneologists, Etc. London: George
Bell, 2nd ser., XI, (March 2, 1861), 169, (March
23, 1861), 236, (June 16, 1861), 477; 4th ser., VII
(Jan. 7, 1871), 3, XI (May 17, 1873), 403, (May 31,
1873), 450, (June 28, 1873), 533; 8th ser., XI,
(Feb. 6, 1873), 106, (March 20, 1897), 237-238.

Northamptonshire Notes and Queries, An
Illustrated Quarterly Journal Devoted to the
Antiquities, Families, Family History, Traditions,
Parochial Records, Folk-lore, Quaint Customs, &c.
of the County. Northampton: John Taylor, VI,
(1896), 75-79.

Porter, Bertha. "Edward Montagu, Second Baron
Montagu of Boughton (1616-1684)." Dictionary of
National Biography, 13, 673.

Rigg, James McMullen. "Montagu, Sir Henry,
First Earl of Manchester (1563?-1642)." Dictionary
of National Biography, 13, 696-697.

Rowse, A.L. "Tradition of British Policy."
Political Quarterly, 10 (Oct. 1939), 489-501.

Stone, Lawrence. "Literacy and Education in

England - 1640-1900." Past and Present, 42 (Feb. 1969), 69-139.

Temperly, H.W.V. 'Tocuments Illustrative of the Powers of the Privy Council in the Seventeenth Century." English Historical Review, 28 (Jan. 1913), 127-131.

Tuberville, A.S. "The House of Lords Under Charles II." Part I. English Historical Review, 44 (July 1929), 400-417.

_____. "The House of Lords Under Charles II." Part II. English Historical Review, 45 (Jan. 1930), 58-77.

Turner, Edward Raymond. "Committees of the Privy Council - 1688-1760." English Historical Review, 21 (Jan. 1916), 545-572.

Walcott, Robert. "The Later Stuarts (1660-1714): Significant Works of the Last Twenty Years (1939-59)." American Historical Review, 67 (Jan. 1962), 352-370.

Zagorin, P. "Court and the Country: A Note on Political Terminology in Earlier Seventeenth Century." English Historical Review, 77 (April 1962), 306-311.

INDEX

STUDIES IN BRITISH HISTORY

DATE DUE